MW00617080

EVERY

NATION

HAS ITS

DISH

EVERY NATION HAS ITS DISH

BLACK BODIES & BLACK FOOD IN TWENTIETH-CENTURY AMERICA

JENNIFER JENSEN WALLACH

The University of North Carolina Press

CHAPEL HILL

© 2019 The University of North Carolina Press

All rights reserved

Designed and set in Alegreya HT Pro with Treadstone and Kapra display
by Kristina Kachele Design, llc
Manufactured in the United States of America

The University of North Carolina Press has been a member of the Green Press Initiative
since 2003.

Jacket illustration: *Interior View of Dining Hall, Decorated for the Holidays, with Students
Sitting at Tables at the Tuskegee Institute*, Frances Benjamin Johnston, photographer,
ca. 1902; courtesy Library of Congress Prints and Photographs Division.

Library of Congress Cataloging-in-Publication Data
Names: Wallach, Jennifer Jensen, 1974– author.
Title: Every nation has its dish : black bodies and black food in twentieth-century America /
    Jennifer Jensen Wallach.
Description: Chapel Hill : The University of North Carolina Press, [2018] | Includes bibliographi-
    cal references and index.
Identifiers: LCCN 2018023985| ISBN 9781469645216 (cloth : alk. paper) | ISBN 9781469645223 (ebook)
Subjects: LCSH: Food habits—United States—History—20th century. | African Americans—
    Food—History—20th century. | African Americans—Social life and customs—20th century.
Classification: LCC GT2853.U6 W35 2018 | DDC 394.1/208996073—dc23 LC record available at
    https://lccn.loc.gov/2018023985

Portions of chapter 2 appeared in Jennifer Jensen Wallach, "Dethroning the Deceitful
Pork Chop: Food Reform at the Tuskegee Institute," in *Dethroning the Deceitful
Pork Chop: Rethinking African American Foodways from Slavery to Obama*, edited by
Jennifer Jensen Wallach (© 2015 University of Arkansas Press; reproduced with
the permission of the University of Arkansas Press, www.uapress.com).

Portions of chapter 7 appeared in Jennifer Jensen Wallach, "How to Eat to Live: Black
Nationalism and the Post-1964 Culinary Turn," *Study the South*, July 2, 2014, https://
southernstudies.olemiss.edu/study-the-south/how-to-eat-to-live/; © Jennifer Jensen Wallach.

MIX
Paper from
responsible sources
FSC   FSC® C013483
www.fsc.org

For Mike and Augie. Always.

CONTENTS

FIGURES

ACKNOWLEDGMENTS

This book had its genesis during a series of leisurely lunch conversations in the late 1990s with my mentor and friend Robert Paul Wolff. Bob never batted an eye when I wanted to talk about this project and supported my growing belief that untangling the food politics of a past moment was an intellectually significant undertaking. I still owe him a tremendous intellectual debt, as I do other current and former members of the Department of Afro-American Studies at the University of Massachusetts. I appreciate in new ways the things I learned from Bill Strickland, Ernie Allen, Manish Sinha, Steve Tracy, John Bracey, Esther Terry, and Jim Smethurst.

I have continued to benefit from the advice and encouragement of equally supportive colleagues and mentors ever since, including those who offered me feedback as this project developed over the years. I had the opportunity to present portions of my research at the Texas Food Writers Salon, at meetings of the Culinary Historians of New York and the Southern Historical Association, at the Summersell Center for the Study of the South, and at the University of North Carolina's State of the Plate Conference. I am grateful for the feedback from the participants in all of those events, especially Elizabeth Engelhardt, Scott A. Barton, Josh Rothman, Michael Innis-Jiménez, and Marcie Cohen Ferris. I also benefited from helpful advice offered by Anthony J. Stanonis, Ted Ownby, Sara Camp Arnold, and John T. Edge, who each read a portion of this manuscript. I am grateful to the editorial staff of *Study the South* and the staff at the University of Arkansas Press, including Mike Bieker, David Scott Cunningham, Charlie Shields, and Melissa King, who have enriched my life and my ability to contribute to the field of food studies in many ways.

Other scholars who have offered me support and inspiration include Jeannie Whayne, Regina A. Bernard-Carreño, Helen Zoe Veit, Megan Elias, Jeffrey Pilcher, Adam Shprintzen, Meredith Abarca, Rafia Zafar, James McWilliams, Krishnendu Ray, Carol J. Adams, Carrie Tippen, John Hoenig, Colter Ellis, Kristin Burton, Robert Caldwell, Priscilla Ybarra,

Harland Hagler, Elizabeth Hayes Turner, Todd Moye, Rita Reynolds, David Kaplan, Amanda Milian, John David Smith, John Ferling, Jodi Campbell, Christopher Johnson, Agatha Beins, Andrew Torget, Marvin Bendele, Gretchen Hoffman, Rebecca Sharpless, and Fitz Brundage. Thanks additionally go to Jon Sisk and Larry Malley for offering me wonderful editorial advice over the years. I am also grateful to the Food Studies Mentoring Group in the Department of History at the University of North Texas, whose members include Nancy Stockdale, Sandra Mendiola García, Rachel Moran, Clark Pomerleau, Marilyn Morris, Kate Imy, and Michael Wise. They have made my life richer, both intellectually and personally. I admire them all for being not only accomplished scholars but also caring, empathetic human beings. Thanks also go to Rick McCaslin, Harold Tanner, Steve Cobb, Christy Crutsinger, Michael McPherson, and the UNT Office of Faculty Success for providing funding for food studies programming here at UNT. Our group would not exist without them.

I am grateful to Angela Jill Cooley and Psyche Williams-Forson for their enthusiasm for this project and for helpful insights. I took their thoughtful advice seriously, and the book is better because of them. Thanks also go to the wonderful staff at UNC Press, especially to my editor, Elaine Maisner. Elaine helped me find some critical distance from my work, sharpen my arguments, and trim some of the excess from the manuscript. Furthermore, I could not have written the book without the aid of archivists at the Library of Congress, the Schomburg Center for Research in Black Culture, the Atlanta University Center, the Schlesinger Library, the National Archives, the David Walker Lupton Cookbook Collection at the University of Alabama, and the Tuskegee University Archives. I particularly enjoyed the time I spent at Tuskegee. Thanks go to Dana Chandler and to the library staff and volunteers for the guidance and the hospitality, which even included a drive in the countryside and a free lunch. Funding from the University of North Texas in the form of a Research Initiation Grant and a Scholarly and Creative Activities Award and grants from the Southern Foodways Alliance and the Culinary Historians of New York made this travel possible.

I am blessed with family members who are caring enough that they actually read the books I write, regardless of their personal interest in the subject. My thanks go to Jamie Jensen, Aaron Jensen, Gaby Gollub, Brian Wise, and David and Sara Jensen. I am so lucky to have the support of loving grandparents like Janice and Dick Thorson and Aage and Joyce Jensen. I owe a particularly large debt to Carolyn and David Briggs and to

Don and Debbie Wise for offering support on many levels. They have provided unconditional love, childcare, editorial help, beach vacations, home-cooked meals, a steady supply of Oyster Bay sauvignon blanc, and so much more.

Finally, I am grateful for my son, Augustine Jensen Wise, and my husband, Michael D. Wise. Augie, your first two years of life have been filled with activities and challenges that certainly did not make writing this book any easier, but you made it, and everything else, more rewarding. I cannot remember or imagine a reality without you at the very center of my universe. Mike, I would not have written the same book had I not known you. Many of my thoughts and sensibilities have been formed in the process of conversations with you; your influence is everywhere. Thank you for being both my intellectual soul mate (a phrase I scoffed at until I met you) and my dearest companion and friend. When I look back on the period of time when I was writing this book, I will remember being sustained not only by your intelligence and encouragement but also by food you grew and somehow found time to transform into memorable meal after meal, which we ate accompanied by the shrill soundtrack of "Ten Little Humpties."

EVERY

NATION

HAS ITS

DISH

Introduction

In 1924 the African American journalist Lester Walton wrote a letter to his friend W. E. B. Du Bois confessing, "I enjoyed immensely our lunch yesterday—both the lamb stew and our talk. It is difficult for me to say which pleased me more: but the lamb stew was good, wasn't it"?[1] In a friendship that spanned decades, "race men" Walton and Du Bois dined together frequently and conversed on topics ranging from African American artistic productions to the potential role of black activists in the American political system and their mutual interest in developments on the continent of Africa. Given the gravitas of the intellectual and cultural concerns they shared, Walton's claim that he enjoyed the lamb as much as the conversation might seem, at first glance, to be a jocular remark too absurd to be taken literally by scholars seeking to understand the race politics of that particular moment. Indeed, the very framework of intellectual history, which has often been used to document the lives of people like Walton and Du Bois, is designed to foreclose the possibility that two serious men could possibly put the act of fueling their bodies on par with the mental stimulation of exchanging ideas. This tendency to focus exclusively on the cerebral qualities of historical figures can have the unintended effect of severing metaphorical heads from their equally significant corporeal frames. The purpose of this book, however, is to take Walton at his word that the act of consuming that lamb was indeed as meaningful to him as the intellectual exchange that accompanied it and to suggest that his remark can be used as an entryway into a particular kind of historical knowing, which takes seriously the knowledge embedded in the physical sensations of past bodies.

The subject of eating appears frequently in correspondence between Du Bois and Walton, and the men ate together often when they were in New York City at the same time. Read together, their letters reveal a shared understanding of the term "hunger," which they used both as a metaphor to describe a desire for intellectual connection and as a straightforward way to refer to a physical urge that proved even more compelling than the need for conversation. Walton sometimes initiated communication with his friend by asking, "Will you kindly let me know when you expect to be hungry?"[2] Du Bois responded by using "hunger" as shorthand for the intellectual and bodily ritual of a shared lunch. He once ordered Walton to "quit stalling," impatiently telling him, "I have been home for a week or more and am hungry."[3] Another time, he gave his friend more warning of his growing need, informing him, "I am beginning to get hungry."[4] These persistent references to the sensation of hunger serve as a reminder of the often forgotten fact that even great minds are ensconced in bodies, which are relentless in their demands. Because eating is a necessary prelude to everything else, even the most celebrated thinkers must spend an inordinate amount of time daydreaming about lunch.

Although Walton and Du Bois certainly could not afford to ignore the biological imperative of acquiring food, this quest for sustenance was not fueled by grim caloric necessity alone. For these men, the ritual of mealtime—how, what, and where they ate—was also utilized as a performance where they could convey messages about who they were or who they hoped to become. Both men were thoughtful about the art of personal presentation and thus would have arrived at these joint lunches neatly attired and equipped with knowledge about proper dining etiquette designed to highlight their sophistication and sense of dignity. Furthermore, many of the locations where these meals took place were rich in cultural meaning. In 1930, Du Bois proposed that they meet for a "simple" dinner at the Civic Club on East Twelfth Street.[5] Although Du Bois downplayed the significance of the meal itself in his invitation, the proposed meeting place was a symbolically important interracial gathering spot. In 1924, black artistic luminaries and their white and black supporters, including Du Bois himself, had gathered at the Civic Club to publicly usher in the birth of a Harlem renaissance and of a purportedly more race-conscious and militant "new Negro."[6] While dining at such a storied venue, Du Bois and Walton were also invoking the spirit of the event that had preceded them.

Sometimes the items on their plates were also enlisted in the work of sending messages about who the diners wished to become. In 1927, Du Bois ribbed Walton, telling him to save his "pennies" so that he could "afford a first class lunch."[7] Although half in jest, Du Bois's reference to the cost of a nice meal demonstrates the fact that meals then, as now, were frequently used to perform ideas about social status. In 1942, the pair enjoyed a luxurious "feed" at Luchow's, a restaurant that the *New York Times* labeled a "vast gastronomic cathedral on 14th Street." Du Bois and Walton would have gorged themselves on hearty portions of German fare while gazing at mahogany walls, oil paintings, and chandeliers that signified luxury instead of the deprivation usually associated with the plight of mid-twentieth-century African Americans living in a segregated world where they had unequal access to food.[8] As they dined at Luchow's, Du Bois and Walton were well aware of the fact that they were also unsettling a social hierarchy that sought to deny such hedonistic pleasures to black men.

For Du Bois and Walton, the tastes, sounds, and sights of mealtime helped foster a shared sense of identity and purpose that inspired them to enjoy numerous lunches and dinners together over the course of more than two decades. However, for other reflective African American eaters, interactions at the dinner table were not always so harmonious, and the table could also become an emotional space where feelings of competition, frustration, or rage overshadowed the possibility of a heightened sense of connectedness. For many, food practices made up a realm where bodily compulsion was intertwined with a web of competing social, political, and aesthetic considerations.

Writer and producer Terence Winter memorably captured the alternative possibility that food could divide as well as unite people in an imaginative rendering of an early twentieth-century African American family dinner gone awry. In an episode of his award-winning television drama *Boardwalk Empire*, Winter reveals that the dinner table, which served as a site of physical and intellectual empowerment for Du Bois and Walton, could also become a place where antagonistic visions about racial, class, and national identities could come into conflict with one another.[9] In an episode that originally aired in 2011, Albert "Chalky" White, a fictional African American gangster operating in Atlantic City during the era of Prohibition, partakes of an evening meal with his wife, his three children, and a dinner guest. The setting denotes middle-class domesticity and includes a table covered in a white cloth and laden with china, crystal, and carefully arranged food: a roasted duck, homemade biscuits, and a bowl brimming with peas and carrots.

To an impartial observer, nothing about the materiality of the dinner table scene would suggest that either the funds used to purchase the food or the implements used to serve and consume it were funded by proceeds from extralegal activities. Nor is it readily apparent that the Whites are members of a despised racial group only decades removed from the legalized debasement of slavery. The carefully groomed members of the family sit with perfect posture, offering up their bodies as evidence of their refinement, which is also evoked by the elegant domestic interior and the painstakingly prepared meal. It is clear that the bodies surrounding the table, the food destined to sustain them, and the dining accoutrements used to choreograph the meal are all carefully curated and chosen to serve as powerful signifiers of status and of a certain set of values.[10]

Despite the facade of domestic respectability, Chalky's sense that he may not fully belong in the universe he has carefully created is revealed when he snarls at his wife for not serving "hoppin' John," a food he ate as an impoverished child growing up in the South. She coolly responds that this beloved dish is "not proper food" to serve to the guest who has joined the family for dinner. Chalky seethes with indignation when the ambitious young medical student who is courting his daughter smilingly claims that he actually likes the dish, a "type of food" he associates with his grandmother. Nonetheless, it is clear that in the mind of this young man, hoppin' John is a meal linked to the past and not to the present aspirational moment. Although Chalky has worked to assemble the means necessary to construct a dining performance laden with ideas about respectability, he cannot steadfastly enjoy these pleasures. Instead, he sees the public rejection of the beans and rice dish as a denunciation of more than his criminal activities; he interprets it as a personal indictment by family members who possess more cultural capital and as a betrayal of their shared racial heritage. He seems to sense that it is a particular version of blackness, not his illicit occupation, that his family regards as criminal. After being chastised for his "country ways," Chalky defies an unspoken prohibition against invoking the trauma of slavery as he storms out of the house, labeling himself a "field nigger."

Through the seemingly unexceptional act of sitting down for a family meal, the Whites were seeking to create a shared sense of who they were both as a family and as members of a marginalized racial group. By accepting or rejecting the roasted duck, they were sending messages about their understanding of their class and racial status. In the process they were also negotiating the terms of their association with Chalky's criminal activities. Furthermore, they were making statements about their relationships to and identification with the larger nation, whose laws the head of the household routinely violated. Although the blandly American, middle-class dinner menu seemed designed to pave the way for assimilation as full-fledged members of the U.S. nation-state, Chalky's brooding presence and his hostile reminder that he "put the food on the table" reminded the family that both their patriarch's occupation and their racial heritage precluded them from full national belonging.

The dynamics of this brilliantly imagined family meal capture some more of the complexities inherent in the historical task of black identity construction in the decades after emancipation. Although it remains an underexamined cultural and social space, the realm of dining behavior frequently served as an arena where different identities could be assumed, modified, or discarded. This study begins with an examination of the tense politics of African American food habits in the wake of emancipation and ends with an assessment of black food behavior after the end of the classical phase of the civil rights movement. I analyze the various attempts of African Americans who, like the fictionalized White family, used food practices as a means of exploring questions of both national and personal identity, experimenting with different ideas about who they were and who they wished to become. As they made decisions about how and what to eat, they sought control over how their recently emancipated bodies were represented in the U.S. national imagination as they endeavored to shape their individual, corporeal experiences of freedom.

Food is central to the process of identity construction for any group. As the sociologist Claude Fisher has convincingly argued, "The way any given human group eats helps it assert its diversity, hierarchy, organization, and at the same time, both its oneness and otherness of whoever eats differently."[11] For black Americans, foodways became a mechanism that could be used to define their relationship both to a nation-state that offered them only second-class citizenship and to their fellow Americans of African descent. Food habits were a convenient and consistent means of exploring the community's relationship to the U.S. nation-state as well as to a borderless, independent black nation. In the wake of emancipation, conscientious black eaters understood the process of making food choices as one way to perform national ideologies. At the same time, they were also aware that eating good food was one potential means of shoring up their physical bodies. From the era of slavery onward, black people have attempted physically to strengthen themselves in order to fight the degradations of structural racism that aimed to injure black bodies and, later, to ready themselves for the rigors of the variously construed duties of post-emancipation citizenship.

In the late nineteenth century, the project of racial advancement was a multifaceted one as newly liberated slaves fought to have their basic material needs met at the same time that they struggled to devise a variety of markers, tangible and otherwise, of their change in status. Members of the free black community who were scattered around the nation also had to redefine themselves as they saw the difference in station among free and enslaved African Americans disappear, even though racial boundaries remained deeply entrenched. Members of both groups had to construct in opposition to white society a racial identity that also acknowledged real intragroup differences in terms of material circumstances, priorities, and values. Food decisions, among the most quotidian of concerns, offered one important avenue where African Americans could work out these competing ideas about personal and group identity.

Booker T. Washington, one of the most well known individuals to have made the transition from slavery to freedom, was among those who acknowledged the significance that foodways played in his own personal journey of post-emancipation identity construction. Washington's 1901 autobiography, *Up from Slavery*, has been regarded by some as an implausibly equanimous account of his life history due to his assertion, among other things, that slavery was a kind of "school" that improved those who endured it "materially, intellectually, morally, and religiously."[12] In the post-emancipation era, too, Washington claimed that he continued to find morals embedded in menial labor, maintaining that he found great satisfaction in performing mundane jobs such as sweeping a floor. However, by his own account, his youthful adventures in housekeeping paled in comparison to his post-freedom discovery of the power of the bathtub. Bathing was a ritual that Washington declared not only kept the body healthy but also made the bather virtuous and thus clean both inside and out.[13] In fact, in Washington's telling, one of the key contrasts between slavery and freedom was the newfound ability of the freed people to keep their bodies and surroundings much cleaner than they were before. This way of measuring the impact of emancipation might, at first glance, seem underwhelming in light of the plight of freed slaves struggling to navigate a world characterized by racial violence and sociopolitical turmoil.[14] Nonetheless, throughout his narrative, Washington makes a persistent case for the importance of learning tidier, more orderly modes of behavior as a vital facet of the task of racial advancement. One crucial sphere of personal behavior where he traces his own evolutionary development from slavery to freedom is in the area of food practices.

When recalling the bleak dining culture of slavery, he writes,

I cannot remember a single instance during my childhood or early boyhood when our entire family sat down to the table together, and God's blessing was asked, and the family ate a meal in a civilized manner. On the plantation in Virginia, and even later, meals were gotten by the children very much as dumb animals get theirs. It was a piece of bread here and a scrap of meat there. It was a cup of milk at one time and some potatoes at another. Sometimes a portion of our family would eat out of the skillet or pot, while some one else would eat from a tin plate held on the knees, and often using nothing but the hands with which to hold the food.

In this passage, Washington implies that depriving slaves of the resources needed to eat regular meals and to utilize dining implements was not mere thoughtlessness but instead a vital part of the calculated attempt to reduce enslaved people to the degraded status of animals. In this formulation, the evil of slavery consisted not only of the institution's most blatant crimes, such as appropriating labor by force and wrecking families, but also of myriad smaller evils, such as preventing enslaved people from performing the daily rituals that white society used continually to reaffirm their own humanity. In Washington's mind, proper dining etiquette was a vitally important means of asserting personhood, both individually and collectively. Thus it is unsurprising that he claimed that the post-emancipation experience of "having meals at regular hours, of eating on a tablecloth, [of] using a napkin" helped usher him "into a new world," which he deemed "civilized" in contrast to the degradations of slavery.[15] Having the means and the leisure to perform these niceties became an important dimension in his definition of freedom. Although Washington was famously reluctant to speak publicly about the issue of black civil rights, he was outspoken in his demand that other African Americans should be permitted to enjoy the privileges of living in a "new world" of hygiene and decorum. Given these priorities, it is understandable that he later took immense pride in being able to expose his students at the Tuskegee Institute to a "large, beautiful, well-ventilated, and well-lighted dining room . . . tempting, well-cooked food . . . neat tablecloths and napkins, and vases of flowers upon the tables."[16]

For the most part, scholars have failed to analyze seriously the implications of Washington's program of hygienic elevation. A close reading of the work of his primary biographers, Louis R. Harlan and Robert J. Norrell, reveals that cleanliness was an ongoing preoccupation for Washington throughout his life, not only in the pages of his autobiography.[17] Yet many have regarded Washington's emphasis on cleanliness merely as a means of assuring potential white allies both that his program for racial uplift was geared toward personal rather than societal transformation and that working-class African Americans could be taught to conform to middle-class norms of behavior.[18] Others have suggested that Washington's hygienic advice was designed to temper potentially more radical avenues for racial elevation. For example, Patti McGill Peterson has argued that Washington was deliberately creating "a pedagogy of behavior [that] served to brush aside questions from the students about their future place in American society."[19] But even if Tuskegee's educational emphases on such quotidian matters as food and bodily hygiene might look insignificant or even regressive to scholars assessing them generations onward, for Washington and many of his students, the curriculum proved foundational for imagining black identities in the new century.

The practices that Washington extolled (as well as the household items associated with them) have become so naturalized that the circumstances of their construction and the meanings embedded in activities such as washing one's body or wiping one's mouth with a napkin have sometimes become rendered invisible. In failing to take Washington's advice seriously, however, we foreclose the possibility of finding unvarnished insights into one important dimension of the transition from slavery to freedom. Peter Coclanis has pointed to other interpretations of Washington's emphasis upon "cleanliness behaviors," speculating that his fascination with the subject might very well be the outgrowth of "his 'lived experience' in the highly morbid and mortal disease environment of the late-nineteenth century South." Washington, Coclanis suggests, must have realized that the habits he was endorsing could be correlated to better health outcomes and that healthy bodies were a necessary first component for any program of racial advancement.[20] Bridget T. Heneghan has pointed toward a more radical interpretation of the significance of Washington's insistence that freed people had the right to care for their bodies and their homes in the same style that white people did. She argues that Washington understood that material items like toothbrushes had the potential to "civilize" black people not only in the imaginations of white observers but, more important, in their own estimation.[21] Demanding the right to possess and utilize objects needed to perform the rituals of personal hygiene, housekeeping, and dining became a way to perform racial equality and to signify a profound change in social status. Engaging in behaviors that denoted equality resulted, in some significant yet highly personal way, in a means of actually becoming, at least for the duration of the ritual, equal.

In his influential study *The Civilizing Process*, Norbert Elias pointed out that, as the former slave Washington instinctively understood, "nothing in table manners is self-evident." The action of using a napkin, which Washington marveled at upon his first exposure to the ritual, was the outgrowth of a set of customs that were refined and solidified over the course of centuries.[22] From the perspective of a newly emancipated person who had never had access to any but the crudest cooking or eating implements, coming into possession of such items for the first time may have been a remarkable, even life-altering experience that was weighted with symbolism. Washington's decision to extol the virtues of eating at a table covered with a cloth or of eating meals at a regular hour may not have been the cynical attempts of a self-serving race leader to present white critics with a timid platform for racial improvement as much as it was the manifestation of a sophisticated recognition of the significance of being allowed to participate in social rites that could be taken for granted only by those who had never been excluded.

Elias has provocatively suggested that modes of behavior, such as the table etiquette that Washington so admired, that have been slowly codified as markers of civilized behavior have eventually become part of the socializing process whereby children become adults. Because not practicing what a particular society deems as proper behavior is associated with childhood, Elias notes, groups of people that adhere to different norms are sometimes perceived as being childlike, regardless of their chronological age.[23] This observation may help explain why Washington found being deprived of a napkin or a plate while enslaved so humiliating. The act of denying enslaved people the right to participate in the rituals of civilization may have functioned as yet another element of the infantilization process whereby slave owners imagined themselves as paternalistic figures charged with moderating the impulses of a class of perpetual children. Viewed in this light, the action of using a napkin becomes a means to grow up, to spurn dependency, and to assert an equal right to participate in the collectively authored rules of so-called civilization. Thus for Washington, the stakes at the dinner table were high, and the napkin was a powerful symbol.

Washington, like many of the other African American food reformers who are the subject of this book, had a fascination with the social system governing food production and consumption precisely because he believed that unlocking these rules could become one means of advocating for fuller citizenship. Although African Americans technically became U.S. citizens after the passage of the Fourteenth Amendment, for most this legal status was not translated into meaningful incorporation into the body politic until nearly a century after its adoption. The brutal regime of Jim Crow was designed to make sure that African Americans could never advance politically, socially, or economically. Those who wished to practice citizenship in the realms of politics or civil society were met with the barriers of disenfranchisement and segregation, which were reinforced by violence. This dismal state of affairs led many to search for other avenues of national inclusion, particularly in the realm of culture. The mechanisms of white supremacy were far less effective at preventing African Americans from embracing an idealized version of American values and cultural practices than at keeping them away from the ballot box or theoretically shared civic spaces. The realm of foodways, particularly private dining practices that took place away from white scrutiny, became one way that African Americans could assert their right to U.S. citizenship without risking the ire of those who would renounce their right to participate in more conventional modes of political behavior.

Throughout modern history, ideas about a shared culinary tradition have played a large role in the construction of various national identities. The idea of a peculiar, national way of eating has been variously used, as Alison K. Smith argues, to "introduce a nation to its own members . . . to introduce the nation to the outside world . . . to preserve the memory of a nation."[24] In the case of the formerly enslaved, the idea of a national cuisine, along with its attendant food practices, was used as a means of asserting a right to belong. While celebrating the napkin and the tablecloth, Washington was proclaiming his right to eat in a style befitting a citizen. As a later chapter of this book will reveal, Washington extended his culinary agenda to include a demand that African Americans be given the opportunity to ingest what he considered to be the actual foodstuffs of Americanization, high-status menu items like beef and wheat bread. In eating carefully selected foods and following a rigid code of etiquette, Washington, along with numerous allies in his project of culinary elevation, was performing a rite of cultural citizenship. The association that he made between food habits and national belonging set a precedent for a variety of black attempts to use the dinner table as a space for acting out various ideas of U.S. national identity.

Food habits have been used as a means of constructing not only national identities but also racial ones. As Rachel Slocum has observed, "Producing and maintaining racial identity is dependent, in part, on holding on to food habits and tastes, which are themselves imagined as cuisines belonging to racialized groups or nations."[25] Although Washington advocated primarily for foodways of inclusion, in the coming decades other African Americans used food practices as a way to celebrate or advocate for their exclusion from U.S. culture. Rejecting foods or food practices that were coded as "American" became one way that some African Americans, including those who touted the virtues of consuming a racially specific "soul food" diet beginning in the late 1960s, could reject the flawed promises of U.S. citizenship and create an alternative and explicitly racialized culinary identity. This book also documents the various attempts of politically conscious black eaters to reject American ideas about proper food behavior just as strongly as Washington—at least at most moments in his political career—embraced them. These black culinary nationalists revived, invented, or adopted ideas about racially specific ways of eating in order to create a meaningful alternative to a U.S. national identity.

One of the aims of this book is to explore the relationship between African American food expression and nationalism; however, I am deliberately defining "nationalism" expansively as "a feeling of belonging." Due to the peculiarity of the black experience in the United States, nationalist loyalty was frequently an unstable affective state that shifted not only in accordance to fluctuations of sentimental attachment but also due to pragmatic concerns. As Gary Gerstle points out, "Throughout its history ... [the idea of] American civic nationalism has contended with another potent ideological inheritance, a racial nationalism that conceives of America in ethnoracial terms, as a people held together by common blood and skin color."[26] Although African Americans could make a claim for national inclusion through expansive readings of the Declaration of Independence and the Constitution, they also had to contend with their own historical experiences that revealed that in practice, American "inalienable rights" were reserved for a racially exclusive group. Understandably, African Americans found it difficult to aspire to unwavering fidelity to a nation that had rejected them and similarly challenging to emphasize political and social separatism while also agitating for the full inclusion promised by the elusive ideals of American civic nationalism. Faced with the American national paradox, African Americans have frequently had to maintain contradictory and changing ideas about national identification.

For my purposes, an expressed desire—however transitory—to identify as "American" and to assimilate socially and culturally into mainstream society meets my litmus test for a pro-U.S. civic nationalism.

When identifying the strains of black ethnic nationalism, which are evident throughout the scope of black culinary history, I draw upon the definition used by John Bracey, August Meier, and Elliot Rudwick in their classic anthology, *Black Nationalism in America*. Bracey, Meier, and Elliot employ the label "black nationalism" widely to "describe a body of social thought, attitudes, and actions ranging from the simplest expressions of ethnocentrism and racial solidarity to [a number of] comprehensive and sophisticated ideologies."[27] They discover nationalist impulses in examples ranging from amorphous feelings of racial solidarity to the concrete actions of would-be geopolitical nation builders. William L. Van Deburg advocates for a similarly broad definition of nationalism, which is also useful for my purposes. Nationalists, he argues, are simply those who place a "high value" upon "self-definition and self-determination."[28]

I am mindful of the charge made by political scientist Dean E. Robinson and others that defining black nationalism as an "affective state, or as any form of racial solidarity," may, in some instances, strip the concept of some of its explanatory significance.[29] Robinson calls for a definition of nationalism that goes beyond feelings of pride and is also programmatic. According to stricter definitions of black nationalism, would-be members of a black nation must show their fidelity through actions designed to bring about a black political entity or, at least according to Robinson, "black administration of vital public and private institutions."[30] Nationalism of this variety, thus, is not just something a person feels; it is associated with a certain set of actions, which can vary depending on the particular political context.

My working definition of nationalism allows for a nationalism of sentiment, which may not be linked to a concrete political agenda, but in agreeing with those scholars who emphasize the idea of nationalism as a practice, I too argue that nationalism should be conceptualized as not only something that people believe or feel but also as something that people can *do*. However, my emphasis is not on the public, political arena but on the more personal ways that nationalism can be exhibited. I am interested in examining not only the affective nationalism that influences the figurative heart but also nationalism as it is exhibited in the literal, physical human body.

As Benedict Anderson has famously observed, nationalism is and must be an act of imagination "because the members of even the smallest nation will never know most of their fellow-members, meet them, or even hear of them, yet in the minds of each lives the image of their communion."[31] The willful and emotional act of belonging, which can be charted among groups who hold a shared narrative of their history, originates with numerous small acts of individual imagination, which are sustained through a series of choices—some of which are affective or intellectual, while others are more active. This study examines a set of daily activities—those of producing, preparing, and consuming food—and conceives of them as political activities. Throughout African American history, national identification has been expressed through political mobilization, rhetorical expression, and cultural outpourings—the arenas where scholars have usually looked for black nationalist expression—but nationalism can also be seen as a bodily practice. Nationalism is not merely an abstract ideology but may also be thought of as something that a person does or, as the case may be, undoes by manipulating his or her body. Historically, African Americans have used the biological process of food consumption to demonstrate, challenge, construct, and perform a range of beliefs about their relationship to both the U.S. nation-state and to the stateless, imagined black nation. By choosing to eat or to reject certain foods, black Americans have manifested physiological loyalty to or rejection of the U.S. nation or to a separate black nation as represented by the foodways associated with each group.

While foods themselves can be used as powerful symbols to signify a sense of cultural affiliation, I wish to look beyond what certain foods meant to also examine what consumers believed these foods actually did to the physical body as they were ingested, digested, and excreted. In so doing, I too am participating in Kayla Wazana Tompkins's quest to investigate moments when "acts of eating cultivate political subjects by fusing the social with the biological, by imaginatively shaping the matter we experience as body and the self."[32] By paying attention to the embodied experiences of U.S. national or black national eaters, it is possible to begin to contemplate the way that national sentiment was physically expressed and personally experienced within black bodies. Black food expression was, after all, both performative and potentially transformative.[33] In writing about performance, I am drawing on Erving Goffman's definition of performance as "all activity of a given participant on a given occasion which serves to influence in any way any of the other participants."[34] The process of deliberately choosing what and how to eat could be orchestrated to show members of the dominant culture or fellow group members who the eater imagined himself or herself to be. However, conscientious eaters also had further aspirations beyond trying to influence how others viewed them. They hoped that the ingestion of particular foods could actually help physically transform the body of the individual eater into the image he or she projected. In aggregate, black bodies could reflect what Pierre Bourdieu referred to as a "materialization of . . . taste" as their shared food culture was "turned into nature, that is, embodied."[35]

Responding both to external compulsions and to the pull of individual agency, African Americans have used eating practices to discipline their bodies for political purposes. Anderson's definition of nationalism as a manifestation of shared "communion" is a particularly apt conceptualization of this process if we think also about the Christian ritual of communion. Coreligionists perform their shared feelings of affinity through the action of ingesting the symbolically significant meal of wine and bread together in order to further cement their group ties. Thoughtfully chosen food, with its power to transform the bodies of those who consume it, can potentially make ideology more material. Group belonging of whatever variety, when expressed at the table, can transform membership from a matter of emotional or intellectual affinity into a transformative physical activity as shared food becomes a part of the body of each person who consumes it.

In this, as in most studies about the process of culinary identity construction, the temptation to quote Jean Anthelme Brillat-Savarin's irresistible 1825 declaration "Tell me what you eat, and I shall tell you what you are" is strong.[36] Brillat-Savarin has clearly articulated the drive behind much of the scholarship in food studies, which is animated by a belief that the decisions about what people consume can yield insights into their culture, values, aspirations, and anxieties in a way that few other kinds of human behavior can. Nothing is more fundamental than the human need for nutritional sustenance. Regardless of time or place, no human issue has been as pressing as the problem of how and what to eat. That being said, this, like all aphorisms, is too simplistic. Group and individual identities—as expressed through food choices or any number of forms of expression—are generally far from stable. Food choices often reveal the conflicts, ambivalence, or obstacles people face in defining who they want to be or who they are becoming. The process of identity construction and the related question about national identification as they unfold at the African American table are dialectical issues. In 1903, Du Bois encapsulated the conundrum of black identity in his famous discussion of double consciousness. He summarized what he regarded as the central problem in the psychic quest to construct a stable African American identity, writing, "One ever feels his twoness,—an American, a Negro; two souls, two thoughts, two unreconciled strivings; two warring ideals in one dark body, whose dogged strength alone keeps it from being torn asunder."[37]

The tension between the oppositional positions of identifying as "an American" or as "a Negro" is evident throughout African American food history. An examination of the attempts to resolve this central tension through bodily, culinary discipline yields insights into how black Americans coped with the dilemma of living in a nation that would not grant them full citizenship rights. Sometimes African Americans prepared and ate foods designed to demonstrate their worthiness and interest in full inclusion to the U.S. body politic. Sometimes they ate foods designed to reject the country that had spurned them and to create an alternative black national identity. And sometimes they ate foods that reflected competing national affiliations at the same meal.

As Bracey, Meier, and Rudwick make emphatically clear, different black political ideologies, and by extension politically influenced food behavior, "are often not sharply delineated, nor are they mutually exclusive categories. . . . Moreover, nationalism and racial integration as ideologies or as programs have often coexisted in organizations, in theories, and in the minds of individual[s]."[38] Thus U.S. nationalism and black nationalism are not necessarily oppositional poles. Drawing upon Robinson's claim that "nationalists share conventional assumptions common to their historical period," we might argue that in the American context, these competing concepts of national belonging are often inextricable.[39] Even the most boldly articulated black nationalist sentiment bears the imprint of the broader culture from which it emerged.

Black culinary history is a history of both protest and accommodation, of both race pride and an aching desire for acceptance. It is a history of both conscious deliberation and unintentional actions that reveal a great deal about the worldview of individual eaters. The study of black food habits as reflections of political convictions highlights the fact that temptation to categorize black intellectuals into competing ideological factions, an always flawed undertaking, becomes even more difficult when we begin to think of bodily practices as manifestations of belief systems. In general, historical black food practices must be characterized as being more improvisational and pragmatic than inflexible and purely idealistic. A serious examination of individual food activities as a form of political practice reveals the ideological inconsistencies of eaters whose appetites sometimes overcame their political resolve. Furthermore, a history of African American eating practices emphasizes the embodied similarities among individuals forced to navigate the same social world, including individuals such as W. E. B. Du Bois and Booker T. Washington, who are often portrayed in the historical literature as being archrivals.

This book seeks to complicate existing intellectual histories of African Americans in a long twentieth century beginning at the end of Reconstruction not just by focusing on the thoughts of notable black figures but also by concentrating upon their bodily experiences as they prepared, consumed, and ate carefully chosen and symbolically resonant foods. Returning again to Du Bois's articulation of the concept of double consciousness, it is important to note that he claimed that the "warring ideals" of being an American and a Negro simultaneously occupied "one dark body." He acknowledged the vulnerability and changeability of that body with his assertion that "dogged strength alone keeps it from being torn asunder."[40] In this famous passage, Du Bois implicitly disavows a thoughtless adherence to a Cartesian mind-body dualism that has dogged so much of the historical interpretation of prominent intellectuals. It has been a common mistake to consider the historical significance of towering figures like Du Bois as consisting of pure, disembodied thought.[41] Although it would be impossible to forget that Du Bois occupied a racialized body that was socially set apart as inferior, we seldom stop to contemplate the particularities of his bodily experiences, and by extension those of others, to remember that he felt hunger and pain, experiences that shaped the contours of his thought. Anthropologist Tim Ingold has offered a useful challenge to the tendency of scholars throughout both the humanities and the sciences to conceive of human beings either as biological organisms or as socially and culturally constructed persons without effectively reconciling the interplay of these two components. Ingold's solution to this conceptual dilemma is encapsulated in his insight that "the person *is* the organism." The human being, Ingold argues, can be best thought of "not as a composite entity made up of separable but complementary parts, such as body, mind, and culture, but rather as a singular locus of creative growth within a continually unfolding field of relationships."[42] Du Bois, like all humans, was aware of and to an inevitable extent guided by the realities of his biological fragility, an awareness of which is revealed in his acknowledgment that black bodies were regularly at risk of being "torn asunder."

Because modern theories of race were built upon ideas of corporeal difference among people, there is a certain amount of irony embedded in the fact that so many histories of racialized people depict their subjects as being disembodied. The social constructionists who spent the better part of the twentieth century rightly chipping away at the notion of real biological distinctions, emphasizing instead the social and cultural mechanisms behind the race-making project, often inadvertently managed to disembody their subjects in the process. Sociologist Bryan Turner argues that an unintended consequence of dethroning the idea of essentialized racial bodies has been to "side-line . . . the living, sensual practical body by concentrating on the social categories by which embodiment is assembled."[43] The end result of this suppression of the "lived body," Turner speculates, may be an inability to "clearly articulate the problems of human suffering, pain, and misery."[44] The ways that the individuals under consideration here sought to care for and feed their all-too-frail human bodies reveal a great deal about the nature of their lived experience as we seek to understand how they navigated the precarious terrain of sustaining their black bodies in a society that did not value their physical integrity. In my emphasis on food and the body, I am responding in part to Roy Porter's challenge to those working in the historical profession to endeavor to understand "how particular individuals and cultures . . . have ascribed meaning to their limbs and organs, their constitutions, their flesh." "What," Porter asks, "is the emotional and existential topography of skin and bones?"[45] When African Americans made deliberate, thoughtful decisions about what to eat, what to avoid, or how, when, and where to consume food, they did so, in part, in deference to their own predilections and as an outgrowth of their own beliefs about how these behaviors would affect their physical sense of pleasure, propriety, or well-being. Food was the fuel that sustained the black bodies that managed to persist even in the face of society that sought alternately to exploit or to devalue them.

One of the central though not always explicitly acknowledged themes in African American history is the tension between systematic attempts to control black bodies for the financial and psychic benefits of white supremacy and the attempts of African Americans to resist bodily domination and to assert ownership—either individual or collective—over black corporeality. The most elemental staging area of this conflict is at the dinner table, where decisions about how and what to feed these contested bodies are made. An emphasis on food and food expression allows us to renew our attention to black bodily experiences and to think about racial embodiment not from the perspective of biological race-makers who scrutinized African American bodies in order to impose evidence of somatic difference and inferiority but from the felt perspectives of African Americans themselves. Many black eaters used food consumption both as a way to perform ideas about racial and national identity and as a way to transform their bodies in deference to their cultural and political ideals.

One of the striking characteristics of the African American impulse toward culinary reform in the twentieth century is the fact that the mandate to eat thoughtfully was directed at every segment of the black community. Food activists maintained that politically conscious African Americans were obliged to weigh the symbolic and health-related implications of their food choices, from childhood to the grave. They agreed that both the black elite and the working classes should aspire toward improved habits. Furthermore, both men and women were charged with playing a role in the communal project of "eating right."[46] Since the market revolution, American ideology had relegated most of the work of constructing a national diet to a separate women's sphere; however, black culinary activists regarded the task of food reform as too significant to be reductively gendered.

The fact that Booker T. Washington and W. E. B. Du Bois, the most well known racial spokesmen of the era, each devoted considerable energy to the cause of dietary improvement demonstrates the significance of this issue as a key political priority. Nonetheless, even though race-conscious eaters sought to inculcate the entire community with the idea that food choices were significant, gendered assumptions about social roles still played a part in dictating the precise tasks that men and women were to undertake. Andrew Warnes convincingly argues that Washington and Du Bois shared the point of view that the intellectual work of writing (and, by extension, of speaking) enjoyed a "cultural supremacy" over the practice of cooking, proclaiming that both men "accepted the prevailing characterization of cooking as a functional, inartistic practice and of writing as a passport to political awareness, high culture, ambition, and upward mobility."[47] Warnes makes a compelling case that "Western, patriarchal assumptions that have undervalued the 'female' culture incarnated in the culinary arts" may have emboldened these men into a joint dismissal of the intellectual and creative skills inherent in the art of *cooking*; however, it is clear that Washington and Du Bois remained unified in their belief that the act of *eating* was of enormous political concern. Both men proffered dietary advice under the tacit assumption that their role in the labor of culinary reform was primarily an intellectual one and that female cooks would be charged with most of the physical drudgery of carrying out their recommendations. In this regard, Washington and Du Bois shared a great deal in common with white food reformers like Sylvester Graham and John Harvey Kellogg who similarly saw themselves as the source of the culinary ideas that the labor of others would make material.

My examination of the intertwined subjects of black nationhood, black bodies, and black food begins in the late nineteenth century with the struggle of a relatively small group of upwardly mobile African Americans to define a set of food practices that they hoped would help establish their cultural sophistication and, by extension, their worthiness for first-class U.S. citizenship. In chapter 1, "Creating the Foodways of Uplift," I discuss how self-consciously respectable middle-class eaters aspired to dining practices that emphasized modernity, elegance, and food selections that did not bear the historical taint of slave rations. I situate the maneuverings of members of this group within the wider context of other Progressive Era attempts at food reform, which were often coordinated by self-proclaimed "domestic scientists" intent on practicing culinary social engineering. I demonstrate that uplift-oriented black eaters drew inspiration from their white counterparts but inevitably had an ambivalent relationship with white activists who were steeped in racism, conscious and otherwise, and who promoted, among other things, a rigorous training program for domestic servants, an occupational role that few post-emancipation African Americans were willing to celebrate.

I then move, in chapter 2, "Booker T. Washington's Multifaceted Program for Food Reform at the Tuskegee Institute," to a particular case study of one uplift-oriented attempt to transform the black diet. In addition to preaching the "gospel" of using napkins and tablecloths, Washington micromanaged the dining plan for students and teachers at Tuskegee, advocating for their right to consume beef and wheat. These high-status food items served as symbols of Americanization that were in particularly short supply in a region where less coveted pork and cornmeal appeared, often to the exclusion of other foods, on regional dining tables. Washington encouraged the cultivation of performatively middle-class food practices both for the benefit of observers intent on gauging the status of black acculturation as well as for the private benefit of his students, whose bodies he hoped these foods would benefit. Washington, like the respectable eaters described in chapter 1, drew inspiration from white domestic scientists and the latest nutritional information of his day, but he subsumed the importance of following conventional dietary wisdom to the importance of black self-sufficiency. He advocated for an elastic food politics that would prepare his students for full incorporation into the U.S. nation-state, should the privileges of citizenship be forthcoming. At the same time, he also taught them to contemplate the possibility of black economic nationhood in the face of continued exclusion. Washington's fabled rival W. E. B. Du Bois shared his contemporary's belief that food was a tool of bodily, and by extension racial, elevation. Although the historical scholarship has seemed to endlessly explore the differences in the political philosophies and personalities of these two race leaders, it has tended to ignore some core similarities both in their ideas about proper racial food practices and in their own individual embodied experiences. Each man took his health seriously and ate thoughtfully as a way to protect himself from the potential physical degradations of white supremacy.

In chapter 3, "W. E. B. Du Bois, Respectable Child-Rearing, and the Representative Black Body," I examine Du Bois's food politics by closely scrutinizing the health-related advice he gave to his daughter, Yolande. This chapter demonstrates that Du Bois and many other middle-class race leaders, self-anointed or otherwise, took great pains to control their children's diets and to impart the significance of making thoughtful food choices. Du Bois considered black bodies, particularly those of the elite members of the black community, as exhibits of black equality and saw the task of preserving the black body as one not only of enormous individual concern but of significance to the advancement of the entire race.

Chapter 4, "Regionalism, Social Class, and Elite Perceptions of Working-Class Foodways during the Era of the Great Migration," explores the class tensions inherent in the middle-class project of reforming black food habits, demonstrating that working-class African Americans frequently did not share the certainty that foodways could be used as an avenue for citizenship and doubted many of the assumptions embedded in the project of cultural elevation subscribed to by black food reformers. One of the issues at the heart of the culinary tensions among members of the black community was the emerging question about whether there was a distinctive African American way of eating that was separate from mainstream American food culture. In the context of the Great Migration, "southern" food often became labeled "black" food in the northern cities that served as the terminus for black migrants. This transformation took place much to the consternation of black food reformers who, on the whole, resisted the idea of essential black cultural practices.

The carefully curated program for proper food behavior advocated by middle-class reformers faced an even greater challenge during the First World War. In chapter 5, "World War I, the Great Depression, and the Changing Symbolic Value of Black Food Traditions," I demonstrate that the push for voluntary rationing during the global conflict rendered foods like beef and wheat, which were once of enormous symbolic significance to black food reformers, as unpatriotic. Black food reformers had to choose between performing a U.S. patriotic food identity that demanded conservation and sacrifice and continuing to shun foods like pork and corn that were associated with the plantation South and thus with the history of slavery. Assimilationist eaters generally chose U.S. patriotism, a choice that inevitably muted some of the earlier antagonism that members of the middle class had shown toward the iconic southern foods they associated with the history of slavery. Ultimately, the economic pressures of the Great Depression worked to mute the machinations of even the most ardent food reformers as the community's emphasis shifted from what to eat to the even more dire problem of having enough to eat.

The last two chapters of the book look at transformations in the politics of African American food expression during the era of the civil rights movement. Chapter 6, "The Civil Rights Movement and the Ascendency of the Idea of a Racial Style of Eating" begins by examining the symbolic significance of the sit-ins at restaurants and lunch counters throughout the South as black protesters asserted their right to eat iconic American food items like hamburgers and to drink the symbolic beverage of Coca-Cola on equal terms with their fellow citizens. I find that at the same time that many demonstrators became disillusioned with the only partially fulfilled promises of the civil rights movement, the alternative concept of a black national culinary identity emerged in the form of "soul food." Southern food practices were rebranded as an essential black culinary production, and eating dishes like collard greens and chitterlings become a means of expressing fidelity to the idea of a stateless black nation. Yet, for some of the most ardent culinary nationalists, the concept of soul food later began to be seen as culturally and historically problematic. Beginning in the late 1960s, a new group of culinary radicals sought to distance themselves from the soul food tradition, which had become increasingly associated with bad health and open to criticism due to its linkages to the cuisine of slavery. In chapter 7, "Culinary Nationalism beyond Soul Food," I explore the culinary imagination of a new group of radical food reformers who advocated for the rejection of both traditional American foods and the soul food menu. Their largely vegetarian diet was designed to dissociate themselves from the foodways of slavery as well as from the ethos of domination associated with carnivorism. They hoped that their healthful eating practices would strengthen their bodies to prepare themselves for a concerted program of black nation building.

In aggregate, these stories of culinary reform, retrenchment, and negotiation serve as a reminder that historians' unconscious tendency to privilege public representation over private, felt experience brings with it the unintended consequence of distorting the way that historical subjects conceived of their own existence. The proceedings, position papers, typescript speeches, and other remnants of the quest for what was sometimes framed as racial advancement and at other times as racial revolution have been successfully used to create scores of compelling intellectual histories of activists who vied against white supremacy, as well as against each other, in their quest to change the contours of the American caste system. This study seeks to complement and complicate these narratives by following several generations of conscientious black eaters from the classroom or the convention hall to the dining room, from the field or the factory floor to the kitchen. In doing so, we discover that the physical work of nourishing their bodies was not incidental to the political work of social reform but rather a constituent component of the program of racial and national transformation. Through the process of making food decisions and through the bodily labor of digestion, African American food reformers were performing work that was both cultural and biological as they fought to reshape the world, beginning with their own bodies.

Creating the Foodways of Uplift

Mary Church Terrell, the daughter of a successful black businessman and the wife of a prominent lawyer and judge, could have afforded the luxury, rare in the African American community, of not having a professional occupation. However, her wide-ranging set of intellectual interests and a deeply felt sense of obligation to fight for social justice pushed her beyond the confines of the separate sphere. Prior to her marriage in 1891, Terrell worked as an educator at both Wilberforce University and the M Street High School. Later, she served as the first African American woman on the Washington, D.C., school board. She was also a charter member of the National Association for the Advancement of Colored People and the first president of the National Association of Colored Women. She took her public role as an activist and as a "race woman" seriously, devoting a vast amount of her time to giving lectures and writing essays advocating for full civil rights for both African Americans and women. Nonetheless, despite her tremendous professional obligations, Terrell still labored under the expectation that she was also responsible for ensuring the smooth operation of her household. She juggled her paid work and her activism with a belief that her most significant responsibilities were domestic ones. Before attending to other tasks, she believed that she first had to "discharge my duty to my family."[1] One of the primary obligations that women of Terrell's generation were beholden to was, of course, making sure that the members of their households were well fed.

Beginning at the age of six, Terrell attended boarding school and then continued her education until she earned a master's degree from Oberlin College. During the decades she was a student, she ate most of her meals in school cafeterias. While at home on vacation, she ate food prepared by a family cook who did not tolerate the presence of a curious young girl in the kitchen. Thus, upon reaching adulthood she still had very little exposure to the mechanics of shopping for ingredients or preparing a meal.[2] Well aware of the societal expectation that she should have mastery over the culinary realm during her married life, she made learning how to cook a top priority after her marriage.

Terrell privileged reading about the topic over direct observation. Her approach to learning the skill was not only indicative of her own predisposition toward formal education but also reflective of a historical moment when many well-educated women who had found it similarly impossible to cast off the gendered expectations of housekeeping sought to elevate their status by framing these tasks as a serious intellectual undertaking, as "domestic science." Not having the culinary folk wisdom of a mother or a grandmother to call upon, Terrell's method of self-training was self-consciously modern and scientific. She recalled that she "studied all the new notions," "made a business of keeping up with the housekeeping times," and attended lectures given by professional domestic scientist Sarah Tyson Rorer.[3] Terrell chose Thanksgiving as the moment for making her debut as a home cook, setting out to "set such a dinner before my husband as no experienced cook could surpass." It was no accident that she chose this symbolically significant meal, a ritual of American belonging, to perform simultaneously the social roles of citizen and wife.[4]

Although eventually Terrell became proficient in the kitchen, her first significant culinary undertaking was something of a disaster due to the fact that she did not know how to operate a cumbersome iron stove. After calling upon a friend for advice, she finally managed to get the holiday meal onto the table at ten o'clock in the evening, hours after she planned to serve it. Although she regarded her first attempt at cooking as rather an embarrassment, her menu choices reveal something about the kind of cook she would later become. Because she came of age as a cook at a moment when industrial foods were ascendant, it is unsurprising that Terrell turned to a product cookbook produced by Crisco shortening to help guide her.[5] She optimistically chose to make an ambitious-sounding dish called the "Queen of All Puddings," a choice that indicated her investment both in creating an elegant meal and in the new scientific cookery of the era. Her version of the dish, a popular lemon-flavored custard that was topped with meringue, utilized newly marketed Crisco shortening in place of the traditional butter.[6] This new factory-produced vegetable shortening was advertised as being "uniformly pure" and thus became a favorite among domestic scientists who advocated for a style of cooking that they described as being both hygienic and modern.[7] By choosing the recipe, Terrell was aligning herself with the sensibilities of those who endorsed industrial foods like Crisco as symbols of culinary progress.

Although Terrell floundered during this early cooking misadventure, in the future she was in the enviable position of being able to hire domestic servants to assist her. By employing help, Terrell was making a profound challenge to the stereotype of servile African Americans. Through her own example, she was able to unsettle white assumptions about caste demarcations and reframe servitude as a class issue as she ran a household where both the employers and the hired help were members of the same racial group. However, even when employing other people to assist with household tasks, Terrell never abdicated a sense of personal responsibility for overseeing the domestic chores, recalling, "There were numerous things about the home which, like other women, I had to attend to myself."[8] These chores included not only the work of cooking food in the kitchen but also the selection of the kinds of foods served in her household.

Terrell believed that proper dining choices were of far greater significance than just making sure the members of her household had adequate nourishment. Food choices were a reflection of status and values, and for that reason more than just particular menu items were on display during mealtime. When writing her autobiography in 1940, Terrell, who "dreaded having company like a toothache," still remembered with great shame failed dinner parties that had taken place decades previously.[9] For example, she recalled her overwhelming embarrassment when her cook served an oyster stew that "was so badly curdled it looked for all the world like dishwater" to the composer Samuel Coleridge-Taylor.[10] These missteps mattered because ultimately she could not make a firm distinction between her public work fighting for civil rights and her private work of making sure that her household functioned smoothly. Instead, she saw these tasks and her corresponding social roles as being intertwined. Terrell, like many other members of her social circle, staggered under expectations of personal perfection. Negligence in any of her undertakings, she believed, could reflect badly not only upon her but also upon other members of the race.

The Strategy of Racial Uplift

||||||||||||||||||||||||||||||||||||||||||||||||||||||

During the period of Jim Crow, many African Americans, like Terrell, regarded the realm of culture as an important facet of the struggle for civil rights and embarked on the uphill challenge of trying to convince white racists of their shared humanity. To use the parlance of this group, they strove to "uplift" their race, in part by adhering to strict standards of public decorum. Every decision that a "race man" or "race woman" made, ranging from sexual behavior, to styles of elocution, to recreational activities, to choices in clothing and personal hygiene, could be seen as an opportunity to demonstrate worthiness of first-class citizenship.[11] The dinner table is an underexamined but significant space where Mary Church Terrell and other middle-class African Americans could act out these codes of behavior, practicing what Evelyn Higginbotham refers to as "the politics of respectability."[12] For African American race leaders who could afford the luxury of some degree of dietary choice, decisions about personal consumption were not made individually or casually but with race-conscious care.

Given the virulence of racial animosity during the era, proponents of the politics of respectability must have suspected that they could not effectively blunt the impact of racism merely by adopting middle-class norms of behavior. Yet for those who desired assimilation and full national incorporation, the strategy of respectability could represent an optimistic alternative either to the perils of more overt forms of protest or to the defeat of acquiescence. As W. Fitzhugh Brundage notes, those who embraced the ethos of uplift "represented an assertion of the will and agency of blacks to define themselves."[13] This project of self-definition ultimately and perhaps also inevitably made a more lasting impression on the black community than upon the rest of society. The primary impact of the strategy of uplift was psychic, individual, and internal rather than structural, societal, and external. The performance of respectable behavior was more likely to influence the ability of an individual to cope with the trauma of racism than it was to affect either the power structure or white racial attitudes. Self-consciously respectable black Americans could, after all, exert control over their own actions, but they could not ensure that white society would notice their efforts or, if they were indeed paying attention, interpret them in the manner intended. However, even if the rewards of respectability were generally felt inwardly, the orientation of the practice was necessarily external as proponents of the philosophy sought to challenge—both for their own personal benefit and for the edification of others—the hurtful stereotypes that enveloped them.

Creating the Foodways of Uplift

Respectable eaters created their ideas about proper food behavior at least in part in response to the complex and often contradictory set of stereotypes about black food habits that permeated American culture in the late nineteenth and early twentieth centuries. They set out to challenge contradictory depictions of African Americans as either dim-witted but loyal servants or lazy, cunning food thieves. The agenda of uplift at the dinner table was similarly designed to counter ubiquitous representations of gluttonous black people with outsized appetites for watermelons and chickens as well as for foods like opossums or raccoons, which were associated with rural southern poverty and deemed loathsome by middle-class white consumers. These representations, which ranged from distorted images of cheerful, bandanna-wearing black cooks in advertisements to the performances of culinary racial difference by voracious eaters wearing blackface on the vaudeville stage, were designed to help make the case that African Americans were destined for subservience and irredeemably inferior. As a consequence they were considered unworthy of full citizenship rights.[14]

In order to counter these representations, respectable eaters hoped to demonstrate a sophisticated, scientific, and performatively American sensibility. They challenged the idea of a perpetually servile black population by advocating for an upwardly mobile style of eating that demonstrated cultural sophistication and class status. They defied the stereotype of black gluttony by approaching cooking and eating as intellectual tasks, designed to gratify the mind as well as the body. Furthermore, they confronted representations of black culinary inferiority and difference by culturally distancing themselves from the food habits of the enslaved and by asserting their right to consume modern, purportedly more hygienic industrial foods.

Domestic Science and the Limits of Interracial Cooperation

Because white cultural productions provided much of the animus for the foodways of uplift, it is somewhat ironic that white social reformers also provided some of the inspiration for African Americans' program of culinary self-improvement. Respectable eaters like Mary Church Terrell drew motivation both from the philosophy of racial uplift and from ideas of white Progressive Era reformers who also believed that the quest to change food habits could become an important dimension of a project for even greater social transformation. Just as black food reformers hoped that by improving their food habits they could unsettle some of the underpinnings of white supremacy, many white progressives similarly believed that if they could temper unruly personal appetites, they could also solve a variety of other social ills. Since tackling racism was seldom part of the agenda of white progressivism, there were limits to the nature of interracial alliances that could be built around the issue of food reform.[15] Occasionally black and white food reformers worked in tandem, but more frequently they worked on parallel food reform projects on opposite sides of the racial divide.

At the turn of the twentieth century, the most determined white food activists held a seemingly limitless faith in the idea that a proper diet not only could ensure the physical health of compliant eaters but also could improve their moral character. Dogged food reformers marshaled current knowledge about nutrition alongside their deeply held beliefs in their own culinary superiority to create the bland prescription diets they believed could cure alcoholism, save marriages, and prevent crime.[16] Jacob Riis, the muckraking author of the 1890 landmark book *How the Other Half Lives: Studies among the Tenements of New York*, was one who thought that proper food habits could cure alcoholism, which he believed was rampant in poor communities. He claimed that a cooking class was the "best temperance sermon."[17] White domestic scientist Sarah Tyson Rorer, whose lectures played a large role in Mary Church Terrell's culinary training, concurred, maintaining that the "hankering of the ill-fed stomach drives men to drink."[18] Allegedly, indifferently prepared meals could also imperil domestic stability. Legendary settlement house worker Jane Addams recalled a tearful interview with a woman whose husband allegedly planned to leave her because of her lackluster domestic skills. Six months after enrolling in a cooking course she reported having created a "united and happy home" on the basis of improving her cooking competence alone.[19] Cooking instructor Pearl Idelia Ellis imbued food habits with even more power over individual behavior, warning that improper diets would result in laziness and poor study habits in children whose malnourished bodies would tempt them into participating in criminal activities.[20]

Members of white ethnic groups found themselves on the receiving end of much of the culinary proselytizing of the era. Food reformers not only promised that improved diets would heal sick bodies and troubled souls but also argued that proper food behavior was a mandatory prerequisite of American citizenship. For example, Addams praised the potential that culinary training had to help recent arrivals assimilate into U.S. culture. "An Italian girl who has had lessons in cooking at the public school,"

Creating the Foodways of Uplift

claimed Addams, "will help her mother to connect the entire family with American food and household habits."[21] Progressive Era reformers situated this training in proper food behavior at the front line of their effort to transform immigrant families into "American" families.

In 1890, a group of Bostonian activists embarked on one of the most ambitious attempts to Americanize the palates and later, it was hoped, the rest of the bodies of recent immigrants when they founded the New England Kitchen. This establishment sold inexpensive meals that were designed to ameliorate working-class poverty and to encourage recent arrivals to radically change their food habits, replacing dishes from their countries of origin with Yankee cuisine, such as oatmeal, beef broth, and Boston baked beans. The Anglo-American diet that they viewed as a vehicle of assimilation was a bland one and served as a metaphor for the transformation they hoped immigrants would make as they became neutral and inoffensive members of the nation who could compliantly blend into the "melting pot."[22] Because most of the reformers who sought to Americanize newcomers were mired in racism that depicted African Americans as unassimilable, black Americans were seldom the target of these efforts at culinary outreach. Nonetheless, many black food reformers derived inspiration from the core idea of these initiatives, which claimed that food habits could be used as a means of performing nationhood and of asserting their rights to belong as first-class American citizens.

Increasingly, many food reformers, both white and black, began to label themselves as "domestic scientists," a wistful and hyperbolic phrase designed to frame cooking and the other mundane chores of housekeeping as intellectual and skilled undertakings. According to Helen Zoe Veit, this posturing language also enabled women to conceive of their efforts as "vital public service, crucial to the health of American citizens and the American nation."[23] The language of domestic science allowed women to claim membership in a respectable profession whose efforts were of great personal and also civic significance, and they could do so without ever completely leaving the separate domestic sphere. As we have seen, even professional women, like Mary Church Terrell, felt tremendous social pressure to juggle their careers alongside a nonnegotiable commitment to a variety of domestic responsibilities.

Massachusetts Institute of Technology domestic science instructor Ellen Swallow Richards and others hoped to offer their students strategies for managing both roles as they offered them intellectual validation and practical skills. Although Richards was by all accounts a true believer in the importance of scientific domestic training, it is worth noting that she could not have become a faculty member at MIT teaching any other subject. She was able to insinuate herself into the all-male enclave of MIT only because she was willing to couch her interest in chemistry in the gendered language of household chores, something she did ably in her 1881 book, *The Chemistry of Cooking and Cleaning*.[24] For understandable reasons, the fact that Richards and others were able to use domestic science as an unlikely tool to fight against discrimination and exclusion offered a compelling example to black food reformers, who also hoped to break down societal barriers.

White food reformers acted out of a variety of motivations, which ranged from the altruistic, though intrusive, goal of helping working-class immigrants better themselves to more self-centered ones. Not only did some advocate for the professionalization of domestic science because the enterprise created jobs for the middle-class women who could teach the subject, but also others hoped to establish domestic science training programs in the hope that such efforts might rectify a shortage of household servants, thus decreasing their own gender-specific homemaking burdens.

For example, the Women's Educational and Industrial Union, which was founded in Boston in 1877 to promote the "educational, industrial, and social advancement" of women, worked both to scientifically train domestic servants and to find employment opportunities for them. Would-be domestic servants and motivated homemakers could sign up for an extensive training program where they would learn the latest techniques of household management. Graduates could take advantage of the services of the organization's Domestic Reform League, which hoped to match potential employers with domestic workers. From the perspective of the middle-class members of the organization, the "servant problem," as the shortage of household help was known in the parlance of the day, was particularly severe in Boston.[25] For example, between April 1 and August 1, 1907, the union members in charge of job placement were able to fill only 28 percent of the requests they received for cooks.[26] Despite the dearth of willing domestic employees, organizers of the Domestic Reform League were surprised to discover that white Bostonians were reluctant to hire black servants. The organization was able to secure positions for only about half of the black women on its roster who were seeking work assignments, a fact that highlights the difficulties black food reformers had in embarking on interracial projects of culinary uplift during an era of extreme racism.[27]

In the context of the time, the Domestic Reform League, in trying to place black domestic employees in positions, however unsuccessfully, was notable for its attempts to transcend racial barriers. White progressive reform efforts often excluded the needs of the black working class. This was largely true of the settlement movement, which included dietary reform in its mission to help assimilate white immigrants during the late nineteenth and early twentieth centuries. Settlement houses provided beneficiaries with wide-ranging support, including a variety of educational and recreational programs and assistance in securing necessities such as health care and childcare. Although working-class African Americans could certainly have benefited from these services, Elizabeth Lasch-Quinn claims that white reformers excluded them because they saw "African American culture as severely deficient" and thus beyond the purview of their assimilationist mission. Whether attributed to innate racial characteristics or interpreted as the outgrowth of the deprivations of slavery, these perceived cultural differences meant that black people were seldom aided alongside disadvantaged whites.[28] Because they were excluded from or poorly served by many white progressive food reformers, black food activists worked to create their own institutions, generally relying on the progressive movement for intellectual inspiration rather than for tactical support.

Uplift through Scientific Housekeeping

Motta Simms, who served as a director of the food department at the Tuskegee Institute, was one black food reformer who used her training in domestic science to try to create opportunities for black students who were underserved by white initiatives. A graduate of Spelman College, she also held a degree in home economics from Fisk University and a graduate degree in the field from Columbia University. In the 1930s she devised a program to train highly skilled black cooks who she hoped could transcend the barriers of discrimination and secure jobs not only as domestic servants but also in better-paying professional kitchens.[29] While designing her curriculum, she visited "the new, most modern White House kitchens . . . and leading hotels, tea-rooms, and dining rooms" seeking inspiration. By modeling her efforts after those of the White House, she implicitly considered herself and those she trained as first-class citizens. By shrinking the distance between the test kitchens at a small black college in rural Alabama and the well-equipped and generously funded kitchens used to create meals for the first family and their illustrious guests, she made a claim for equal culinary citizenship.

Emphasizing the political potential of culinary work, Simms and other black food reformers promoted programs in nutrition and cooking, which were sponsored by educational institutions, churches, and civic organizations. These educational and vocational training courses were the natural outgrowth of a widespread community interest in education that manifested itself most intently beginning in the Reconstruction Era but predated it as well.[30] Because enslaved people were forbidden to learn to read during the antebellum era, literacy became a symbol of freedom, and the importance of educational opportunities became a unifying value among members of the black community throughout the class and ideological spectrums.

Vocational training in the art and science of cooking also melded particularly well with the ascendency of the industrial training movement in the late nineteenth and early twentieth centuries. Proponents of industrial education designed curricula to educate working-class children who had been forced out of the workplace due to new regulations restricting child labor.[31] Traditionally, formal schooling had been devised to develop the cultural literacy of students, but increasingly intellectual pursuits were framed as the provenance of those who could afford the luxury of contemplation. As Sol Cohen explains, advocates of industrial education argued that "for the children of the masses[,] the whole system of public education had to be reshaped along vocational lines to help them better adjust to the life they were destined to lead."[32] This rationale appealed to progressive reformers who wished to alleviate some of the harshness of poverty while still supporting the status quo. Graduates of vocational programs were theoretically prepared to find steady employment that would sustain them without giving them the opportunity to advance beyond their class station. Although many progressives excluded African Americans from their charity work initiatives, many still regarded them as ideal candidates for vocational training.[33] Fearful of post-emancipation idle black hands, they reasoned that freed people could participate in industrial training as a path toward slightly improving their skill set and their economic outlook without seriously disrupting the caste and class structure.

Black supporters of the domestic science curriculum capitalized on the belief that members of their community were good candidates for industrial education and appealed frequently for financial support from the proliferating number of governmental entities and philanthropists who endorsed hands-on training as a way to create a working class that had both useful skills and modest ambitions. For example, Booker T.

Creating the Foodways of Uplift

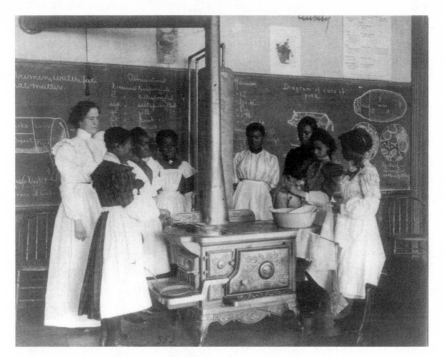

African American students learning to cook in Washington, D.C., ca. 1899.
(Photo by Frances Benjamin Johnston; Library of Congress LC-USZ62–26380)

Washington, founding principal of the Tuskegee Institute, became well known for his ability to extract donations from white donors who supported his institution's programs in industrial education. Unable to meet operating expenses with either tuition funds or the scant support offered by the institution's home state of Alabama, Washington kept the institution afloat through his skillful and constant fund-raising efforts. For example, in the 1914–15 school year he managed to erase the institution's severe budget deficit after securing $188,506.29 in donations.[34] Through adept maneuvering, Washington and other proponents of industrial education could frame their efforts as being modest and practical while they subversively embraced, as in the case of domestic science, the intellectual dimensions of their pursuits.

Uplift eaters effectively straddled this divide, framing food reform as both practical and intellectual. Respectable eating held broad appeal both for black supporters of industrial training and for critics who favored a more diverse array of educational opportunities. As a result, black women could enroll in domestic science courses at the famed Hampton and

Tuskegee Institutes, which proudly identified with the tradition of industrial education, as well as at historically black liberal arts colleges and universities such as Fisk and Spelman, institutions that prided themselves in the intellectual and professional development of their students rather than in providing practical, occupational skills.

Although courses in domestic science proliferated and were sponsored by a wide variety of black civic organizations and educational institutions, some race leaders were ambivalent about the value of these programs, fearing that white Americans might not be able to differentiate between a college-educated black domestic scientist and a black domestic servant. In her autobiography, Mary Church Terrell offered one model for how a middle-class black woman might endeavor to manifest an interest in domestic science while also refuting the idea that black people constituted a class of perpetual servants. Terrell was, of course, an educated woman who made no qualms about her intellectual interest in scientific cooking, a pursuit she considered different from mere domestic drudgery, which she hired domestic servants to help her perform. W. E. B. Du Bois, a well-known skeptic of the virtues of industrial education, was worried that the nuances of such a position might be lost upon white observers and thus had reservations about the wisdom of advocating for domestic science training programs. He doubted that training African Americans to become even better servants could lead to opportunities for social or economic advancement. He noted with despair that in U.S. society, "Negro and 'servant'" were "synonymous terms," and he expressed his fear that servant training programs, however lofty the language they used to describe the tasks of housekeeping, would do little to challenge this association. Given the paucity of job opportunities for African Americans, Du Bois ultimately supported the idea of training programs for servants, hoping against hope that such programs might elevate the skill set and thus the social status and pay grade of the graduates. However, he was adamant there should be nothing racially exclusive about these initiatives and wanted domestic science training programs for servants to serve as a racial equalizer, ushering in a day when "both blacks and whites [could] enter more freely into service without a fatal and disheartening loss of self-respect."[35]

Despite these understandable misgivings that even college-level domestic science programs served merely as training programs for servants, most black food reformers ultimately embraced the idea of domestic science as a possible tool for racial elevation. At the very least, the jargon of scientific cooking offered a means of challenging the pernicious stereotype that black people cooked by instinct while white people were better suited to scientific culinary training.[36] Respectable black eaters sought to emphasize the fact that reason guided their food choices, not some mystical and racialized culinary instinct. Correspondingly, supporters of domestic science programs were careful to accentuate the fact that cooking skills and food knowledge were not inborn racial attributes but rather the outgrowth of research and training, which benefited black and white pupils equally.[37]

Although the vast majority of black Americans, including those who worked in domestic service and those who worked in other occupations, did not receive formal training in the subject, interest in the principles of scientific housekeeping became widespread within and outside the academic realm. Culinary reformers urged consumers to scrutinize their eating habits more closely, a development that led to a growing demand for what became labeled "pure food." In the late nineteenth century, Harvey Wiley, director of the Chemical Division of the U.S. Department of Agriculture, began campaigning for federal legislation outlawing the adulteration of manufactured food products, which were frequently contaminated by poisonous preservatives and inexpensive fillers. Aided by the popularity of Upton Sinclair's gruesome exposé of the practices of the meatpacking industry, which was published in novel form as *The Jungle* in 1906, "pure food" advocates declared legislative victory when the Pure Food and Drug Act, which outlawed the sale of adulterated foods in interstate commerce, was passed that same year.[38] Ironically, "pure food" legislation actually worked to benefit industrial food companies, some of which had actually been guilty of selling adulterated products.[39] Capitalizing on the mood of the moment, manufacturers seized on the popularity of the pure food campaign to promote their products, claiming that food produced in factories was free from the contaminating impact of the human hands that handled food prepared in smaller-scale operations. These large companies often enlisted well-known cooking school instructors like Sarah Tyson Rorer to endorse their products, and they created product cookbooks, such as the Crisco pamphlet Mary Church Terrell used to make the "Queen of All Puddings," to tout their wares.

"Purity" became a stand-in word for foods that were produced outside of the home and were thus, at least theoretically, subject to federal regulation. Processed foods developed in laboratories and made in factories using the latest equipment were depicted as modern, optimally nutritious, and high-status. According to Aaron Bobrow-Strain, the food reformers' creed stated that "industrial food is pure food, and pure food is the foundation of social progress."[40] Pure food reformers set out to aid Americans in creating meals that not only would demonstrate scientific sophistication but also would reflect concomitant ideas about American progress, which was thought to be driven by technological prowess.

African American adherents to the strategy of uplift enthusiastically joined in the conversation about pure food, publicly championing contemporary ideas about modern and scientific eating. The 1914 Negro Yearbook labeled "pure food" one of its "three graces of health" and furthered the reigning fascination with the idea of "purity" by adding pure air and pure water to its list of necessities.[41] In an obvious response to reader interest in the subject, the Chicago Defender and other key black newspapers dispensed seemingly endless advice about housekeeping and health concerns, urging readers to eat thoughtfully, slowly, and hygienically.[42] A Defender editorial in favor of pure food and improved hygiene in poor neighborhoods ominously warned, "The farmer who neglects to clean his milk cans endangers the lives of children fifty miles away." The author claimed that it was up to individual citizens to stop the infanticidal farmer by supporting pure food reform efforts designed to protect "the state's most valuable possession—the lives of the children."[43]

According to the evangelists for pure food, the best way to clean up the food supply was to shift the responsibility for distributing hygienic foods from the farmer to the laboratory. Thus, African American students at the Tuskegee Institute were expected not only to advocate for but also to learn how to produce scientifically sound, pure foods. Two photographs in an article written by Booker T. Washington titled "Twenty-Five Years of Tuskegee" illustrate how the institute hoped to equip their students to become modern food preparers. A photo of a smiling elderly African American woman wearing humble, homemade clothing is captioned "An Old Negro Cook Whose small income is spent in dues to burial society" is contrasted with the image of a young Tuskegee student wearing a bright starched uniform and placing a syringe inside a beaker of milk. The caption proclaims that she is "learning the principles of hygiene and the use of pure food."[44] Tuskegee prided itself in offering the training necessary to transform old-fashioned farmers and cooks into scientists who would pave the way for racial advancement.[45]

In an age that prided itself on technological innovation, new ways of doing things were considered to be positive reflections on the progress of the nation. In their quest for the factory-created purity promised by indus-

Creating the Foodways of Uplift

trial food producers, domestic scientists proudly used canned and store-bought ingredients, rapidly accelerating the distance between the producers and consumers of the food that was to increase decade by decade in the twentieth century and creating an identity for themselves and those who followed their culinary advice as modern eaters. By enthusiastically adopting these new methods, African American reformers could make a case for fuller incorporation into the U.S. nation-state.

Subversively, by claiming the mantle of "purity" during an era when the pseudoscience of eugenics had rendered them racially impure, African Americans could also use their food habits to challenge the underpinning of the entire social order. As Angela Jill Cooley argues, for many white people, "pure" food took on a racial dimension as food "fit for white consumption."[46] When white consumers demanded pure products, they did so to preserve and perform their superior racial status. When black consumers made the same demands for "purity," they were also working to disempower the idea that only white bodies could be pure, and when black bodies absorbed "pure" foods, they were symbolically laying claim to some of the privileges of whiteness. However, an unspoken truth behind black endorsements of "pure" food was that relatively affluent, urban African Americans had the greatest access to the factory-produced foods that signified modernity and cleanliness in the contemporary imagination. Thus, in the end, it was primarily members of the black middle class who could aspire to ingest the symbolic privileges of food purity.

Many black reformers, including Mary Church Terrell, found additional reasons to support the idea of food purity while participating in contemporary discussions about "euthenics," a corollary philosophy to eugenics. While eugenics emphasized selective procreation for the sake of optimizing desirable characteristics in the gene pool, euthenics, in the words of one of its more outspoken proponents, Ellen Swallow Richards, stressed "developing better men now" through improved living conditions.[47] According to Richards, improving the quality and cleanliness of the food supply offered one of the most important dimensions of the path for immediate self-improvement, and by extension national improvement. She warned that unclean food could lead not only to actual disease but also to "lowered vitality" and "lessened work power," conditions that, when multiplied across the entire citizenry, damaged the hope of national progress and prominence.[48] Understandably, these ideas resonated with the idea of uplift, adding the veneer of a universalizing science to a racially specific program for bodily elevation already in place.[49] Although African

Americans, due to their alleged racial inferiority, were excluded from the future utopia offered by white eugenicists intent on developing an idealized population pool, they could openly attach themselves to the project of immediate self-improvement offered by euthenics. Those who wished to transform their food habits in order to make a better case for their worthiness for first-class citizenship could be heartened by Richards's claim that "indifference of the people is today the only stumbling block to national prosperity."[50] Thus respectable eaters could imagine themselves as both uplifting the race and enhancing the future prospects of the U.S. nation-state.

The mandate of respectability bolstered by the doctrine of euthenics empowered members of the black community to see their domestic skills not only as a way to care for their families and fight stereotypes about black cultural inferiority but also as a means of contributing to the well-being of the entire nation. The idea that taking care of one's own body and one's own family was a form of national service was a profound one that contributed to the undercurrent of annoyance many felt at the perpetual association of African Americans and servitude. Du Bois captured middle-class frustration about this mindset in his novel *The Quest of the Silver Fleece.* The narrative chronicles the struggles faced by the founder of a southern school for black pupils who has to circumvent local white interference in her educational mission as she tries to secure funding for the institute. When a group of planters and northern white philanthropists comes to visit the school, they demonstrate only a tepid interest in her work. Although they arrive for their scheduled visit late and leave early, they do, however, briefly linger in the cooking department. One of the visitors conjectures that the school must supply the majority of cooks for the county. The school's administrator responds to this guess affirmatively, saying, "Largely . . . the county, you know, is mostly black."[51] The white observers are incapable of understanding her implication that the cooks trained at the school use the skills they learn to make food for themselves and their families, not just for the local southern aristocracy. In carefully preparing foods in their own homes, black cooks continuously challenged the unthinking white assumption that black people existed to serve the white population and did not have dietary needs or preferences of their own.

Performing Race and Class in the Kitchen

IIIIIIIIIIIIIIIIIIIIIIIIIIIIIIIIIIIIIIIIIIIIIIIIIIIIIIIIIIIIIIIIIIIIIIII

Aware of these assumptions, many black women felt tremendous pressure to excel in their domestic responsibilities. Messages urging women to take these tasks seriously were widespread. Writing in the *Chicago Defender* in 1915, Mrs. F. Fletcher dramatically proclaimed that "the economical, scientific, and artistic housewife is the greatest woman in the world." Mindful that race women often participated in a number of social and charitable activities, she admonished them to remember that their families should be their first priority: "Into whatever field of labor our women may go, and whatever her social duties, she remembers that her first duty is to manage the cooking and her home."[52] Those who followed Mrs. Fletcher's advice hoped that by serving family meals that were both scientifically sound and elegant, they were benefiting their race and their nation. However, they also made dining decisions that they hoped would shore up the health of themselves and their families. Although some discussions about proper food behavior were public and thus could be constructed in part for the benefit of the white public who might, inadvertently or otherwise, stumble across these conversations, family meal times were also private affairs. Respectable eaters endeavored to feed their families meals that they regarded as nutritious, modern, and hygienic, even when no one was watching. Dining performances not only could serve as important public rituals but also were embedded with important private meanings. Those who saw food practices as a marker of assimilation and an important rite of citizenship could perform an American identity at their own dinner table if they wished, free from immediate discrimination and the scrutiny of naysayers.

Members of the rarefied group who could afford the time to cook thoughtfully or the resources necessary to hire help could also aspire to serve meals designed not only to fuel the bodies of those who consumed them but also to feed their own sense of cultural equality with, if not superiority to, those would denigrate black food habits and table etiquette. Historian Glenda Gilmore notes that Sarah Dudley Pettey, an 1883 graduate of Scotia Seminary for women and the wife of an African Methodist Episcopal bishop, used the table in her North Carolina home to reflect the couple's social standing as she served elegant foods such as "roast bear, lobster cutlets, and Russian salad with sauce tartare and provided finger bowls."[53] Food studies scholar Psyche Williams-Forson similarly notes that Charlotte Hawkins Brown and other black educators of her ilk used food in an attempt to "impress upon the larger society that black women were indeed 'ladies' of decorum and manners, worthy of societal respect, honor, and nationhood."[54] Thus Brown advocated for polite dinner conversation, aesthetically pleasing meals, and delicacy when handling messy foods, such as those containing bones or seeds.[55] According to Brown, the ideal meals for guests included items from the domestic science canon. She suggested, for example, "Stuffed Tomatoes in Aspic," a classic dish that appeared, among other places, in Fannie Farmer's famous *Boston Cooking-School Cook Book* as a perfect dish for a buffet luncheon.[56] In general, Brown's meal plans called for fussy items like bonbons and canapés as well as various dishes that were "decorated," "frosted," or (her favorite descriptor) "stuffed."[57] Although Brown's culinary suggestions did always take economy into account, for many respectable eaters the dictates of culinary uplift reigned even when finances were strained. Sisters Sarah and Elizabeth Delany reported that they "took great pride in preparing and serving meals for company." They recalled that "while we didn't have the best china, you'd be surprised with what you can do with fresh flowers and pressed linens." They took such pride in entertaining in as elegant a style as their income would allow that they kept a journal recording what they had served at each meal so as to avoid repeating dishes twice for the same guest.[58]

African American recipe writers often described various foods prepared and eaten by black diners as "dainty," a term that could readily be applied to Charlotte Hawkins Brown's meal suggestions. Laura Shapiro decodes "dainty," a description commonly used by the most aesthetically minded domestic scientists, arguing that it "was used to temper any implication of drudgery and to give housework an important boost upward on the social scale."[59] During an era when white society denied black women the status afforded to middle-class white women, who were depicted as being innately virtuous and delicate, it is understandable that columnists for black newspapers would wish to challenge this disregard by publishing numerous "dainty" recipes, which could be used to highlight the feminine attributes of black women while also offering the reminder that black people were consumers of fine foods and not merely the servants who prepared them. "Dainty" eaters could enjoy painstakingly elaborate foods and still avoid the stereotype of black gluttony. Dainty foods, because they were prepared with care by someone with the time to devote to their preparation, were always considered to be delicate markers of an elevated class station regardless of their calorie count.

A 1908 recipe for "Dainty Potatoes" in the *Washington Bee* instructed its class-conscious readers about how to make a showy version of mashed potatoes. The recipe dictated that portions of potato should be molded into small spheres, and each orb should be carefully inserted into a lettuce cup and then garnished with sliced eggs and parsley.[60] This dish was designed to elevate eating beyond that of bare necessity, transforming it into an act of creativity that exemplified a sense of refinement and leisure. "Dainty Potatoes" and other fussy and labor-intensive dishes were among the most prized dishes on the uplift table. Dishes like this could be decoded to reveal a great deal about the eater. Not only did "Dainty Potatoes" signify that the eater had the time and resources to adorn a plain food for the sake of enjoyment, but the dish also called upon many of the most popular, domestic science–approved cooking and serving techniques of the day. It was bland enough not to alarm proponents of an insipid and homogeneous American style of eating, and it featured favorite contemporary cooking and serving techniques. Cookbooks like Fannie Farmer's iconic *Boston Cooking-School Cook Book* often endorsed garnishes that would alter the appearance of simple foods without vastly changing their flavor. Farmer's book contains no shortage of uses for embellishments like lettuce leaves, parsley, and boiled eggs.[61]

"Dainty" foods and self-consciously modern foods were important in the uplift diet because they offered direct challenges to what many regarded as the backward-looking cuisine of slavery. When creating the uplift cuisine they would serve both at home and in public, respectable eaters had to engage with a constant dialogue between the modern, domestic science–approved way of eating they aspired to and the past of slavery, when most African Americans were forced to make the most of limited and repetitive rations. Just as the black middle class was loath to see blackness and servitude conflated in the white imagination, they were also mindful of the ramifications of endorsing a style of eating that would bring with it reminders of a past they hoped to transcend (if their ancestors were enslaved) or dissociate themselves from (if they were not).

For this reason, uplift-oriented eaters were always more likely to reference Massachusetts than Mississippi in formal dinner settings. In 1911, Rosa Richardson of Baltimore hosted a dinner to honor members of the black fraternal organization the Order of Calanthe, where she served fried chicken, a food associated with southern cooking and thus, in the minds of many uplift-oriented eaters, with slavery. Although most enslaved people would have eaten such a delicacy only rarely, by the twentieth century fried chicken was becoming a powerful signifier of a racially specific style of eating. The popular culture of the era was rife with caricatured images of black people stealing and relishing the bird, a state of affairs that later led Williams-Forson to label the "historical relationship between chicken and black people . . . [as] one of the many linchpins of white racist propaganda that claimed black inferiority."[62] Given these negative associations coupled with her continuing desire to serve poultry to her guests, Richardson endeavored to serve the popular dish while still adhering to the dictates of respectable eating. She distanced herself from the potential implications of embracing a food item associated with the South and with slavery by serving it, according to her menu, "Boston style."[63] Although Richardson did not leave any clues behind explaining how fried chicken from New England allegedly differed from its southern cousin, she clearly hoped that this geographical reorientation would also neutralize negative stereotypes about a black obsession with this food item. She was not the only resident of Baltimore to attempt to remove fried chicken from its regional culinary roots. A 1931 article in the *Baltimore Afro-American* containing suggestions for a Fourth of July menu recommended the dish for the occasion, claiming, "So many sections of the country lay first claim to fried chicken and gravy as their traditional best dish . . . that with continental migration it has become the popular sectional treat everywhere."[64] Thus fried chicken was reimagined as a national and not a regional specialty, as a universal rather than a racially specific meal, which was also a patriotic dish suitable for a celebration of the nation's origins.

While some attempted to rebrand symbolically potent foods like fried chicken to make them suitable for the uplift table, others avoided—at least publicly—consuming foods negatively associated with the South or with purported black taste sensibilities. Harlem Renaissance luminary Claude McKay dramatized respectable anxiety over consuming such foods in his 1928 novel *Home to Harlem* through the character of a New York–based chef who "had a violent distaste for all the stock things that 'coons' are supposed to like to the point of stealing them." In his mind, the negative cultural work performed by foods like fried chicken could not be undone by attempts to unmoor them from southern regional cooking.[65] His efforts to dissociate himself from white stereotypes of larcenous black people with huge appetites meant that "he would not eat watermelon, because white folks called it 'the niggers' ice cream.' Pork chops he fancied not. Nor corn

Creating the Foodways of Uplift

pone. And the idea of eating chicken gave him a spasm."[66] A 1928 article appearing in the *Baltimore Afro-American* gave scientific and not just cultural validation to the dietary preferences of McKay's chef. The headline unambiguously proclaimed, "Poor Diet Causes High Death Rate: Pork, Greasy Foods, Cornbread, Peas Constitute Faulty Diet."[67] Thus respectable eaters not only were told that they risked giving credence to racial stereotypes if they dined on southern food but also were warned they might be irreparably damaging their bodies if they indulged in the iconic dishes of southern regional cuisine.

The combined factors of white stereotypes claiming that black people had coarse, oversized appetites and the fear that eating too much of the wrong foods might sicken black bodies meant that McKay's chef and many other respectable eaters viewed hunger with caution. Because uplift-oriented African Americans worried that wrong food choices could reinforce racist ideas about black consumption patterns, they generally wished to emphasize discernment and denial rather than the sensual pleasure of food. Nannie Helen Burroughs, a staunch proponent of bodily restraint as a tool for racial improvement, founded the National Training School for Women and Girls in Washington, D.C., in 1909 in order to provide vocational training for black women who lacked other educational opportunities. She used her platform as the director of the school to preach the "Gospel of the Bible, Bath, and Broom," arguing that "life should not be reduced to meat and drinks, gluttony . . . social vice and intemperance." Instead, she proclaimed, "The sanctity of the body must be preached by the Negro Church as the basis of morality and the best expression of an efficient religion. It must teach that taking care of the body is as much a part of religion as faith and trust in God."[68] Thus for Burroughs, the stakes of disciplining the body were especially high, transcending both the temporal fight against racism and the earthly need to nourish physical bodies and entering into the spiritual realm. Controlling one's appetite was both a worldly and otherworldly obligation, a duty that served the individual, the race, and—most important—God.[69]

To emphasize the significance of spiritual needs over bodily ones, students at the National Training School had to attend Sunday school *before* breakfast. Burroughs managed to convert at least one freshman to the wisdom of this kind of reprioritization. This acolyte cheerfully proclaimed, "I didn't know I could have so much religion before breakfast and really enjoy it."[70] However, even those students who did not instinctively approve of Burroughs's culinary regime were forced to prioritize both their studies and church attendance above meeting any but the most minimal of dietary needs. Students were required to come to the school's dining room "on time or not at all" and upon arrival were granted only half an hour to eat.[71] This emphasis on quick and minimal food consumption was reinforced by the school's extensive domestic science curriculum, which taught students about the essential nutritional components of individual foods, forbade eating between meals, and generally encouraged them to see food as a functional necessity to be consumed in moderation rather than as a source of hedonistic pleasure.[72]

Burroughs was hardly the only proponent of respectable food practices to advocate for eating selectively and not too much, a strategy designed to vanquish the specter of the black glutton. A 1915 column in the *Chicago Defender* warned, "More people are killed in this country by over-eating than by starvation."[73] Elizabeth Delany, who had been born in North Carolina in 1891 and later became the second woman licensed to practice dentistry in New York State, performed her respectability not in terms of what she consumed but rather by abstention. As a centenarian, she proudly declared, "I have never been *drunk* in my life."[74] Others used food practices to keep their dignity intact by tightly controlling not only what they ate but also where. To avoid the humiliation of being denied food service, being forced to order food from a back window, or being relegated to takeout or outside seating, African Americans who traveled during the Jim Crow era were certain to pack ample food supplies so that they could provide for their own needs and avoid having their dignity trampled upon in the sphere of public dining.[75] In so doing, they managed to meet their bodily needs for sustenance without allowing white observers to watch them scramble for food amid degrading circumstances. The physical appetite was not allowed to supersede the demands of maintaining personal dignity.

It is important to note that respectable eaters not only sought to control the ravages of the appetite to challenge the presumptions of white racists and to bolster the health of their individual bodies but also made particular food choices as a way to send messages about their status and values to other members of the black community. Ironically, at the same time that food practices were used to minimize racial distinctions, they were also utilized to help draw class boundaries within the community. When Mary Church Terrell set up a system of respectable housekeeping, she anticipated being observed by whites intent on finding evidence of racial inferiority and also by working-class members of the black community. Terrell became the first president of the National Association of Colored

Women in 1896, an organization that adopted "Lifting as We Climb" as its motto and rationale for the efforts of middle-class members of the organization who hoped to influence working-class members of their community to adopt the particular tenets of their program of cultural elevation. Although uplift-oriented eaters hoped to transform the black community by virtue of their good examples, the performance of respectability was often more effective at drawing intraracial class demarcations than it was at chipping away at racial barriers. As Kevin Gaines points out, although the philosophy of uplift was, on one hand, geared at "collective social aspiration" aimed at improving the lot of the entire race, the ideology often became mired in a kind of class warfare perpetuated by a "racialized elite" who sometimes portrayed "class stratification as race progress."[76]

While working-class African Americans like those whom Nannie Helen Burroughs attempted to train were sometimes told to rein in their appetites, more elite members of the black community were often given the collective permission to indulge theirs as a means of demonstrating their sophistication and status. Novelist Dorothy West, who was born into Boston's small black upper middle class in 1907, explored turn-of-the-twentieth-century African American food practices that were primarily designed to erect class barriers in *The Living Is Easy*, a novel set in Boston.[77] The status-conscious character Cleo Judson attempts to demonstrate her social worth not by abstaining from too much food but by serving elegant food to a carefully curated list of guests. Cleo had begun her life as an impoverished member of the black working class, but in the course of the book she marries a black businessman who had made a small fortune by cornering the market on bananas. Due to his shrewd ability to manage his grocery business, he is able to grant her access to a life of material comforts, which she utilizes to perform a new class identity.

Intent upon impressing her guests, Cleo hosts an elegant party with a feast that evokes the city of Boston, where she lived as an adult, instead of the southern cuisine of her childhood home. The table was laden with "a large boiled lobster, its meat removed and replaced." The meal not only contained high status food items but was also elaborately staged: "A grapefruit, dotted all over with toothpicks, the ends of which were capped with diced ham and tongue, had been placed at one end of a platter, and at the other a large cucumber, pricked with toothpicks to resemble a porcupine, lay lengthwise, its scooped-out center filled with red seafood sauce."[78]

The cucumber porcupine and the other carefully staged dishes that she served at the party were not designed to persuade white society of black equality. Instead, her close attention to detail was meant to impress the members of the black bourgeoisie who attended the event. West's characterization of how her upwardly mobile protagonist leveraged showy displays of food in the name of social advancement indicates a multifaceted politics of respectability. Not only were respectable food practices designed to gain white acknowledgment of black humanity and refinement and to increase the health and sense of self-worth of the respectable eater, but they also served the function of working to establish one's social status within the black community. In a social world where gaining white approval for one's actions was unlikely, members of the small black middle class often looked inward, toward other members of the community, for approbation. Indeed, throughout the era of uplift, members of the aspirational or actual black middle class paid a great deal of attention to what they ate and how it was served in order to preserve their own class status at the same time that they used these tactics for the more amorphous goal of fighting against racism.

The elaborate meals served at black social and political gatherings throughout the era were designed to serve the multifaceted agenda of uplift. These feasts were frequently described in great detail in black newspapers so that those who were not privy to such repasts could still have the satisfaction of vicarious enjoyment and elevation. For example, readers of the *Colored American* were given a detailed account of the menu served at a 1903 dinner in honor of the black journalist T. Thomas Fortune, which included little neck clams, olives, salmon, trout, beef filet, claret, and Roquefort cheese, among other luxurious food items.[79] Even those who would never be invited to a dinner in honor of a race leader could aspire to create meals worthy of T. Thomas Fortune at home, thanks to the proliferation of recipe columns in black newspapers.

When respectable eaters loaded their dinner tables with food that they regarded as dainty or modern, they did so performatively. Their food practices were designed to demonstrate their humanity and sophistication to white observers while helping preserve their individual health and allowing them to assert their class status within the black community. When crafting both the food practices that they would participate in at home and the domestic science curricula they hoped would educate the rest of the race, respectable eaters maintained a shared insistence that food was not merely a means of nourishment but also a powerful symbol that could perhaps be leveraged to transform the social order. The next chapter reveals that no less a race leader than Booker T. Washington put food reform at the center of his agenda for race progress. Scholarly discussions about the slippery and complicated politics of Washington's program for racial uplift have not yet taken into account the centrality of his detailed vision for dietary reform. Washington, like many of the contemporaries discussed in this chapter, saw food habits as a means for cultural advancement that could lead to greater incorporation in the U.S. body politic. However, Washington's pragmatism also led him to explore an alternative, subversive set of black nationalist possibilities for racial food reform as he urged black Americans toward a program of culinary self-sufficiency that he hoped would blunt some of the excesses of white racism should full national incorporation never be forthcoming.

Booker T. Washington's Multifaceted Program for Food Reform at the Tuskegee Institute

On April 25, 1901, the students at the Tuskegee Normal and Industrial Institute, located in eastern Alabama, ate soup, roast beef and gravy, asparagus tips on toast, stewed corn, and blackberry pie for their midday dinner.[1] This spread was more abundant and varied than the meals that most of the black working-class students were accustomed to eating. This repast also featured an ingredient that was in particularly short supply in the southern larder: beef. Significantly, beef, which was rarely eaten by other working-class rural Alabamians, was frequently served for one or more of the three daily meals at Tuskegee. Its recurrent appearance on the table was at the personal insistence of the principal, Booker T. Washington, whose thoughtful dining choices were an outgrowth of his complex vision for racial uplift.

Washington's ideas about proper eating habits were influenced, in part, by Progressive Era food reformers who believed that food could serve as a vehicle for social change and assimilation. However, although Washington was intrigued by their ideas, he never completely subsumed local African American food traditions to the dictates of outside specialists. He continually advocated for a food system managed by and for black people. He believed that food practices were an important means of preparing the black population for first-class citizenship, if racism could be ameliorated, or for independent racial sustenance, if it could not. During Washington's tenure at Tuskegee, which began in 1881, he helped create a food culture that paid homage simultaneously to the high moral tone of progressive food reformers and to an African American culinary heritage rooted in slave culture. Although Washington was intrigued by the possibility of using the table as a space for acting out the politics of assimilation, ultimately he believed that the problem of subsistence was far more pressing.

Building Ties to the National Domestic Science Movement

Throughout his life, Washington demonstrated a sustained interested in familiarizing himself with the latest scientific information about nutrition. He was influenced by progressivism's faith in science and by the belief that giving students "technical and scientific knowledge" would enable them to first "supply the immediate wants of the body" but eventually lead them to "that higher atmosphere of truth, virtue, love and unselfishness."[2] The body, though demanding in its physiological need, was also a portal for reaching larger psychological and political goals. He corresponded, at least briefly, with white food reformers who shared his beliefs that scientific knowledge could be used for the betterment of individuals and of society at large and that proper eating habits were a reflection of one's moral virtue; correspondents included Fannie Farmer, the "mother of level measurements"; John Harvey Kellogg, director of the famed Battle Creek Sanitarium; and the chemists Ellen Swallow Richards and Wilbur Atwater.[3]

Washington cooperated particularly closely with Edward Atkinson, the inventor of the slow-cooking Aladdin Oven, a wooden box lined with tin that was heated by a kerosene lamp. Atkinson, a Boston businessman, developed this fuel-efficient cooking mechanism specifically to benefit the poor, who he hoped would use the device to tenderize cheap cuts of meat.[4] Atkinson frequently narrated a story about meeting Washington during one of the Tuskegee founder's fund-raising trips in the Northeast. Atkinson claimed that Washington told him that black people in the South lived on a poor diet of "hominy, corn meal, and bacon" in large part because "Alabama beef is so tough."[5] Atkinson reported that he responded to this dilemma by giving Washington detailed instructions about how to construct large Aladdin Ovens at Tuskegee, which he promised could tenderize the stringiest cuts of beef. Washington took his advice, and the institute built large Aladdin Ovens that were eventually used to cook a hundred pounds of beef at a time, along with other foods ranging from baked beans to sweet potatoes to rice pudding.[6] The ovens remained in use at Tuskegee at least through 1910. Not only were they used to aid in meal preparation for students and teachers, but instruction on how to best utilize the technology became a part of the cooking school curriculum.[7]

The Tuskegee experiment with the Aladdin Oven most likely represented the most widespread usage of Atkinson's invention outside of New England and may have been the most successful large-scale implementa-

Washington's Food Reform at the Tuskegee Institute

tion of the invention anywhere. The Aladdin Oven had a number of problematic characteristics, which meant that most users deemed it unsuitable as a sole cooking device. Unlike the iron stove, it could not be used to provide a source of heat for a household. Neither could it be left unattended for fear of fire. It cooked food slowly and thus could not be used to fry foods or to boil water. It was difficult to operate for the uninitiated, who often destroyed it due to operator errors.[8] Given the fact that most users of the device deemed it impractical and cumbersome, the Tuskegee commitment to the technology is notable and indicative of the strength of Washington's determination to implement the latest scientific advancements and to link his work at Tuskegee to the work of domestic scientists elsewhere.

Atkinson was so thrilled by Washington's adoption of the Aladdin Oven that the inventor asked Washington to construct a large prototype and to display it at the 1895 Cotton States and International Exposition to be held in Atlanta.[9] The oven ultimately appeared there under other auspices because Washington wound up participating in the event as a speaker rather than as an exhibitor. He delivered his "Atlanta Compromise" speech at the exhibition, rising to national prominence after promising black patience on civil rights issues and emphasizing the need for gradual economic advancement instead.[10] Intriguingly, the historical event when Washington became famous as a race leader bent on interracial compromise could have been a quieter moment had Washington chosen to present himself as a face of modern home economics rather than as a general spokesperson for southern African Americans. However, these two personas may not be as oppositional as they appear at first glance. The range of Washington's choices when determining how to craft a public personality demonstrates the complexity of his uplift philosophy as well as his unflinching belief that racial uplift and better food practices were inextricably linked.

Washington's interest in making connections between his race advocacy and the national conversation about domestic reform was encouraged by advice he received from J. L. M. Curry, agent for the Peabody Education Fund and the Slater Fund for the Education of Freedmen, foundations that provided financial support for the institute. In 1894, Curry supplied Washington with a grant to hire "some competent and trained woman to give her attention to household improvement."[11] Although Washington had a strict policy against hiring white faculty for fear that whites would be given credit for the success of Tuskegee, he bent those rules to hire Alice J. Kaine, a white home economist from Wisconsin, who made several extended trips to Alabama with the mission of improving domestic life on campus.[12]

Kaine's racial status and the significance of her work to the mission of Tuskegee were reflected in her salary. She was paid eighty dollars a month in addition to room and board, a figure that was twice the remuneration an average woman teacher received.[13] She was charged with a variety of tasks, including giving advice on how "the cheapest food consistent with health [could be served] at the smallest possible costs," and was given broad authority to implement her program, a situation that led to inter-personal difficulties with some permanent members of the faculty.[14] Kaine had an expansive vision of her duties, believing it was her obligation not only to impart knowledge about home economics but also to try to create what she deemed "a better moral atmosphere at the school," a task that she considered difficult because, in her estimation, most Tuskegee students came from homes "void of discipline."[15]

Her sense of both self- and racial superiority was not something Kaine was able to hide from Washington. When she wrote to him accepting the position, she did so with the caveat that she had never worked with "the colored people." She had, on occasion, attended their "Schools and Churches." However, visiting black community spaces was an activity that she regarded as "one of my hobbies—that is all."[16] Washington, however, had pragmatic reasons for cooperating with Kaine and for inviting her to practice her "hobby" of taking an interest in the disadvantaged at Tuskegee. Her presence pleased white donors and built a bridge between the work at Tuskegee and advancements in domestic science elsewhere.[17] Kaine, for example, shared Washington's enthusiasm for the cumbersome workings of the Aladdin Oven, boasting to its creator that beef cooked with it was "as deliciously tender as spring chicken."[18] It seems likely that his connec-tion with Kaine and other white food reformers encouraged Washington to value beef not only as a nutritious food but also as an instrument of civilization.

Kaine was likely influenced by the New England Kitchen, an endeavor discussed briefly in chapter 1, which encouraged late nineteenth-century immigrants to eat "American" food.[19] The kitchen staff sold inexpensive dishes like beef broth and beef stew, promoting them as tools of assim-ilation and symbols of citizenship.[20] In the 1890s, some white domestic scientists began bringing these ideas southward. For example, Anita J. Atkinson worked to promote "soups and stews, *a la* New England Kitchen," to African American students at Atlanta University. Atkinson argued that displacing "the principal diet of fat pork, hoe cake, pone, hominy and molasses" was a prominent part of what she regarded as her civilizing mission in the South.[21]

The Symbolic Significance of Beef and White Bread at Tuskegee

The foods these reformers promoted had obvious English culinary antecedents. The partiality for beef was certainly rooted in traditional English preferences, making the meat a convenient symbol for proponents of an Anglo-accented American culture.[22] In this context, this form of animal protein soon became associated with civilization and whiteness. Prominent nineteenth-century neurologist George M. Beard proclaimed, "Savages who feed on poor food are . . . intellectually far inferior to the beef-eaters of any race."[23] Building upon this observation, some reformers believed that beef consumption could transform the eater from the inside, priming him or her for full incorporation into the U.S. nation-state.

In addition to adhering to the mandates of contemporary culinary assimilationism, the beef that appeared on the Tuskegee table in the form of roast beef, veal cutlets, beef gravy, and liver and onions may also have been a reflection of the fact that Washington and other members of the Tuskegee staff shared some of the culinary prejudices of self-consciously refined African American eaters who wished to dissociate themselves from foods like pork that were evocative of slavery or of southern regionalism. Washington criticized those who subsisted primarily on "grits, meat [pork], corn bread" and urged black southerners to "throw off the old habit and not grow into the slavery of using a certain thing on the table because it has been used that way generation after generation."[24] He attempted to frighten his audience into dietary compliance by arguing that African Americans had a high mortality rate because they consumed not only fatty pork but also what he called "knickknacks": cheese, crackers, cake, and pie. He told his students they were fortunate to have avoided those pitfalls, claiming, "You are five times more healthy and stronger by eating [the] clean, fresh beef" served at the institute.[25]

Washington traveled as much as six months of the year raising funds to support Tuskegee, but he kept close tabs on the daily operations of the institute while he was in town.[26] He also monitored campus life while he was away, encouraging beef consumption even from afar. Tuskegee staff members sent him detailed updates about campus life, including daily menus served in both the students' and teachers' dining halls. In 1899 he wrote to an administrator from New York complaining that the students were "having too much fat meat; you will notice that they had bacon and gravy for two meals."[27] Beef appeared with regularity on the Tuskegee menus despite the fact that the institute had difficulty in maintaining a profitable herd of cattle. In 1906, the farm superintendent reported that the school was losing $300 a month attempting to raise beef. Rather than turning to another form of animal protein, E. T. Atwell, the institute's business agent, resorted to purchasing beef from large meatpacking companies.[28] The consistent inclusion of beef on both student and faculty menus was clearly a calculated decision and an unusual one, given both the difficulty the institute had in raising cattle and beef's status as a luxury item in a region where pork was the least expensive and most widely consumed protein.[29]

The mystique of beef-eating at Tuskegee was likely enhanced by the meat's relative scarcity in the South. Compared with pork, beef was harder to preserve in a form nineteenth-century Americans found palatable, and it was perceived by many as a luxury item well into the twentieth century. As late at the mid-1930s, only 12 to 14 percent of the meat consumed by rural southerners was beef.[30] Thus, the beef that was served at Tuskegee was a luxury item for rural southerners of both races. The Tuskegee students who dined on beef were actually subverting the racial order by eating a product most local whites could not afford.

Outside of Tuskegee, the majority of rural African Americans likely never or rarely tasted beef. The federal Department of Agriculture sponsored a study of the foods eaten by African Americans in Alabama in 1895 and 1896 and determined that rural African Americans consumed salt pork as their prime—if not only— form of animal protein.[31] Although the researchers who conducted the study regarded black residents of Alabama as almost universally "improvident . . . [having] very little ambition," they believed that those who lived the closest to the Tuskegee Institute showed some degree of moral improvement.[32] Beef consumption was one implied measure of civilization and refinement in the report. Only one respondent consumed beef during the period of the study, and he was a carpenter who worked at Tuskegee.[33]

Although beef was seemingly the most symbolically significant food appearing on Tuskegee tables, the principal also valued white bread, which he hoped to serve alongside the humbler regional staple of corn bread. By the turn of the twentieth century, cornmeal had become a food deeply associated with the South, with poverty, and with slavery. Washington's uplift-oriented food politics meant that he wanted to help campus community members distance themselves from these associations and to be sure they also had access to breads made from white flour. The South produced little of this coveted grain, but improved transportation networks steadily brought down the price of this imported luxury, an increasingly popular, high-status food by the twentieth century.[34]

Although cornmeal had become an American staple beginning in the colonial period, it had been consumed somewhat reluctantly as an allegedly inferior substitute grain for wheat. The early modern Europeans who first colonized what was to become the United States arrived on the continent already valuing light-colored leavened bread made from wheat above loaves or flatbreads made from rye, oats, or beans that were more readily available to the lower classes in Europe. Because they brought this preference with them, they quickly cataloged corn as yet another inferior grain and enshrined wheat, which was initially a scarce commodity in the Americas, as a higher status grain. This characterization of wheat bread as being somehow superior to other varieties remained steadfast in the American imagination throughout the coming centuries.[35] Although many Americans learned to become fond of corn bread, most middle-class, self-consciously refined eaters considered it an inadequate substitute for wheat bread.

Because Washington was aware of the symbolic significance of wheat bread, wheat biscuits and yeast-leavened "light bread" appeared frequently on the tables in the teachers' dining room in particular. Washington was attuned to a variety of culinary nuances and did not consider all baked goods made from wheat as being equally desirable. In keeping with the food prejudices of his day, Washington thought that cold yeast-leavened bread was more healthful than warm wheat biscuits, and he demanded that "plenty of cold light bread" should appear on the teachers' table and that they should not be confined to "hot soda biscuits," a lower status and allegedly less healthful wheat bread.[36]

Although the dietary preferences of the teachers sometimes took precedence over the students' desires, Washington hoped to serve the favored grain as frequently as possible to students as well.[37] Always attuned to the smallest details of running the school, in 1898 Washington determined that it would cost only an additional $1.04 to make wheat bread instead of corn bread for the evening meal in the Tuskegee dining hall.[38] Sometimes, due to budgetary concerns, when the students did receive coveted wheat bread at their evening meal it was served as a main course and not as an accompaniment to a larger meal. There were times when bread and sorghum syrup made up their entire supper.[39]

Washington not only kept track of how frequently wheat bread was served at Tuskegee but also monitored the quality of the product when it was served. In 1898 he sent a staff member in the boarding department an actual sample of the bread that the students had been served at the midday meal, chastising him for poor quality control and claiming that "such cooking is not only a great waste but it is very injurious to the health of the students."[40] Even when students did not have the opportunity to consume wheat at their regular meals, the cooking school students always learned how to prepare it, alongside other grains. Beginner students learned how to make "breads without yeast; biscuits; cornbread, sweet and white potato bread; graham and oatmeal; [and] muffins of each of the above flours," and more advanced students learned to make highly prized light bread with yeast.[41]

Although the beef and wheat bread served at Tuskegee reflected an understanding of the dietary preferences of white domestic scientists who tended toward the uncritical embrace of Anglo-derived food preferences, Tuskegee food practices were not created purely for the benefit of a white audience. In compiling publicity for the institute, Washington published some Tuskegee menus, surely with the knowledge that his efforts at food uplift would meet with the approval of many white food reformers. However, identical meals were also served at the institute daily with no fanfare.[42] Washington and his staff at Tuskegee clearly believed that the diets he recommended were of intrinsic value to those who consumed them in the proper fashion, regardless of who was watching.

The members of the Tuskegee Women's Club hosted a lecture series in 1898 titled "Suitable Foods for Different People." Lecturers gave advice about which foods would best meet the purportedly different nutritional needs of various groups of people, ranging from invalids to those who did physical labor.[43] These lectures reflected the core Tuskegee belief that food choices and social station were linked. By choosing high-status, domestic scientist–approved foods for the shared Tuskegee table, Washington was implying that his students and staff had the same nutritional needs and the same right to enjoy luxurious food items as the white-educated classes. His insistence that the Tuskegee community be given access to beef and to wheat bread amounted to an implicit assertion of physiological and, by extension, social and political equality.

Dining Etiquette and Racial Uplift

||||||||||||||||||||||||||||||||||||||||||||||||||||||||||||||||

While specific ingredients like beef and wheat maintained their symbolic significance at Tuskegee, Washington did not limit his ideas about ideal food habits to the selection of ingredients alone. Notions about proper presentation and etiquette were also indispensable elements of the local food culture. When young Washington, who had been born into slavery, arrived at the Hampton Normal and Agricultural Institute in Virginia in 1872 to receive the education he craved, he recalled being struck by revelations about a more gracious way of living that transported him into a "new world." He claimed that he was introduced to the practices of "eating meals at regular hours, of eating on a tablecloth, using a napkin."[44] In his narration of his own life, Washington recalled that being allowed to participate in these seemingly unremarkable rituals was life-changing. He made sure that his own students would learn similar lessons about proper food etiquette. For Washington and his staff, proper food behavior consisted not only of eating healthful, "civilized" ingredients but also of practicing good table manners.

Economic realities dictated that the members of the Tuskegee community did not always eat as well as Washington hoped they could. The quality and diversity of food items available varied in accordance with Washington's recent success in raising funds and in collecting tuition, in response to the seasonal availability of some ingredients, and as a result of the relative success or failure of the institution's farm. However, Washington and the Tuskegee staff believed that the politics of racial uplift could be practiced at mealtime regardless of which menu items were being served.

Thomas Monroe Campbell enrolled in the institute in 1899, during what was apparently a lean time in the dining hall, and reported being appalled at menus that consisted of little more than "heavy corn bread . . . a little syrup in a saucer, and some salad greens cooked with little or no meat."[45] His first meals at Tuskegee bore little resemblance to the abundant 1901 feast described at the beginning of this chapter. However, he was surprised to learn that he was expected to dress for dinner, regardless of how humble the meal itself might be. In order to help him prepare for his first Tuskegee dinner, his "class brother" generously loaned him a shirt collar and tie and told him to shine his shoes before entering the dining hall. This ritual proved to be a difficult adjustment to Campbell, who found the

A scene from the Tuskegee Institute dining hall, ca. 1902. (Photo by Frances Benjamin Johnston; Library of Congress LC-DIG-ppmscd-00085)

expectation that he change his work clothing before mealtime a cumbersome but required part of life on campus.[46]

For Washington, appearances mattered. He used visual cues—such as a dining hall filled with African Americans dressed impeccably for dinner—to send messages about black dignity and equality that worked to contradict the humble and patient persona cultivated in his writing or in his face-to-face interactions with would-be white supporters of his initiatives. Marlon B. Ross argues, "Though rhetorically [Washington] presents himself and his protégés as humble, ordinary and contentedly mired in the muck of the menial Black Belt Labor, Washington *does* portray his own body, and those of his colleagues and students, in upwardly mobile fashions whenever *visual* representations of his enterprise are at stake."[47] The care Washington took in curating the visual representation of black bodies is evident in scores of carefully staged photographs of well-groomed Tuskegee students studying, working, and eating on campus.

The expectations for proper dining etiquette did not end with the sartorial requirements. Students who were late to meals at Tuskegee

Elegantly attired Tuskegee students serving a meal outdoors sometime between 1890 and 1910. (Library of Congress LC-USZ62–137808)

were not permitted to eat, and proper table manners were to be observed at all times.[48] Washington's third wife and the "Lady Principal" of Tuskegee, Margaret Murray Washington, approvingly noted that one of the ways that Tuskegee students judged each other was on "the niceties of table-training." She encouraged students to criticize one another for lack of refinement, noting that these critiques "play no small part in the development of students."[49]

In what was partially an attempt to construct an unthreatening vision of African American advancement for the benefit of white donors and partially a reflection of a wistful belief that adherence to middle-class standards of decorum might eventually open the door to fuller incorporation into the U.S. body politic, Washington frequently focused his attention on the private rather than the public sphere. He proclaimed, "The Negro has had to learn the meaning of home since he learned the meaning of freedom. All work which has to do with his uplifting must begin with his home and its surroundings."[50] Intriguingly, his time frame for the racial uplift that was to begin at home was more rapid than he implied in his carefully worded public statements on the subject, including his famous declaration at the 1895 Cotton States and International Exposition that "it is at the bottom of life we must begin, and not at the top."[51]

In order to demonstrate his humility, Washington told the white readers of his autobiography, *Up from Slavery*, about the first makeshift kitchen and dining room at Tuskegee, which was a basement that students dug themselves. He described using carpenters' benches for tables, cooking outdoors over a fire, burned food served at erratic hours, and squabbles among students over the scant supply of dishes.[52] In retrospect, he somewhat preposterously claimed, "I am glad that our first boarding-place was in that dismal, ill-lighted, and damp basement," speculating that better accommodations would have made them "stuck up."[53] However, Washington does not reveal how quickly the less-than-adequate conditions were remedied. He implies a slow evolution when in actuality a modern facility was erected in less than a year.[54] He did not intend for the faculty or student body to eat in that makeshift facility for long.[55] Behind his public, humble demeanor, which bore the desired fruits of much-needed white philanthropic dollars, was hidden a more radical agenda for domestic reform.

Washington wanted to be judged on his domestic accomplishments, both in creating impressive dining and living spaces for his students and in maintaining his own home, The Oaks, which was situated next to the campus. Completed in 1900, Washington's fourteen-room, five-bath Queen Anne style home was handsomely decorated and furnished to convey a public face of African American refinement for local whites and visiting philanthropists as well as for Tuskegee students, who were charged with emulating the Washingtons' domestic sensibilities.[56] Students assigned to work at The Oaks lived on the third floor, gaining firsthand impressions of Washington's personal desire to create living spaces that conveyed "from kitchen to parlor a delicacy, a sweetness and refinement that made one feel that life was worth living."[57]

The students who were responsible for making life at The Oaks adhere to Washington's standards learned, as all Tuskegee students did, according to Carla Willard, "*to be* served, as well as to serve."[58] Although the vocational training that Washington advocated for would seemingly have trained his students to be merely cooks or waiters and not the employers or customers who were waited upon, their education actually prepared students to fulfill both roles. The Tuskegee pupils who were taught the art of cooking and serving doled out simple, cafeteria-appropriate meals to their fellow students in the dining halls on campus, but at The Oaks they also had the opportunity to prepare and serve more elaborate cuisine to distinguished members of their own race. This performance prepared students for roles beyond that of becoming domestic servants to white people. While serving fellow African American diners, students could more easily imagine themselves in the future role of dinner party guest and not just that of perpetual cook or waiter.

In 1910, to celebrate Washington's return to Alabama after a European tour, students served the institution's Executive Council in the president's home an elegant meal:

> Blue Points
> Sauce
> Brown Bread Sandwiches
> Consomme   Cheese Straws
> Olives   Cheese   Radishes
> Swedish Timbales   Mushrooms
> Broiled Halibut   Tartar Sauce
> Bread Sticks   Cole Slaw
> Brown Hashed Potatoes
> Orange Sherbet
> Birds on Toast   Jelly
> Green Peas   Rolls   Candied Potatoes
> Tomato Salad
> Ice Cream   Lady Fingers   Bon Bons
> Wafers   Cheese
> Black Coffee[59]

The menu choices demonstrate, once again, an insistence that high-status food items were not out of place on African American tables. Luxurious Blue Point oysters, imported from New York, also showed that Tuskegee was connected to the national market economy. Their appearance at the feast indicated that Tuskegee students had been well trained in current dining and cooking conventions and thus were demonstrating their possession of cultural capital befitting first-class citizens. Paul Pierce, superintendent of the food exhibitions at the St. Louis World's Fair and author of *Dinners and Luncheons: Novel Suggestions for Social Occasions*, would have concurred with the decision of the Tuskegee students to serve Blue Point oysters, "a favorite first course in season," followed shortly after by consommé, believing as he did that "a heavy soup will so far cloy the appetite as to render one indifferent to the rest of the dinner, while a clear soup refreshes, and prepares one for the enjoyment of the succeeding solids."[60] Their recipe for "birds on toast" may have been adapted from the recipe for "Reed Birds on Toast" that appeared in the influential 1887 *White House Cookbook.*[61] They may also have culled the recipe for Swedish timbales, cheese straws, and other items from Fannie Farmer. The second edition of her *Boston Cooking-School Cook Book* had appeared in 1906, four years before this Tuskegee meal.

The care with which the feast was planned represents the Tuskegee belief that the stakes at the dinner table were high. Culinary missteps could reflect badly on the race and thus impede racial progress. In 1906, Washington wrote Margaret Murray Washington and complained about aspects of a formal dinner service that were not up to his high standards. He noted, "The tomatoes were served in soup plates. There were no fresh flowers on the table. The girls did not wear caps. The menu card was cheaply gotten up, it was cheap paper poorly cut, and the writing was not in attractive form."[62] Two days later he again chided his wife for the lack of cleanliness and organization in the school's cooking facilities, noting, "I have very seldom been more disgusted than when I visited the small model kitchen. . . . The whole thing needs serious attention."[63]

In Washington's mind, food practices were about more than obtaining adequate nourishment.[64] Mistakes at the table, such as using the wrong plate or creating an unattractive menu card, provided evidence of poor character and could not be overlooked. Students were charged with paying careful attention to the practices of cooking, eating, and serving because proper food habits would prepare them to assume the rights of first-class citizenship should they be proffered. However, equally significantly, Washington wanted black people to take seriously the challenge of achieving food self-sufficiency as a means of becoming less dependent upon white goodwill, should those rights fail to materialize.

Washington Promotes the Merits of Southern Food

Although Washington attempted to intervene in the traditional southern pattern of consuming pork as a primary source of animal protein, his vision for dietary reform did not eschew all traditional southern food items, nor was it inflexible. In the food front, as in all aspects of his uplift philosophy, Washington combined assimilationist and nationalist sensibilities. He believed that food could be used as a tool to demonstrate black worthiness for full incorporation as citizens, but he ultimately valued self-sufficiency far more than adherence to contemporary ideas about proper food habits. Furthermore, although Washington performatively ate meals that were coded as high-status or as quintessentially "American," he also publicly indulged in items that would never have been served in the New England Kitchen. Even though Washington worked to diversify the food offerings in the Tuskegee dining hall and hosted elaborate dinner parties highlighting a range of menu items at his own home, he did not always follow his own culinary advice. According to his biographer Robert J. Norrell, Washington's favorite personal diet was high in fatty foods, especially pork, and low in fiber.[65] The ever-adaptable "wizard of Tuskegee" managed to exploit the political potential of both embracing and avoiding traditional southern foods.

Washington maintained a lifelong fondness for opossum, a low-status regional food. In 1914, he invited the teachers of Tuskegee to a "'Possum & 'tater Supper and Candy Pulling," an old-fashioned meal that certainly had antecedents in slavery when small game was used to subsidize monotonous, minimal diets.[66] Occasionally, he sent friends or associates shipments of opossum, giving, for example, a gift of the animal to Jeannette Tod Ewing Bertram, whose husband was employed as Andrew Carnegie's secretary.[67] The animal was accompanied by a note that suggested pride in the culinary heritage of southern African Americans with Washington's declaration that "a Southern colored woman knows how to cook the opossum better than anyone else."[68] Thus, Washington's vision for dietary reform was moderated by a persistent regard and affection for some aspects of traditional southern foodways. He did not allow uplift-oriented foods to completely crowd out the comfort foods of his childhood on his table. Nor did he expect the Tuskegee community to adopt the latest dietary advice and trends at the expense of local food traditions. While he advocated for the right of African Americans to enjoy high-status foods that had received the approval of contemporary nutritional experts, he did not discount the value of local ingredients and long-standing dietary habits. Although Washington insisted that dishes long associated with the diet of southern poverty did not predominate in the institution's dining rooms, Tuskegee students ate pork as well as beef and corn bread alongside wheat biscuits.

Washington advocated for the maintenance of southern food practices for reasons of practicality and not just pride and affection. For example, he urged African Americans to eat more black-eyed peas, an inexpensive local food that he deemed "one of the most nutritious foods, when properly cooked." In his advocacy for the legume, he favorably compared it to the "far-famed 'Boston bean,'" an item, like beef, that figured heavily into white food reform efforts.[69] Furthermore, in 1912 he asked members of the boarding department to economize on meal planning and to investigate the possibility of serving "pig feet, ears and so on," which "can be gotten cheap."[70] To Washington, the symbolic significance of the food that appeared on the table was ultimately far less important than the frequently struggling institution's financial solvency.

Washington accused the southern black community of not making the "vital connection between vegetable life and the life that sustains the body," and he advised African Americans to exploit their natural environment in search of food.[71] Fresh local produce was served regularly at Tuskegee. A sample 1902 student menu of beef and gravy, greens, and corn bread epitomizes Tuskegee's hybrid culinary sensibilities. Pork was removed from the classic southern plantation menu, while other southern staples were maintained in a nod to both the past and the future, a divide Tuskegee students were obligated to travel in their journey toward racial uplift.[72]

Culinary Self-Reliance

Although Tuskegee's survival depended upon the largesse of northern white philanthropists, Washington and the Tuskegee staff balanced this reality with an emphasis on black culinary self-reliance. Washington's tiring fund-raising schedule demonstrates how dependent the institute was on aid from the outside, but Washington strove to create a daily environment for his students that shielded them from this reality and emphasized black agency. Food at Tuskegee was to be raised, prepared, and served by and for black people. In 1910, Washington boasted to the readers of *Good Housekeeping* that the young women who learned domestic science by living together in a "Practice Cottage" on campus prepared meals for themselves with food supplies raised on the school farm, including milk, butter, cheese, vegetables, and beef.[73] Achieving such self-sufficiency was a matter of ongoing concern for the staff, which strove to limit dependency on canned goods and to revise menus to utilize foods produced on the school grounds rather than those imported from the outside.[74]

Washington repeatedly ordered the staff to strive for culinary independence. In 1902, he instructed the institute's treasurer, Warren Logan, "to purchase as little in way of provisions from the store as possible." He acknowledged that "it is so much more convenient to open a can of salmon or a barrel of grits than to prepare our own vegetables for the table." For this reason, Washington advocated vigilance on the issue of provisioning, warning, "You cannot prevent the use of store bought goods without constant attention."[75] To help reach these goals, the staff and students of Tuskegee both grew their own produce and preserved it. Workers in the campus cannery put up 5,000 gallons of fruit and vegetables each year.[76] Ideally, Washington hoped not only to produce the food necessary to feed the campus community but also to sell the surplus to help pay the institution's debts.

Although Washington generally commanded a great deal of respect and deference from most of the students and staff at Tuskegee, he faced a surprising degree of resistance from the community as he sought to implement his vision for local food self-sufficiency. Although no one outwardly disagreed with him in principle, he found that few were willing to commit themselves wholeheartedly to performing the specific chores needed in order to achieve culinary independence. Many found the lessons of dressing for dinner and performing good manners easier to embrace than the less picturesque tasks related to producing the food that went onto the table.

Famed agricultural scientist George Washington Carver, who joined the faculty in 1896, was tasked not only with teaching students and conducting research but also with managing the institution's farms. By the late nineteenth century, the Tuskegee farm system consisted of 2,300 acres. Managing the acreage was itself a full-time job. It was also one that Carver, a scientist and not a farm manager by training, was not particularly well suited for and that he deemed less important than his instructional and experimental work.[77] Unsurprisingly, perhaps, given the enormity of Carter's workload and his lack of experience in farm management, the Tuskegee farms frequently lost money. A report from the institution's auditor in 1901 concluded that the farm system lost between $17,000 and $18,000 in 1901, a figure that represented a large increase over losses of between $9,000 and $10,000 in 1900.[78]

Furthermore, although Carver's students were an enthusiastic group and generally fond of their instructor, agriculture was not a popular major at Tuskegee. Many of the students came from farming backgrounds and were seeking a higher education in order to escape their parents' occupation, not to become more skilled farmers. Most Tuskegee students hoped to learn industrial trades, and a large portion planned to become teachers upon graduation. Working on the school farms was, in fact, so unpopular that some instructors used the threat of agricultural labor as a punishment for students who misbehaved.[79]

Thomas Monroe Campbell, who eventually became one of Carver's prize students, recalled, "Dr. Washington knew how unpopular the subject of farming was among both teachers and students . . . so he often emphasized . . . the importance of developing rural life among the Negroes."[80] In his vision both men and women were equally responsible for using agriculture as a means of racial elevation. The faculty and staff in the agricultural department encouraged both female students and local women to raise poultry as a potential means of achieving economic independence. An 1899 article in the *Tuskegee Student* declared, "Any woman of ordinary intelligence can make a good living by raising poultry scientifically. . . . The more independent life a woman can lead, the better it is for her."[81] This message was not an easy sell to many women who wanted to leave manual, agricultural labor behind in exchange for jobs that were coded as being more feminine in the realms of domestic science and education in particular.

Washington attempted to raise the symbolic status of careers in agriculture, in part by honoring the small number of declared agriculture majors. Washington often praised them publicly, asking them to rise during school assemblies—a strategy that at least partially backfired. Campbell confessed that he was initially so ashamed of his status as a student of agriculture that he sheepishly remained seated.[82] Although Washington believed food production was of tremendous practical and political significance, for most of the student body, leaving the fields—and the accompanying associations of slavery and poverty—was of greater symbolic significance.

For Washington, however, black economic self-sufficiency was a cornerstone of his plan of racial uplift. He was absolutely sincere in his famous 1895 public pronouncement that "there is as much dignity in tilling a field as in writing a poem."[83] Although many of his staunchest critics interpreted this as a public dismissal of the significance of black intellectual achievements, Washington saw agricultural labor as an enterprise of both the mind and the body. Students learned the latest scientific information and conducted experiments designed to increase the general pool of knowledge. They were trained not only to consume information but also to generate it in a creative process not altogether different from writing a poem.

Significantly, Washington's vision of black food autonomy was not limited to the education of his students, and the staff at Tuskegee promoted the message of food self-sufficiency beyond the grounds of the institute through a series of outreach programs designed to educate local farm families. Washington sought and received philanthropic support for a mobile agricultural school. The Jesup Agricultural Wagon traveled the countryside around Tuskegee offering local farmers instruction about best agricultural practices and introduced them to recent discoveries made by Carver and his students.[84] The institute also invited local farmers to an annual Negro Farmers' Conference beginning in 1892, where staff taught moral as well as practical lessons. Attendees of the 1900 gathering heard uplift-appropriate messages about economy and specific instructions not to waste money on too much food, "whiskey, cheap jewelry, [and] old buggies."[85] Faculty members urged black farmers to diversify their production and to grow their own food—and not just the cash crop of cotton—in order to reduce their dependency on food purchased on credit at plantation commissaries, which charged high rates of interest.[86] Washington proclaimed that "the Farmer who wants to get out of debt will have large patches of greens, his garden will have something growing in it the year round. His table will be loaded with wild fruits. . . . His potatoes will keep him from buying so much corn meal and flour on credit."[87] Although Washington's advice made good rhetorical sense, there were structural reasons his program was hard to implement, the most notable being that most black farmers were tenants and not landowners and thus generally had very little input on the particular details of land usage. Furthermore, white landowners had every incentive to maximize the acreage devoted to commodity crops and little incentive to make sure their tenants were well fed and thus were reluctant to provide garden space for sharecroppers living on their land. Sadly, most of the attendees at the annual conference faced varying levels of restrictions should they have desired to implement the ideas they gleaned. Out of the 400 people who attended the first gathering, only 23 owned their own homes.[88] In Alabama, as elsewhere in the South, black landowners had much greater freedom to diversify their production and to implement experimental techniques than tenants who worked on land they did not own.[89]

Given the restrictions that tenants had to contend with regarding land usage, the advice proffered by Washington, Carver, and others may not have always been practical, but the theory behind their recommendations was significant, and food autonomy remained one of the most concrete goals of the Tuskegee political program. The Tuskegee mindset, which linked campus concerns to the needs of the broader community, was influential. In 1899, African Americans organized 150 conferences for farmers, which were inspired by the Tuskegee example.[90] The organizers of these events agreed with Washington's insistence that food was a tool of economic independence, which could ameliorate the impact of racism if African Americans became less dependent on white employers and creditors to fill their stomachs. It seems likely that the ability to assert black national culinary independence could have softened the blows of dependency and oppression.

The idea of black food autonomy as a practical and meaningful tool in the struggle against white oppression stood in contrast to the emphasis of most middle-class proponents of culinary uplift whose food activism was primarily cultural in orientation. Reformers of this ilk aimed to influence particular food choices and to mold personal behavior in the hope of demonstrating shared values and thus equality with members of the white middle class. When Washington encouraged his students to eat beef and light bread and to mind their manners at the dinner table, he was wholeheartedly endorsing this strategy. However, even the most optimistic proponents of cultural uplift at the table knew that the strategy of trying to earn first-class citizenship through good behavior would be a slow, laborious approach. Simultaneously, many, like Washington, embraced a complementary but far more radical strategy for racial elevation at the dinner table. It was, after all, possible to make symbolically significant menu selections and to observe rules of etiquette while also seeking to undercut economic ties with the system of white supremacy. Enhancing one's personal sense of dignity and learning to separate one's own sense of self-worth from the negative ideas about blackness perpetuated by white society may have been psychologically freeing, but it did little to challenge structural inequalities. The idea of food self-sufficiency—however unlikely it was to achieve—was designed to bring about real, material change.

Severing as many economic ties from the white community as possible as the black community looked for ways to feed itself also posed a challenge—implicit or otherwise—to the assimilationist goals of most advocates of uplift. It was not much of an intellectual leap to move from framing food autonomy as an African American issue to thinking of it as a separatist, national issue. By aiming to separate themselves, as much as possible, from the U.S. marketplace, advocates for black food independence were flirting with the idea of creating an alternative national system.

The notion of black culinary autonomy, particularly as a necessary precursor to black nationhood, did not begin to reach full maturity until the late 1960s, but clear antecedents for this strategy can be found during the era of culinary uplift. Washington never achieved his dream of being able to produce all the food at Tuskegee that his students and faculty could eat. Invariably, those on the staff of the boarding department had to purchase supplies. Frequently, they bought products from local farmers, a strategy that complemented their desire for racial autonomy and mutual cooperation in the realms of food production and consumption. However, they also regularly purchased food from national suppliers, even products like pork and beef, which theoretically were being produced on school grounds. Furthermore, many common menu items like tea or wheat flour were not produced locally. Thus, it was increasingly impossible for Tuskegee or other black institutions to completely separate themselves from the national market economy. They could, however, try to find ways to leverage their collective economic power at the same time that they paid careful attention to nurturing the health of their bodies and exerted influence over how their black bodies were portrayed to white society.

Because Washington's ambitious dream of black food self-sufficiency remained elusive, most contemporary food reformers emphasized dietary choice and proper dining conduct in their food-related advocacy. As the next chapter reveals, the training that Washington provided the Tuskegee community about what to eat and how to best present and comport the black body was similar to the advice that respectable parents, eager to preserve the physiological as well as psychological health of their children, imparted to their offspring at home. Even W. E. B. Du Bois, one of Washington's most famous and public critics, conveyed instructions to his daughter, Yolande, that echoed Washington's certainty that food choices were of tremendous racial significance. Du Bois, like Washington, dreamed of widespread social and material transformation in the United States, but while waiting for those changes to occur he often shifted his focus to the private but, he believed, interconnected tasks of readying his body and those of the next generation for fuller incorporation into an improved world, should it materialize.

W. E. B. Du Bois,
Respectable Child-Rearing, and
the Representative Black Body

In 1923 the great African American intellectual W. E. B. Du Bois wrote a letter to his twenty-three-year-old daughter, Yolande, begging her to eat her vegetables. He hysterically warned, "It is pain, sickness, and suicide to neglect them."[1] While Yolande was in college at Fisk University in the early 1920s, Du Bois frequently wrote similar letters offering dietary advice and demanding to know what she was eating. Unconvinced that she would heed his instructions on her own, he arranged to have food sent to her. Seemingly no aspect of her daily routine was beneath his notice. When he bought her a soup thermos in early February 1923, he also sent advice about how to clean it. His anxiety about the issue of her food choices was so high that he could not contain his exasperation when he believed that she was not taking his concerns seriously. What started off, at the beginning of the month, as a series of suggestions about what and how to eat devolved into chastisement by the middle of February when Du Bois confessed to being "alarmed at your carelessness with your health."[2]

Du Bois's fatherly affection occasionally encouraged him to soften the edge of his irritation about what he regarded as his daughter's poor food choices. Expressing a momentary awareness that the regime he was suggesting might be too arduous, he promised Yolande that with the right mindset she could learn to appreciate such an abstemious lifestyle: "You can," he assured her, "easily learn to like [vegetables]."[3] However, whether or not she learned to enjoy the foods that her father deemed as lifesaving medicine, Du Bois endeavored to convince her that it was her duty to eat them. Furthermore, he clearly believed it his fatherly prerogative to give her dietary advice, regardless of her reception to his overtures, even after she reached adulthood.

Du Bois's concern about his daughter's dietary choices had both a public and a private dimension. He certainly believed that if Yolande would eat what he regarded as a proper diet, she would be happier and healthier. He also, no doubt, welcomed the prospect of reducing the burden of his own parental worries should she comply with his program. However, he also thought that the significance of her food choices transcended the concerns of the Du Bois family unit. He maintained that Yolande, as a member of the black elite, was obligated to set a good example that would inspire other members of the race toward personal and, by extension, group-wide improvement. Du Bois was resolute in his belief that dietary reform began at home, but he was hardly alone in his conviction that good parenting and good eating were intertwined aspects of the work of racial uplift. When Du Bois ordered his grown daughter to eat her vegetables, he knew that the spirit of his admonition would receive strong support from other middle-class African Americans who were equally concerned about the political importance of the food choices that would be made by future generations.

Respectable Child-Rearing at the Dinner Table

In 1920 Edward S. Green, an African American federal employee living in Washington, D.C., published the *National Capital Code of Etiquette* to impart advice to his fellow black citizens about the rules of proper behavior. He regarded the social graces, including knowing how to dress, how to conduct oneself in a variety of social settings, how to craft dignified correspondence, and how to behave at the dinner table, as the greatest among his "SECRETS OF SUCCESS."[4] Respectable readers likely took the advice proffered by Green, a college-educated professional who traveled in one of the most elite African American social circles in the country, seriously. The example he set seemed to epitomize his belief that good behavior would yield social rewards.[5]

Green insisted that good manners should not only guide one's behavior in public but should form the basis for harmonious interactions at home as well. The rituals of life were to be carefully choreographed beginning at the domestic breakfast table. According to Green's imagination, the father in an ideal respectable home would appear at the table already dressed for work in an office, his shoes shined, his collar gleaming and white, his tie straight. The mother of the household, who smelled faintly of a muted floral scent, would flutter around in a morning gown of a style and color best suited for her body type. The children would be attired in nicely tailored, good-quality clothes. The son of the household would greet his parents with a smile and a kiss, while the daughter cheerfully helped her mother put the finishing touches on the meal. The father, who was well trained in the art of conversation, would be talkative and cheerful, sparing his family from an appearance of "the early morning grouch." The mother's chatter would be similarly light and uplifting as she deliberately avoided conversation about the "small, petty and vexatious annoyances of domestic life."[6] When it was time to eat, everyone would sit erectly with their napkins carefully arranged on their laps. Their meal would be elegant and consist of several courses. They would begin with grapefruit and cereal before moving onto a more substantial course of shirred eggs and toast. Then, holding their forks in their left hands, each person would gingerly cut small pieces of broiled lamb chop. Transferring their forks to their right hands, they would deliver these delicate morsels into their mouths. In case anyone could find room to consume more, french fried potatoes and warm rolls would also be served.[7]

Green's instructions for proper behavior indicated that he did not view the private space of the household as a place of relaxation and refuge. Each family member was to follow elaborate rules about what to wear, what to talk about, and how and what to eat. They were not at liberty to uphold ideas about respectability in public and then to embrace a less rigid code of behavior when in private. The rules were identical in each sphere because "carelessness at home" might breed bad habits that would be hard to break.[8] In her etiquette guide for young people, educator Charlotte Hawkins Brown agreed, claiming that the home should be "a school for developing and practicing the fine art of manners."[9] Respectable black children quickly learned that even if dressing and speaking well did not necessarily earn one respect on the street, this behavior would reliably earn plaudits at home.

Much of the drive to abide by the dictates of respectability was in fact motivated by parental concern about how to best train children. As Willard Gatewood points out, parents in elite black families were careful to model "self-culture."[10] Parents showed children by example what they should value and how they should behave, emphasizing both intellectual and bodily discipline. Children, it was hoped, would learn to value uplift-appropriate interests such as literature and music by following their parents' example. They would also learn how to carry themselves with poise and confidence and how to best care for their corporeal needs.

Historian Jennifer Ritterhouse gives insights into the significance of Green's insistence that rules of etiquette applied everywhere at all times with her analysis of the dictates of what she calls "respectable child rearing." She claims that "respectable black child rearing emphasized the need for individual blacks to define or redefine themselves in the public eye. . . . Respectable child rearing also had the additional function of teaching children to be self-defining in their own minds."[11] The rules of respectability not only taught children behavior designed to negate the hurtful stereotypes perpetuated by white supremacists but also encouraged the development of an alternative universe were rationality reigned. The black home could be imagined as a sanctuary not because it was a safe space where the apparatus of respectability could at last be discarded but precisely because good manners could reign in that tightly controlled environment. Watchful parents could create consistent rules, routines, and expectations that could be maintained outside of the direct reach of the destructive power of white supremacy.

Respectable child-rearing practices were designed in part to ameliorate racism by creating model citizens who might be less targeted by the enforcers of white supremacy because they knew how to behave in a way that would not draw undue attention to themselves. Parents hoped that their lessons in proper behavior would enable their children to survive in the unpredictable world outside of the family home where even small missteps could have extreme consequences. Going beyond the very real concern with the physical safety of black children, respectable parents desired that the satisfaction wrought by learning how to behave well could also serve as a buffer against the psychic wounds imposed by racism. Children learned how to find pride and satisfaction through good behavior, regardless of how white society treated them. Since cooking and eating are among the most necessary and constant of daily rituals, the realm of food habits provided a continuous training ground for uplift-orientated parents.

Sarah ("Sadie") and Elizabeth ("Bessie") Delany, the daughters of an Episcopal minister who was also the vice principal of Saint Augustine's School in Raleigh, North Carolina, were raised under a strict uplift-oriented regimen. They recalled being subject to daily inspections by their father. They were not to leave the house unless they were clean and tidy because "we carried the Delaney name and he wanted us to look respectable when we left the house."[12] Dressing well was important because it indicated that they knew how to adhere to social conventions and because it demonstrated that they were well cared for at home. For respectable children, food behavior was supposed to be as impeccable as their attire. Historian Stephanie Shaw summarizes the importance that uplift-oriented parents put upon proper food decorum with her observation, "Woe betide anyone caught eating on the street."[13] Food consumption was supposed to be dignified and restrained. Eating on the street could be messy and, worst of all, could signal impatience, greed, or want on the part of the eater who could not wait for the opportunity to eat discreetly and privately. Civil rights leader Septima Clark recalled learning a hard childhood lesson about the rules of dignified consumption after her mother spanked her when she tried to pick up a bag of candy that a little white girl had dropped.[14] Clark's mother refused to allow her to give off the impression of hunger or need or to demonstrate that black people were willing to accept cheerfully scraps of food that white people regarded as unfit for their own personal consumption.

Like Clark, Sadie and Bessie Delaney learned how to eat properly from their mother. They recalled that although their father took pains to ensure that their outward appearance was pleasing, it was their mother who made certain that they ate well. She strove to prepare food free from contaminants and loaded with nutrients. Testifying to the wisdom of their mother's approach, the sisters later recalled that they were "healthy compared to most children." Her attention to the details of nutritional science was uncommon in their social circle, and the sisters observed that she was "ahead of her time about vitamins and minerals and things like that."[15] Mrs. Delaney may have felt isolated as she educated herself about the latest advancements in home economics, but unbeknownst to her daughters, ideas about nutrition were beginning to have a broad impact on the practices of respectable child-rearing. Although good manners and elegant meals made up an important dimension of respectability training, because good behavior and fine food could be used to demonstrate black cultural capital for the benefit of both black and white observers, increasingly most food-related child-rearing advice was focused upon how to eat to achieve good health.

Uplift-oriented parents like the Delaneys strove to teach their children proper food habits not only because they could use training at the table to model good manners and restraint but also because they were charged with the great responsibility of making sure the youngest members of the race were well nourished and healthy enough to grow into the next generation of race leaders. As in the case in the Delaney household, mothers generally bore the largest responsibility for monitoring their children's diets.

In 1897, Nannie Helen Burroughs reminded her fellow churchwomen of the importance of this mandate, claiming, "It is a mother's duty to try and give her children wholesome meals and an attractive home." If a mother failed in this quest, the consequences, she warned, were severe: "Many a bad habit has been acquired because the meals did not contain all the necessary nourishments for the system. Chewing, smoking, and oftentimes drinking can be traced back to a poor dinner."[16] E. Azalia Hackley, author of the 1916 advice manual *The Colored Girl Beautiful*, agreed, raising the stakes for black womanhood even higher when she declared that the "colored mother is the health officer of the race as well as [of] her own posterity." Mothers should, Hackley urged, "study up on the kinds and amounts of food to give children." She warned that the consequences of mistakes in the task of food selection were enormous, arguing that children should not be "fed the coarse, greasy food which coarsens the instinct, or may make them gluttonous, which will abuse the stomach and cause unnatural heat that may wreck them morally. Instead, [the mother] advocates the light brain forming food to lift them above the dominant animal tendencies."[17] Thus in Hackley's dire scenario, poor food could not only damage the physical health of children but also injure their moral character and inhibit their intellectual development.

Armed with the belief that the consequences for feeding children improper foods was high, race men and women sought ways to distribute this message to members of the community who they feared might not already be subject to the exacting dictates of respectable child-rearing. For example, Harlem public health advocates hosted a well-publicized nutrition class for children in 1926. The organizers of the program likely hoped to correct nutritional deficiencies and attitudes about food among children whose parents had neither the means nor the interest to implement a strict program of culinary uplift at home. Attendees were schooled in the "ten commandments" of healthy living, which included the recommendations that they eat fruits and vegetables, drink large quantities of milk, and avoid tea and coffee, the persistent bane of contemporary childhood health reformers. In an attempt to institutionalize nutritional advice and to employ peer pressure to make children take their training seriously, graduates of the class became members of the "Carrot Club." The slogan of the honorary organization was "Carrots make you beautiful. Eat them!"[18] Interestingly, the conflation of health and beauty in the motto was not uncommon in the programs of many uplift eaters. Theoretically, eating well could also improve the physical appearance of those who took the dictates of nutritional science seriously. Because visual cues were the basis of much of the turn-of-the-twentieth-century race-making project, the idea that eating well could enhance physical beauty was a powerful one.

In her etiquette guide for young women, Hackley emphasized the importance of personal appearance. "We read character from the physical form," she argued; "the corners of the mouth, the manner in which one eats . . . every movement has a special meaning."[19] Writing at a moment when caricatured depictions of African Americans with exaggerated lips and noses were commonly displayed in popular culture, she was on the lookout for ways to disempower these distorted ideas about black physicality. She warned against developing both physical and moral attributes that might reinforce these stereotypes. First and foremost, she warned young women against the detrimental impact of having "thick lips and a leaking mouth," a condition that referred both to a corporeal attribute and to an ethical failing. She argued that thick lips, which she regarded as a beauty flaw, became more pronounced when one engaged in the unrespectable behavior of grinning too widely or talking too much. According to Hackley, both dignity and beauty demanded that members of the race should keep their mouths "shut most of the time."[20]

On June 17, 1911, the *Chicago Defender* presented a syndicated column that proclaimed that what parents allowed their children to put into their mouths could negatively impact their appearance. Not only could excessive talk lead to the appearance of a disproportionately large mouth, but unwise food consumption could also make the orifice more prominent. Citing evidence from an unnamed health authority, the author gave the dire warning that starchy foods could give children a large "starch chin" or an unsightly protruding "potato lip." The stakes for making food decisions on behalf of one's children were particularly high, the article warned, because although food could not change the appearance of the adult face, children were far more malleable.[21] Thus food, imbued as it was with properties to enhance health and shape facial features, was seen as a powerful resource at the disposal of the respectable parent who might be powerless to effectively subdue the impact of white supremacy but who nonetheless should be looking for other ways to ensure the well-being of their children.

Eating Right according to the *Brownies' Book*

The issue of proper food behavior was of such significance to respectable parents that the theme was featured frequently in the pages of the *Brownies' Book*, a children's magazine that W. E. B. Du Bois edited during its brief run in 1920 and 1921.[22] Du Bois conceived of a clear mission for the magazine, which was in keeping with the dual facets of respectable child-rearing: to teach children to behave properly and to enhance their own feelings of self-worth.[23]Although the title of the magazine likely was intended, in part, to give an affirmative nod to the skin tones of its readers, its namesake was also the Scottish and English mythological "brownies" who surreptitiously performed household chores in exchange for food. Inside the pages of the *Brownies' Book*, subscribers were somewhat similarly gifted with insights into what the editor regarded as proper food practices.

Above all, the magazine advocated for making careful food choices and for dietary moderation. A thoughtful and restrained approach to food consumption would, it was hoped, reflect personal discipline and good manners. Furthermore, carefully monitoring one's intake would ensure good health. In November 1920, in the recurrent column called "The Judge," written by Jessie Fauset, she renders a judgment saying that children "do not need candy three times a day."[24] A March 1920 article, "To Mother," tellingly compares spoiled children to rotten apples and spoiled Brazil nuts. The unnamed columnist warns parents not to indulge their little morsels by "giving them all the candy they want." The writer acknowledged the temptation to spoil young children as one means of compensating for the racial discrimination they were destined to face in the future.[25] Although gluttony might temporarily assuage parental guilt over bringing children into an unjust world and the comforts of a full stomach might dull the impact of racist slights in the short term, the overindulged black body was susceptible both to illness and to moral lapses.

According to the *Brownies' Book*, children could be forgiven a few dietary indulgences, but culinary excess must be abandoned upon reaching adulthood. In fact, dietary restraint is framed as a key marker of having reached maturity, and the magazine encouraged its readers toward dietary evolution. In Peggy Poe's 1920 story "Pumpkin Land," the protagonist Happy's age is not given, but he is described as being "not very big" precisely because he still liked candy.[26] In an April 1920 column titled "What Is the Most Fun?," a grown-up cautions young Annie to adopt a

Du Bois, Respectable Child-Rearing, and the Representative Black Body

more mature attitude toward food than that of candy-loving youngsters like Happy, proclaiming, "Eating is certainly a Joy. Consider once,—fried chicken, biscuits, and chocolate-covered nuts, and *Pie*. BUT don't over-eat. If you do, then when you get grown up you'll have a sort of perpetual tummy-ache, which people call dyspepsia."[27] Childish dietary choices, readers were advised, could breed grown-up consequences. A February 1920 article titled "Food for 'Lazy Betty'" warns that sluggish or sickly children were likely suffering from eating the wrong quantity and type of food. These choices were consequential precisely because "lack of nourishment for the child . . . produces the listless, inefficient grown up."[28]

Because the consequences of feeding one's child too much food or improper foods were allegedly so dire and could affect them throughout their lives, anxieties about proper diets for children ran high. A column in the *Chicago Defender* titled "Doughnuts" indicates that these warnings had penetrated the community deeply enough to inspire something of a backlash. The unnamed author of the article urged parents to tone down their obsession with achieving respectability at the nursery table. The writer told the story of a coddled child, raised "on the blandest, the most nutritious, the most digestible of foods," who went to visit his grandmother "who was of the former generation which knew no germs." Unenlightened about the latest information concerning modern nutrition or about the respectable mandate for dietary moderation, the elderly woman fed her grandson pie, jam, and doughnuts. His little stomach rebelled against the rich food, but instead of criticizing the grandmother and endorsing a carefully modulated cuisine of uplift, the columnist chastised the parents for coddling the child to his detriment. The stomach, the author maintained, needed to be trained to digest doughnuts for the good of the child who needed to be toughened up in order to survive in a difficult world.[29]

This attempt to lessen the stakes at the dinner table, however, went unheeded by the editor of the *Brownies' Book*. Throughout his life, and long after his daughter, Yolande, reached adulthood, Du Bois continually exemplified the attributes of the excessively vigilant parent caricatured in the *Defender*. He paid careful attention both to his own food consumption habits as well as to what Yolande ate. Du Bois's actions serve as a revealing example of the practice of respectable child-rearing at the dinner table.[30] Although nearly every conceivable aspect of his intellectual life has been thoroughly examined by scholars, there has yet to be much scholarly attention paid to Du Bois's thoughts on a topic that was frequently on his mind: how and what to eat. Evidence of his ongoing interest in diet and nutrition can be found in various places throughout the corpus of his writing, indicating that Du Bois believed that what people ate (and by extension what they told their children to eat) was hardly incidental but of tremendous personal, social, and political significance.

Du Bois's Representative Black Body

When Du Bois became a parent and began tutoring his daughter about appropriate food choices, the advice he imparted was the outgrowth of decades of contemplation about the subject. He demonstrated an interest in eating right from an early age. As a twenty-three-year-old student at Harvard University, he wrote an essay for his English 12 class titled "Frightened" in which he confessed that he feared becoming ill, a state he hoped to avoid by deciding to "hustle about a bit and frequent the 'gym'" while also making the commitment to "eat like a confirmed dyspeptic." The dyspeptic diet Du Bois planned to adhere to was likely one low on processed food and animal protein and thus in keeping with the dietary advice proffered by contemporary food reformers such as John Harvey Kellogg, who promoted, among other things, dry breakfast cereal as a cure for the condition.[31] Du Bois was interested in a healthful diet and exercise regime because, he confessed, he was not "quite ready to depart from this world of ours yet, with all of its sorrows, disappointments, and dyspepsia."[32]

By framing his concern about dietary reform in terms of his wish to avoid dyspepsia, Du Bois revealed the extent to which he was a product of the culture in which he lived. Historian Harvey Levenstein describes the ailment as "a catch-all term for stomach pains, upsets, and disorders of all kinds," which became "the bane of the mid- and late nineteenth-century middle-class male."[33] The campaign Du Bois waged against dyspepsia during his early adulthood was thus also, in a sense, a means of asserting a feeling of national belonging. In both the contemporary popular media and in medical publications of the era, health writers often mournfully referred to the United States as "a nation of dyspeptics."[34] As he created a regime designed to spare his body from this affliction, his was also affirming the Americanness of his body due to his shared vulnerability to the national scourge. Although the society Du Bois lived in had declared his African American body separate and distinctive, his very physicality told a different story. When Du Bois became swept up in fear of having what Levenstein has labeled a "trendy disorder" that was "part fact and part fiction," he was responding to the same dietary and social cues that affected the bodies of numerous other urban, college-educated Americans.[35]

Du Bois's commitment to bodily, dietary discipline was a lifelong one, and his famously neat personal appearance was the physical manifestation of calculation, effort, and concern about both his health and his body image. In 1917 Du Bois joined the Life Extension Institute, an organization that was founded in 1913 with the commitment to "disseminate life-saving knowledge, which is to be supplied by savants from all parts of the world."[36] Former president William H. Taft was the first chairman of the LEI, and the staff and supporters of the organization included eminent business figures, public health experts, and prominent physicians. For an annual fee, members received a thorough annual medical examination, comparative health reports every two years, and regular urinalysis testing.[37] Du Bois later recalled that he joined the LEI not because he was sick but because he was well and wished to remain so, indicating that his attitude toward maintaining his health was consistent and proactive.[38] Remarkably, Du Bois remained a dues-paying member of the organization for more than thirty years, keeping his membership current at least through the early 1950s.

Despite his obvious ongoing faith in the reputation of the physicians at the LEI, Du Bois was not content to receive medical advice from that organization alone. He frequently sought opinions on the state of his health from a number of medical professionals, and he routinely submitted the LEI reports to his own private physician, Louis Wright, a fellow Harvard alumnus who was the first African American to hold a staff position in a New York City municipal hospital, for further scrutiny.[39] Du Bois's approach to maintaining his physical health not only was preemptive and active but seemed to be, at times, almost obsessive. He quizzed his doctors over slight imperfections in his test results, and he tirelessly tried to reconcile competing medical advice.[40]

Although Du Bois's health reports were generally positive, the one concrete recommendation that he did receive from the LEI in 1922 was that he embark on a program of "gradual reduction." He was advised to "somewhat restrict" his "intake of the more fattening foods, as butter, cream, eggs, breadstuffs, sweets, pastries, etc."[41] He received this recommendation on the basis of a physical examinations in 1922 that found that at a height of five feet six inches and a weight of 164.5 pounds, he exceeded what LEI regarded his ideal weight by slightly more than 20 pounds.[42] The advice from medical professionals inspired Du Bois to follow a strict dietary regiment. Like most uplift-oriented eaters, he worked hard to restrain and subdue his appetite.

Du Bois likely worried about the problem of weight reduction not only because he wished to preserve his health and to refute the stereotype of the black glutton but also in deference to a growing national obsession with a slender body type. The stereotypical dyspeptic body, which Du Bois fought to stave off, was a corpulent one.[43] Katharina Vester argues that in the mid-nineteenth century, dieting became popular among middle-class men who, like Du Bois, worked in sedentary occupations and began to worry that their bodies had become "too soft and feminine" as a result.[44] For Du Bois, who had a strongly defined sense of what an assertive, politically active, dignified "true manhood" should look like, the idea of occupying a feminized body was no doubt unsettling.[45] Although Gilded Age dietary advice manuals often gave women instructions about how to gain weight in order to appear plump, healthy, and maternal, for men of the same era, the cultivation of a slender, fit frame became a means of demonstrating one's masculinity, self-control, and even, in an age of national imperial aspirations, racial superiority.[46]

Increasingly, a large body size became associated not only with digestive troubles and femininity but also with other poor health outcomes as new medical research began to link excess weight to diseases like heart disease and diabetes. Helen Zoe Veit demonstrates that the idealization of the thin body, for both men and women, accelerated during the era of World War I when Americans were asked to conserve food so that surpluses could be diverted to feed troops and hungry allies. The fascination with thinness took hold, and by the 1920s it was common for middle-class Americans to count calories and embark on reduction plans.[47] Given the wartime conflation of abstemiousness at the table with patriotism, losing weight soon became not only a pragmatic way to guard one's health but also a way to perform one's national identification. The patriotic body was a slim one, and the slender frame became a signifier of both nationalism and moral rectitude. Given the broad symbolic register he had to draw upon, it is unsurprising that Du Bois began to consider body size to be an external way to gauge one's health, character, and, at least to some extent, one's belief system.[48]

Just as Du Bois had once been swept up in the late nineteenth-century crusade against indigestion, he took the new century's growing obsession with weight loss seriously. In his quest to influence the shape of his body, Du Bois not only considered the wisdom of traditional medicine but also demonstrated an open-mindedness to alternative ideas about health. In the summer of 1926, Du Bois visited Edmund Devol, a New York homeopath, to receive dietary advice.[49] Although there is no record of precisely what instructions Devol gave Du Bois, homeopathic medicine has a long tradition of treating food as both a potential cause and a cure for a variety of ailments. In the 1920s, homeopaths speculated, for example, that cancer might be caused by the ravages of the modern diet. Patients concerned with preventing cancer and otherwise preserving their health were frequently advised to avoid consuming animal products, alcohol, and coffee.[50] Devol's program may have been similar to the dyspeptic diet Du Bois experimented with during his undergraduate years. Whatever the nature of the specific advice, it apparently worked, because Du Bois later informed Devol that he was "feeling improved" and "keeping his weight under 150 lbs."[51]

Du Bois's correspondence reveals that his struggle against weight gain was an ongoing concern. Because eating is an essential daily activity, Du Bois must have devoted a great deal of mental energy to deciding what, when, and how much to eat in order to reach his health goals. Almost a decade after he followed Devol's reduction plan he wrote a letter to his friend Alexina C. Barrell lamenting that "at our age the tendency is to eat far too much." However, at that point in his life Du Bois seems to have been satisfied at his ability to avoid succumbing too much to this temptation because he satisfactorily reported, "I am glad to say my waistline is not impossible."[52] By 1938 he once again temporarily achieved a weight goal. In a letter to his wife, Nina Du Bois, he cheerfully reported that he had lost nine pounds and "feel much better." "I am going to try not to fatten up again," he proclaimed.[53]

Du Bois's consistent interest in his health must be viewed not only in light of the fact that he came of age during the era of widespread anxiety about dyspepsia and body size but also in the context of post-emancipation attempts by the medical and social scientific establishment to justify second-class citizenship for African Americans by emphasizing their purported physical pathologies.[54] While Du Bois's own bodily experience revealed that he had much in common with the felt experiences of white middle-class Americans, the racist conventional wisdom of the day asserted that his black body was inherently dissimilar to a white one. In 1896 Frederick L. Hoffman, a statistician for the Prudential Life Insurance Company, published a detailed report for the purpose of demonstrating that black Americans were a poor life insurance risk.[55] Based upon what

Image of a young girl reading, from W. E. B. Du Bois's display at the 1900 Paris Exhibition. (Photo by Thomas E. Askew; Library of Congress LC-USZ62–63574)

he described as the "perfect agreement from widely separated authorities and investigators," Hoffman concluded that "the negro of thirty years ago was physically the equal if not the superior of the white." In the post-emancipation era, he found only "deterioration" and difference.[56] When comparing black and white bodies, he claimed that black bodies were sicklier, shorter, and heavier and had less lung capacity and poorer vision than typical white subjects.[57] In an 1896 article published in the *North Carolina Medical Journal*, Dr. J. F. Miller agreed with Hoffman's assessment that African American health had deteriorated in the wake of emancipation. He claimed that while mental health issues and tuberculosis were almost

Du Bois, Respectable Child-Rearing, and the Representative Black Body

unknown among black people in the antebellum South, both conditions were increasing exponentially at the dawn of the new century.[58]

Given these strong assertions that black bodies fared better when in bondage than they did in freedom, it is understandable that Du Bois would view his own body as a kind of public display that could be used to demonstrate black physical equality. He had also put other black bodies on display while curating the Exhibit of American Negroes, which appeared at the 1900 Paris Exhibition. Du Bois carefully selected a large number of photographic portraits of African Americans, which were presented under the title "Types of American Negroes." These photos depicted African Americans, both male and female, with a wide range of ages and skin tones. Despite this diversity, there is a thread of similarity in these representations. The sitters are all neatly, sometimes lavishly, attired. Their posture is consistently erect, and their visages are composed, serene, and confident. Collectively, these images were designed to refute racist stereotypes about a singular black phenotype and black bodily inferiority.[59] Given his pattern of using representations of black physicality to counter assertions of black bodily degradation, it seems likely that he would have thought of his own body as a kind of animated, perpetual refutation of these same ideas. However, he was faced with the dilemma that although he could discipline his own body and be selective about the photographs he displayed in Paris, he could not control the actions or health outcomes of other African Americans whose bodies sometimes seemed to support the allegations of post-emancipation degeneration.

A close reading of the chapter "Of the Meaning of Progress," in Du Bois's landmark study *The Souls of Black Folk*, highlights the extent of Du Bois's concern about the state of the health of black bodies at the turn of the twentieth century.[60] Du Bois recalled revisiting, after an absence of ten years, an Appalachian town where he had worked as a summer school teacher during his undergraduate years at Fisk. Stephen Knadler has noted that while recounting his trip Du Bois "lingers repeatedly (and almost obsessively) on the unsightliness of the maimed and the diseased as if to add his own anecdotal weight to prevailing statistics about the degeneration of black bodies as a result of their freedom."[61] Indeed, negative and despairing descriptions of bodies that are "blighted," "stooped," "gaunt," "half-witted," and "bow legged" abound.[62] Perhaps unsurprisingly, given Du Bois's own obsession with body size, he was quick to document encounters with bodies that did not conform to his slender ideal. Du Bois not only noted bodies that he deemed too large but also conflated size with specific moral or intellectual failings. He speculated, for example, that "fat Reuben," whom he had not seen for a decade, was likely as "lazy as ever." Similarly, he unfavorably observed that "the Neill boys" were "fat, lazy farmhands" and that "Lana," who was "plump" and "brown," was also "slow."[63] Du Bois demonstrates a clear certainty that moral attributes could have physical manifestations. If people learned to behave better, he believed that they would enjoy positive physical benefits that would spring from their interior transformations.

Du Bois's negative observations about the current state of southern black bodies complemented, in many respects, the judgments of men like Hoffman and Miller who had pronounced the state of health of the race as being woefully deficient. However, unlike white proponents of the theory of black degradation who wrote about the black community in monolithic, racial terms, Du Bois's anxieties about the state of health of the black community took into account regional and class variations. For example, an implied contrast between his healthy northern middle-class body and the deformed working-class southerners he wrote about in "Of the Meaning of Progress" is clear. In a detailed and critical review of Hoffman's study, Du Bois charged that the author used his statistics carelessly without acknowledging that the data he collected "relate[d] to different classes of people and to widely different conditions of life."[64] The fact that Du Bois felt free to casually and unfavorably assess the bodies of "fat Reuben" and others in comparison with his own trimmer frame reveals that although he acknowledged that they shared a designation in the reigning racial stratification scheme, there was an enormous gulf between them in terms of lived experiences, which were embodied both in Reuben's corpulence and Du Bois's own implied corporeal superiority.

The distinctions he made when evaluating the bodies of black people throughout the class spectrum are in keeping with Du Bois's ideas about a "talented tenth," which would represent "the Best of this race." In Du Bois's current strategy for racial advancement, a sliver of the black population was charged with the task of "guid[ing] the Mass away from the contamination and death of the Worst." These "exceptional men," he argued, had managed to escape from the fate of most African Americans. He believed that the ravages of white supremacy often resulted in physical degeneration for the masses.[65] Those who had preserved their health in the face of "contamination," "death," and "disease," the loaded words that Du Bois used to describe the degradation caused by slavery and second-class citizenship, were obligated to teach others how to behave in order to reach better outcomes. Thus the leaders of the race not only were intellectually superior due to their better educational opportunities but had physical advantages too due to their superior health status.

Determined to embark upon a serious study about the state of health of the black community, Du Bois devoted the 1906 session of Atlanta University's Conference on the Negro Problem to the topic.[66] After surveying an enormous amount of data, the conference participants concluded that there were indeed bodily disparities among black and white people. However, they did not interpret these differences as proof that black bodies were unfit for freedom but instead as evidence of severe societal neglect, claiming, "The negro death rate and sickness are largely matters of condition and not due to racial traits and tendencies."[67]

Reflecting the gendered ideas about the division of domestic labor common at the time, Du Bois also expressed concern that most black women were forced to work outside the home due to economic necessity. This state of affairs made him fear that their children might be fed "unwholesome and improper food" in their absence that would harm their future health outcomes.[68] Intriguingly, his notion that mothers were responsible for feeding their children did not stop him from trying to correct what he saw as the dietary mistakes of his own offspring.

Yolande Du Bois and the Somatic Burdens of Racial Uplift

Since body size and the linked issue of proper nutrition were topics that concerned Du Bois greatly, it is unsurprising that this preoccupation influenced his child-rearing techniques. Du Bois expected Yolande, who was born in 1900, to share his same commitment to bodily discipline when it came to food consumption. His fatherly fear about the state of his daughter's health had a specific personal context that went beyond both his lifelong obsession with maintaining a healthy lifestyle and the seriousness with which he approached the task of respectable child-rearing: Du Bois was confronted with the frailty of his daughter's body directly after she had an appendectomy in 1922. His advice, tinged as it sometimes was with an element of panic, likely sprang in part from the prescient fear that she might be subjected to another frightening medical intervention. And indeed, in the spring of 1923, not long after Du Bois wrote her a letter where he sternly admonished her to eat more vegetables, Yolande underwent another procedure designed to cure ongoing health problems, which Du

Bois biographer David Levering Lewis speculates was probably a laparotomy to cure a bowel obstruction.[69] Whatever the cause of Yolande's specific set of health issues, Du Bois had no qualms about attributing the failing of her body—in part—to her own behavior. When worrying both about his health and about the health of his daughter, Du Bois emphasized individual agency and choice, refusing to view either of them as completely helpless in the face of health crises. Instead he demonstrated an ongoing and uplift-appropriate belief that proper behavior could positively influence the functioning of a recalcitrant body.

If Du Bois's relationship with his daughter is indicative of similar exchanges between other middle-class black parents and their sometimes uncooperative offspring, it is clear that the mandate of respectable child-rearing sometimes necessitated discussions about unrespectable subjects—like toilet habits. Du Bois worried not only about what went into Yolande's body but also about what came out, warning her to "drink water (4 or 5 glasses) a day and eat fruit and green vegetables" in order to avoid becoming constipated. Du Bois informed his daughter that nothing should interfere with a daily bowel movement at a consistent hour, not "meals, classes, engagements, study or prayers."[70] This fatherly advice left a lasting impression. When Yolande became a mother, she passed on her father's lessons about regularity to her own daughter. In a 1935 memo to a nurse who was charged with caring for her three-year-old daughter, Du Bois Williams, Yolande insisted that the nurse make sure that the girl went to the toilet to "push" one hour after breakfast and if unsuccessful that she repeat the ritual after dinner and again at supper if necessary, demanding that she produce "one bowel movement a day."[71]

The Du Bois family was hardly alone in their insistence that maintaining regularity was of the upmost importance. Contemporary anxiety about sluggish bowels was widespread. Medical authorities warned that constipation could lead not only to discomfort but also to an epidemic of "autointoxication," as constipated bodies unable to rid themselves of toxins succumbed to their own poisons.[72] In the contemporary discussion about constipation, even more than the mortality of constipation sufferers was at stake; the conversation about blocked bowels revealed a set of anxieties about modernity, nationhood, and gender. While instructing Yolande to regulate this basic bodily function, Du Bois was also encouraging her to perform particular ideas about the person he wanted her to become.

Reformers armed with scientific information and righteous indignation hoped to cure constipation, which they regarded as an unfortunate consequence of contemporary food habits.[73] In 1918, John Harvey Kellogg dramatically opined that constipation was "the most destructive blockade that has ever opposed human progress."[74] In a 1913 column in the *Chicago Defender*, Dr. A. Wilberforce Williams echoed that assertion to his black audience, claiming this "bane of civilization" afflicted nearly everyone at some point.[75] Much as proponents of the theory of black physical degradation identified the Civil War as a stark turning point in the health history of that segment of the population, constipation sufferers traced the origins of the national epidemic to the Second Industrial Revolution that took place at around the same time. The increasing urbanization of the American population and the rapid technological changes in food production meant that fewer and fewer Americans were growing and preparing their own food. The ever-increasing consumption of refined and processed foods allegedly had a deleterious impact on the national state of digestion.[76]

Du Bois's assertion that his daughter suffered from this affliction served as another refutation of the idea of black bodily difference. In succumbing to constipation, Yolande's body was reflecting her social status. Her intestines were not blocked because they were housed in a body unfit for freedom; instead, like other middle-class constipation sufferers, she was supposedly the victim of rapid changes in the food supply. Unlike the infectious disease of tuberculosis, which was commonly associated with working-class African Americans during the time period, constipation was imagined as a middle-class illness.[77]

Since a problematic diet allegedly caused the condition, health advocates claimed that a new dietary program was the best solution to the scourge. While Yolande was an undergraduate at Fisk, a group of health reformers whom James C. Whorton has labeled "the whole wheat crusaders" were actively positing whole grains as a cure for what many regarded as the "mother" of many other diseases.[78] This dietary advice even made its way into the *Brownies' Book*, which advised young black children in 1920 to eat whole-wheat "Graham" bread to cure the ailment.[79] Sufferers from this affliction were, according to contemporary experts on the subject, supposed to draw inspiration from the antebellum teachings of Sylvester Graham, a Presbyterian minister and temperance crusader turned dietary food reformer. Graham claimed that processed wheat flour, with the bran removed, was the potential cause not only of constipation but also of a variety of other disorders.[80] In contrast, Graham viewed whole wheat bread, a coveted Euro-American food since the very beginning of the

American colonial venture, as a particularly healthful food, which doubled as an important symbol of national belonging.[81] Kayla Wazana Tompkins claims that for Graham, homemade bread "signified domestic order, civic health, and moral well being."[82] To eat wheat bread was to perform one's Americanness, and heavy doses of the wholesome grain could be used to bring ailing American bodies back into order.

Significantly, according to Graham, the properties of the food alone did not make wheat "American." The eater—who wished to assert his or her sense of national belonging—had to maintain a proper attitude while consuming the grain. Although under ideal circumstances, whole grains could cure both constipation and a long list of other health-related woes, Graham claimed that sometimes "the vicious habits of some people . . . entirely counteract the aperient effects of the bread." Undesirable traits like laziness and gluttony could destroy the curative powers of this miracle food.[83] In 1916, Dr. Samuel Goodwin Gant agreed, arguing that autointoxication was most common among patients who led a "sedentary, indolent, or dissipated life, whose surroundings are unhygienic."[84] According to this viewpoint, sufferers like Yolande were ultimately to blame for the uncomfortable state of their bowels since they were clearly not virtuous enough to trigger wheat's curative power.

Whorton has noted that constipation sufferers who did not behave properly were stigmatized; "since cleanliness was next to godliness, constipation might be considered immoral."[85] Furthermore, their illness was only one of many potential visible signs of their character flaws. Williams warned the black community that "alimentary disturbances" could become visible in the form of a bad complexion. He advised his readers to "regulate your diet" and "clean out your bowels" in order to remedy unsightly blemishes. Because constipation could be avoided through personal effort, the imperfect skin it allegedly created became an outward reflection of inner failings.[86] Some health authorities took the idea that bad behavior could lead to constipation a step further, arguing that the sickness was both caused by poor conduct and could also inspire it. Not only could undisciplined and unprincipled behavior lead to constipation, but "food intoxication" caused by the lingering impact of poor food that had not been properly evacuated by the body could lead the victims in the direction of "violence and immorality," according to W. R. C. Watson, editor of *Health Culture*.[87] In this context, it is clear why Du Bois regarded Yolande's dietary infractions as so serious. Both her physical health and the health of her character were at stake if she refused to heed his dietary advice.

Intriguingly, Graham claimed that the attitude of the eater was not the only effect on the potency of the bread that was supposed to cure constipation; the miracle substance was also said to be more or less potent depending upon who made it. The bread of U.S. nationhood, according to Graham, could be properly made only by a wife and mother "who loves her husband and her children as women ought to love and who rightly perceives the relations between the dietetic habits and physical and moral conditions of her loved ones."[88] Thus the medical power of bread was tied to the embrace of traditional nineteenth-century gender roles. Only bread made by women firmly ensconced in the separate sphere could produce an effective cure for the "mother" of all diseases. During the Progressive Era, ideas about gender and gender roles were still intertwined in discussions about both the cause and the cure of the illness. Elizabeth Herbert argues that by the time Yolande came of age, the colon had became a "gendered organ" because the medical literature of the day widely agreed that constipation was more common among women than among men.[89]

The idea that Yolande suffered from a "female" affliction and not a "racial" illness was a subversive one. On one level both she and her fellow constipation sufferers were subjected to limiting ideas about female bodily inferiority by suffering from what was being labeled as a predominantly female illness. However, in another sense, her embodied experience countered centuries-old ideas about black female physical difference. Deborah Gray White has noted that beginning with European colonization and the advent of African slavery in what is now the United States, Euro-Americans "constructed the black woman's body as monstrous and grotesque, bestial enough to deem all Africans inferior in contrast to the civility and superiority of the English."[90] Yolande's body, however, announced—although perversely through the avenue of an embarrassing medical condition—her membership in a sisterhood of shared affliction. Her body was not bestial and different from those of her white sisters but was instead equally susceptible to a gendered illness and correspondingly equally capable of becoming cured.

By the time Du Bois wrote to his daughter about her bowel movements, the conversation about wheat bread as a curative food had evolved beyond Graham's thinking on the subject. In the wake of the ascendency of the slender body ideal, food reformers paid careful attention not just to what foods victims of constipation consumed but to what quantities as well. In 1918, Edna Eugenia Lowe, an instructor of female physical education, claimed, much as Graham did, that white flour was associated with constipation while whole wheat offered a potential cure. However, she argued that eating too much food was the primary cause of the condition. Bowels operated the best when a "simple, nutritious diet" was consumed.[91] In her popular 1934 book giving physical fitness advice to women, *Stand Up and Slim Down*, Ettie Hornibrook warned women against the constipating impact of eating "too much bread, far too many buns, crackers, biscuits, and cakes."[92] In her popular 1918 weight loss guide, Lulu Hunt Peters also instructed her female readers to rein themselves in, claiming that consuming "leafy vegetables," which were "low in fat-producing properties," was the best remedy for "sluggish bowels."[93] The virtuous female bakers of the nineteenth century had been transformed into women who were consumers rather than producers of food with large appetites that they needed to control. As Joan Jacobs Brumberg points out in her history of anorexia nervosa, *Fasting Girls*, although both men and women during the Progressive Era were charged with maintaining bodily control, the pressure for women to restrain themselves was particularly high: "Overweight in women was not only a physical liability, it was a character flaw and a social impediment."[94]

According to the conventional wisdom of the day, even scrupulously counting calories was not sufficient for keeping constipation at bay. Kellogg warned that women who wished to free up their bowels also needed to exercise more and to wear loose-fitting clothes that would aid in evacuation.[95] Unsurprisingly, the same society that deemed thin bodies to be more virtuous than larger ones made moral judgments about constipation as well, continuing to argue that the condition had a physical as well as an ethical dimension. Women who did not effectively police their bodies and modify their behaviors by eating the right foods or wearing proper clothing had only themselves to blame for their illness. This emphasis on personal behavior and personal responsibility would clearly have resonated with respectable black eaters who stressed the importance of controlling their own bodies and their own actions at a moment when they could do little to transform the society they inhabited.

Intriguingly, just as Du Bois had yielded to the typical middle-class male anxiety about "dyspepsia" in the late nineteenth century, his daughter's body also seemed to respond to cultural cues as she succumbed to an illness that had been coded female. The experiences of the Du Boises demonstrate that physical ailments—not only the names by which they are labeled but also the symptoms themselves—are products of both natural and social causes. Both father and daughter learned to understand

Du Bois, Respectable Child-Rearing, and the Representative Black Body

their bodily experiences, in part, by using the vocabulary given to them by the medical establishment and other self-proclaimed authorities. Not only did the reigning discourse about constipation give Du Bois a label for his daughter's ailment, but being so labeled likely also influenced Yolande's own embodied experience, possibly making physical symptoms appear or worsen.[96]

In either suffering from or seeking relief from the conditions that they labeled dyspepsia or constipation, father and daughter were revealing to what extent they were—in defiance of contemporary ideas about black bodily difference—products of the culture that produced them. Peter Conrad and Kristen Barker have noted that "medical knowledge some-times reflects and reproduces existing forms of social inequality . . . sup-port[ing] gender, class, and racial-ethnic inequality."[97] This was certainly the case at the turn of the twentieth century, when medical authorities busily documented black bodily degradation, making the self-interested argument that while black bodies had thrived under the supervision of white slave owners, they deteriorated after emancipation. These observa-tions about bodily difference helped perpetuate the inferior position that black Americans occupied in the social order. In defiance of these ideas about black bodily difference presented in the guise of science, Du Bois and Yolande continually asserted their corporeal similarity to their fellow citizens, not their racial difference. Their bodies defied the racializing gaze of the medical establishment.[98] They did not inhabit black bodies that were incapable of navigating the world sans white supervision; instead, their bodies responded to the fear of trendy diseases that were also claimed by members of the white middle class.

Du Bois was sympathetic to the idea that health issues were of social— or more specifically, racial—concern. Healthy, disciplined black bodies reflected well upon the race. His own obsession with body size was both inspired by and legitimated by contemporary advice that increasingly warned women, in particular, not to overeat. Although Yolande suffered from physical afflictions serious enough to require surgery during her col-lege years, Du Bois was insistent upon framing her health as a moral issue as well as a physical one. His fundamental outlook on health and personal responsibility had not evolved much since his own college days, when he had decided to embark on a program of exercise and diet to stave off ill-ness. He was mortified that Yolande did not seem to exemplify a similar set of internal motivations to manipulate her body. Determined to provide external pressure in the place of the internal compulsion that he thought was missing, Du Bois warned Yolande that if she neglected his advice to eat well, she was, in effect, committing suicide. It was her responsibility, as a young black woman from a respectable household, to take control of her body to the extent she was able and to coax herself back into health through force of will by dedicating herself to a strict corporeal regime. Du Bois chided, "Neither your mother, nor your physician, nor I can make you well and happy. That is your job."[99]

Keeping herself well and happy and modeling a physique that, in her father's mind, constituted a physical manifestation of inward discipline and dedication were not easily mastered by Yolande, at least not to Du Bois's satisfaction. They were also not subjects that her father was willing to drop, even after she reached full-fledged adulthood. In 1935, although Yolande had already been married, divorced, remarried, and had a child, he was still monitoring her weight and eating patterns, finding both in need of improvement. In 1935 he wrote to his daughter, who was by then a schoolteacher in Baltimore, warning her that as a woman in her thirties, her window for self-improvement was closing: "Not much change or improvement can be expected of ordinary persons who pass forty." He urged her, once again, to be mindful about what she consumed: "You do not realize how much you eat of flesh-forming substances. . . . You have a tendency to be fat. . . . You have got to change. . . . If you don't . . . it means suffering and death."

Repeating the same refrain he began during her college years, Du Bois told Yolande that her health was her responsibility and as such was a reflection of her degree of moral virtue. To make the case that she was not being responsible, he presented evidence, presumably supplied by Yolande's mother, Nina, of her dietary transgressions, accusing Yolande of consuming too much cream, bread, potatoes, butter, gravy, and candy. He ordered her to "stop this surreptitious munching all day" and to "eat mainly fruits and vegetables without seasoning." To add another layer of shame to the situation, Du Bois promised that he would send a copy of the letter to Louis Wright, the family physician, to enlist him in the project of trying to get Yolande to change her food behavior.[100] By involving another member of the black community in this private matter, Du Bois revealed his belief that individual behavior was of group-wide concern. In urging his daughter to eat a proper diet and to avoid becoming constipated, Du Bois was advising her to adopt what historian Stephanie Shaw has referred to as a "socially responsible individualism."[101] She was supposed to pay attention to her personal development, both intellectually and physically, in large part so that she would be better prepared to aid other members of the race in their collective quest for advancement.

As intrusive and condescending as Du Bois's dietary advice to his daughter may seem in contemporary hindsight, there can be no doubt about the sincerity of his belief that his recommendations, if heeded, would help his daughter and, by extension, the rest of the black community. It is also worth remembering that Du Bois subjected himself to the same degree of scrutiny. Yolande, who clearly did not wholeheartedly embrace her father's regime, seems to have allowed her father a certain amount of latitude in advising her because of their familial relationship. However, as the next chapter reveals, respectable eaters frequently disseminated similar dietary advice outside of the context of the nuclear family. Middle-class food reformers who, like Du Bois, were certain of the superiority of their culinary ideals seldom limited the recipients of their advice to their sons and daughters. Instead, the respectable eaters who are the subject of the next chapter offered a comprehensive critique of the food habits of the entire black working class.

Regionalism, Social Class, and Elite Perceptions of Working-Class Foodways during the Era of the Great Migration

"The Watermelon Dance," a children's short story written by Peggy Poe in 1920, features her cheerful reoccurring protagonist "Happy," a young boy who lives in rural Georgia. In this episode from his fictional childhood, Happy, who claims to like watermelons the "best of all things on this part of the world," uncontrollably gobbles the last watermelon of the season. While committing this act, he is directly defying his father, a small farmer, who planned to take the watermelon to market to sell in exchange for a new hoe. After Happy slices into the watermelon rind, the seeds inside expand, come to life, and threaten to kidnap Happy and his friends until the family cow inadvertently disrupts the sinister scene. The inaptly named "Happy" is plagued by both guilt and terror as he learns the heavy-handed lesson that respectable children should obey their parents and learn to tame their appetites.[1]

This instructive story appeared in W. E. B. Du Bois's short-lived children's magazine, the *Brownies' Book*, which was designed by members of the black intelligentsia for the purpose of inculcating children with the values associated with the respectability project. As chapter 3 reveals, the contents of the magazine certainly reflect Du Bois's ideas about which lessons concerning consumption should be imparted to African American children. However, the contents also inadvertently reveal elite attitudes toward working-class food practices. Young readers learned how to critique the "undesirable" behavior of the less privileged and that they had a solemn duty to try to reform the habits of those who were recalcitrant about acquiring the lessons of uplift.

Most readers of the *Brownies' Book* would have understood that Happy's decision to indulge in a stolen watermelon was a particularly shameful act because of the prevalent stereotypes proclaiming that black people had an unnatural and outsized affection for that particular fruit. However, they would also have been trained to presume that this faux pas could be explained as an outgrowth of his ignorance as a poor, rural southerner. In contrast to the members of Happy's family, who were economically insecure enough to worry about the fate of their last watermelon, most of the fictional children who inhabited the pages of the *Brownies' Book* dined on abundant and luxurious foods like roasted chestnuts, duck, and commercially manufactured candies.[2] The 1920 tale "Turkey Drumsticks," written by the magazine's managing editor, Jessie Fauset, gives insights into the editorial team's vision of an ideal respectable childhood diet. The children in Fauset's story enjoy a Thanksgiving table laden with a roasted suckling pig, a turkey, ham, cranberry and quince jelly, vegetables, and oyster dressing.[3] These items, which include the iconic U.S. holiday dish of roasted turkey served alongside the more cosmopolitan quince, were selected to conjure up a much wider set of culinary associations than that of the humble watermelon that Happy enjoyed to his detriment.

The *Brownies' Book* and the Problem of Southern Food

The culinary diversity represented in the magazine's food imaginery was designed, in part, to refute the idea of a singular African American style of eating. Although Du Bois wanted to use the magazine to help instill pride in the "history and achievements of the Negro race," this goal did not include cultivating the idea of a distinctively black vernacular food culture, a concept that Du Bois disavowed. He told Isaac Beton, secretary of the Pan-African Congress, that unlike some other peoples of the African diaspora, "there is no national dish for the colored people." However, although Du Bois did not make a case for a racial style of eating, he did note class distinctions, claiming disapprovingly that the "black laborer" had a "tendency by heritage . . . towards fats and starches."[4] Within the pages of the *Brownies' Book*, the dietary class distinctions that Du Bois acknowledges are often framed in regional terms. Rural southerners frequently stand in as representatives for the black working class, and the southern diet is presented as flawed and in need of improvement.

In the world of the Brownies, there is no "black" diet that culturally unifies the entire race. However, there is a distinctive southern diet, which is to be transcended or reformed.[5] Most contemporary African American food reformers insisted upon describing the prototypical southern African American diet in regional rather than in racial terms. This was in part because many respectable eaters did not consume a southern-inflected diet themselves and thus would have been alienated by the thought of a racial way of eating that excluded them. Furthermore, and even more significantly, members of this group were leery of ideas about racially essential cultural expressions that might contravene a political agenda that emphasized the abilities of former slaves to learn the rules of a society that had formerly excluded them. Because so many respectable eaters associated southern cuisine with slavery and poverty, they logically concluded that consuming a bland, homogeneous, and performatively American national cuisine was one means of symbolically transcending these conditions, and they were critical of members of the race who did not fall sway to the allure of culinary reform.

Unsurprisingly, a children's magazine designed to educate the next generation of black children captured many parents' anxieties about the meanings embedded in southern food culture. In a story titled "The Quaintness of St. Helena," Julia Price Burrell offers a pointed critique of southern eating habits as different and inferior, an approach that is emblematic of much of the magazine's portrayal of southern regional food culture. In partial deference to the ideas of race loyalty and unity, Burrell expresses admiration for the residents of the sea island St. Helena due to the high percentage of independent landownership among the group. However, this positive and politically significant attribute hardly seems to offset the flaws she identifies, which include ill health, an inability to learn Standard English, and a faulty diet. She proclaims that the sea island fare of corn and pork augmented with rice, sweet potatoes, and syrup from locally grown sugarcane is not only spare but also technologically backward. The sea islanders, Burrell insists, foolishly "prefer their antiquated methods of farming to improved scientific ideas which are demonstrated before their very eyes!"[6] Because they had not adopted an unspecified set of modern modes of food consumption and production, which Burrell implicitly endorses, she regards the inhabitants of St. Helena's methods as backward and in need of culinary reform.

A macabre story by Lillian A. Turner, "How Lilimay 'Kilt' the Chicken," suggests that regional and cultural differences could have potentially lethal consequences. Lilimay, a young girl from "a grassy valley of middle Ohio in a country district of New England descendants," is traumatized on a visit to the South when a relative tells her to "kiver" a sickly chicken. The little girl tearfully obeys what she misheard as instructions to kill (rather than to "cover") the tiny bird. All of this trauma could have been avoided, the story implies, if rural southerners bought their food at the market instead of raised it and learned to stop speaking in regional dialect.[7] A story titled "The Chocolate Cake" by Pocahontas Foster reveals a similar sense of anxiety about the possibility of transcending cultural divisions in the black community, but in this story the consequences of the inter-cultural misunderstandings are less traumatic for those involved. When the protagonist, Gwendolyn, is sent to visit an aunt in the South, she is thrilled at the prospect of eating iconic southern foods like fried chicken and biscuits.[8] However, Gwendolyn has a severe falling-out with her aunt after she fails to follow instructions and makes cake frosting out of bitter, unsweetened cocoa. In the mind of the young girl, this intergenerational and interregional dispute seems catastrophic. However, when her father picks up his chastened daughter to bring her back home, he does not scold her for the mistake but instead remarks, "I don't believe I want you to cook any way. I think I'd rather have you study music."[9] The relieved narrator agrees with this suggestion, relegating fried chicken and the skill of cook-ing to her country relatives while deciding to participate in the uplift-ap-propriate pursuit of high culture.

In contrast, in "A Criss-Cross Thanksgiving," Augusta Bird provides a template for the possibility of interregional culinary unity and of south-ern culinary uplift. Bird imagines a harmonious southern Thanksgiving where these cultural barriers have at last been transcended thanks to the efforts of southerners who have learn to embrace the gospel of respectable food habits. An African American mother promises her son, a young New Yorker, a "real Thanksgiving" in Virginia. He imagines being served tur-key, cranberry sauce, roasted pig, pumpkin and mince pies, and chestnuts, a menu that does not contain any self-consciously southern markers.[10] The reformed southerners who are to host this uplift-appropriate meal live in what Bird describes as a "suburban" home, having successfully learned to straddle the cultural extremes represented elsewhere in the magazine by the city or the country.[11] Bird's decision to describe a menu laden with the foods of the fabled New England feast such as turkey, pumpkin, and cranberries without including any dishes denoting regional distinctive-ness was designed to emphasize the potential Americanness of all African American eaters and to offer hope for the eventual culinary transcendence of unrespectable black eaters.

The tangled themes of race, region, and class explored through the medium of food in the *Brownies' Book* are indicative of widespread cultural clashes within the black community over these issues. By looking at the lessons respectable eaters hoped to teach their children, we are also gaining insights into the kind of instruction that middle-class African Americans wanted to impart to working-class members of their community. They hoped to train this group to behave in a manner they deemed appropriate, tutoring them by means of personal example, much as they would their own children. However, it should come as no surprise that although respectable eaters had a captive audience in the form of their own offspring, at least while they were young and dependent, it was far more difficult to capture the attention of working-class African Americans. Members of this group were often alienated, not only by the implication that they needed to be taught how to behave but also by the idea that their cultural practices were in need of improvement.

Southern Traditions

IIIIIIIIIIIIIIIIIIIIIIIIIIIIIIIIIIIIII

While these class and regional conflicts could sometimes be transcended in the imaginary world of the *Brownies' Book*, these dynamics were more resistant to tidy resolutions in the outside world that the magazine hoped to influence. Controversies over the desirability and meaning of southern cuisine remained at the heart of conversations about respectability at the table. Food reformers consistently advocated against the idea of a distinctively black style of eating, which they feared would reify ideas about innate racial differences and work to emphasize the essential otherness of African Americans at a moment when progressive activists were framing food reform as a vehicle to perform assimilation and national belonging.

By the early twentieth century, the industrialization of the American food supply was leading to the minimization of regional dietary differences as technological innovations in both food processing and in transportation networks freed many American eaters from the necessity of eating seasonally and locally and made once-scarce food items cheaper and more readily available. Respectable eaters generally embraced these changes and seized opportunities to eat industrially produced foods and greater quantities of symbolically resonant "American" foods like beef and wheat. However, in spite of these transformations, certain identifiable regional inflections continued to mark the southern diet as distinctive. On the whole, poorer rural Americans, many of whom lived in the South, changed their diets more slowly than those with the greater means to purchase a variety of store-bought goods. Under these conditions, culinary conflicts among respectable eaters and southern African Americans who had not fallen in line with the philosophy of uplift erupted frequently as upwardly mobile African Americans tried to intervene in the traditional eating practices that they regarded as problematic.

Although they were a vocal group, the respectable eaters who were ambivalent about the meanings embedded in the practice of consuming a southern regional diet constituted a tiny minority of the black population. The most outspoken food reformers had achieved a relatively high degree of formal education and resided either in urban centers or in the north. They were candidates for membership in the ranks of W. E. B. Du Bois's idealized, educated "talented tenth" of race leaders. On the surface of things, Du Bois's idea that 10 percent of the population should achieve an education in order to be better equipped to lead the rest of the black community seems to be a relatively modest goal. It was, however, actually a wildly optimistic one. By Du Bois's own count, only 100 African Americans graduated from northern colleges and universities between 1895 and 1900, and slightly more than 500 graduated from southern black colleges during that same time. A 1900 Atlanta University study counted a total of 2,331 black college graduates between 1826 and 1899.[12] Out of a total black population of 8.8 million people in 1900, this group was statistically insignificant. Furthermore, although black food reformers were disproportionately based in urban areas and in the North, in 1920, 85 percent of African Americans still lived in the South, largely in rural areas where they were concentrated in low-paying jobs in the agricultural sector.[13] Thus, although respectable eaters were a vocal group, their number was small in comparison to the large number of southern-style eaters whose cuisine they hoped to reform.

Most African American southerners, particularly members of the working class, ate some variation of a regional southern diet that had been rendered problematic in the *Brownies' Book* and elsewhere. This style of eating was inevitably reminiscent of the diet of slavery due to the fact that southern regional cooking both during slavery and post-emancipation contained corn and pork as its cornerstones. Respectable black eaters grappled with the legacy and meanings of these core foods, which had inarguably played an enormous role in fueling the machine of American slavery.

In his groundbreaking study of the antebellum diet, *Hog Meat and Hoecake: Food Supply in the Old South, 1840–1860*, Sam Bower Hilliard argues that in the nineteenth century, "the dominance of corn bread as *the* bread of the South is unquestionable."[14] Very little wheat was grown in the South, making it a relatively expensive luxury that had to be imported from distant markets.[15] Corn, however, was plentiful and quickly became a ubiquitous slave ration. Adult slaves generally received about a peck of corn a week.[16] The single food item most strongly associated with North American slavery is perhaps a simple corn bread made primarily from meal and water. After emancipation, cornmeal continued to be widely consumed in the South. Although its importance diminished somewhat as wheat flour become more available and less expensive due to improved transportation networks and a more efficient milling process, corn was never displaced as a regional staple.[17] In contrast to other regions of the country where wheat was overwhelmingly the preferred grain, at the turn of the twentieth century southerners were, at best, consuming wheat bread and corn bread in roughly equal proportions. The persistent appearance of corn bread on southern tables meant that uplift-oriented eaters were forced to continually contend with the symbolic significance of the grain.[18]

While the next chapter will consider the meanings embedded in corn in greater detail, this chapter will build upon the discussion, begun in chapter 2, about the significance of the other staple of the southern black diet: pork. Pork, particularly the offal and other scraps of the pig, become a particularly contested symbol in the culinary class wars that emerged in the black community in the first decades of the twentieth century. This form of animal protein had become so omnipresent on southern tables that it was often referred to simply as "meat" without any fear of local misunderstandings.[19] Hilliard claims, "If the 'king' of the antebellum southern economy was cotton then the title of 'queen' must go to the pig."[20] Adult slaves typically received somewhere between three and five pounds of salted, fatty pork each week.[21] For most enslaved people, pork was the only meat they received as part of their regular rations. Most other animal protein that enslaved people sampled came in the form of rare holiday treats; small game they hunted in their scant free time; or items pilfered from the slave owners' larders. White southerners typically ate a wider variety of meat, including more beef, mutton, and poultry, than the enslaved, but for this group, too, swine was predominant. As late as the 1920s, a study of the diets of southern farm families in three different states concluded that the average adult ate 138 pounds of pork a year and only about 12 pounds of beef.[22]

Despite the regional dependency upon pork, some southerners were dubious about its health value even before the Civil War, and this skepticism helped fuel the negative connotations of swine consumption that many respectable eaters maintained well into the twentieth century.[23] On the eve of the Civil War, Georgia physician John Stainback Wilson despaired of the fact that "in many parts of this region, so far as meat is concerned, it is fat bacon and pork . . . and that continually morning, noon, and night for all classes, sexes, ages, and conditions."[24] He regarded this diet to be unwholesome, arguing that pig flesh belonged to the "heat producing" rather than the more desirable "muscle producing" class of foods. Pork was easily digested, he claimed, by only the most active people who lived in warmer climes, by workers and not by thinkers, and thus by slaves and not by free people.[25] For those who wished to transcend the negative memories associated with racial slavery and to dissociate the bodily experience of enslavement from that of freedom, abandoning what was widely regarded as a food well suited for slaves seemed like a step in the right direction.

Post-emancipation food formers who wanted to remove pork from the southern table, particularly the less coveted parts of the animal that were predominant in the slave diet, had to contend with the fact that pigs were the most widely available and thus least expensive domestic animal protein at the turn of the twentieth century. For this reason, pork was regularly consumed by those of lesser means. Historian Harvey Levenstein argues that among the well-off, beef was a much higher-status protein as it was considered to be more healthful and easier to digest. Much like black respectable eaters, members of the rising white middle class who sought to replicate the food habits of their economic superiors "shunned fresh and salted pork and deigned only to eat an occasional slice of smoked ham."[26] These negative associations of pork with slavery and poverty meant that this form of animal protein was a potent, negative symbol for upwardly mobile eaters across the racial divide but more painfully so for respectable eaters who were eager to cast off associations with slavery.

Pork and corn endured as such powerful symbols at the turn of the twentieth century precisely because this style of eating remained entrenched among the South's poorest residents. Many African Americans living in the region, particularly those who worked as sharecroppers, bought food on credit and thus were subjected to the limitations of being able to purchase only what those who lent them money would allow.[27] Plantation owners had little incentive to make sure that their tenants had access to

Regionalism, Social Class, and Elite Perceptions of Working-Class Foodways

An African American couple eating a meal in rural Virginia, 1899 or 1900.
(Photo by Frances Benjamin Johnston; Library of Congress LC-USZ62–61017)

any foods beyond those necessary to achieve the merest subsistence. Thus the poorest African Americans generally ate the "three M's diet" of meal, meat, and molasses in large part because those traditional foods, common in slave rations, were still regularly stocked at plantation commissaries to the exclusion of other items.[28]

Much to the consternation of food reformers, however, evidence suggests that, for some, preference came into play alongside necessity in perpetuating the southern diet. Edward Beardsley speculates that the "three M's" had such a tenacious hold on the imagination of the southern working classes because "it was tasty enough and well-suited to a people lacking luxuries like refrigerators and having little spare time for food preparation."[29] A group of social anthropologists who studied black life in the Mississippi Delta in the mid-1930s found that even when landlords allowed their tenants to plant gardens, some neglected to do so because they lacked other culinary ambitions and were acclimated to subsisting on a diet of pork, cornmeal, and "an occasional purchased dish of cabbage or greens."[30]

These poor southerners had acquiesced to the dictates of what sociologist Pierre Bourdieu has referred to as the "taste of necessity" as they acquired through familiarity, resignation, and habit "a taste for what they are anyway condemned to."[31] This acceptance of or even preference for the foods of poverty made the task of food reformers particularly daunting. To transform the black southern diet, respectable eaters not only would have to advocate for the availability of a more diverse set of ingredients but also would have to convince other members of the race to value the lessons of culinary reform.

There is ample historical evidence attesting to the ongoing predominance, whether out of preference or necessity, of a corn- and pork-based diet among southern black people in the decades following emancipation. Aided by researchers at the Tuskegee Institute, the U.S. Department of Agriculture conducted a study of the diets of black people in rural Alabama in 1895 and 1896 that concluded that salt pork, corn bread, and molasses were indeed the fundamental elements of the southern black working-class diet.[32] Furthermore, the Atlanta Neighborhood Union, a social services organization founded in 1908 by Lugenia Burns Hope, the wife of Morehouse College president John Hope, conducted a study of local working-class food habits designed to assess the needs of the community, which also reached similar conclusions about black eating habits. Researchers determined that corn bread and pork were core foods for this group as well. A survey of household visits conducted with 100 families indicated that on the day researchers arrived, members of 67 households had consumed corn bread and 73 had eaten a pork product of some kind, most often bacon.[33] Researchers participating in an Atlanta University symposium also validated this general understanding of the typical southern black diet in a 1908 study of "the Negro American Family," though they did note some culinary variations across the income spectrum. The researchers collected data on the home lives, including the eating habits, of thirteen families. A family residing in a two-room house in the country represented the baseline subsistence diet for African Americans in the region. They ate little besides biscuits, corn bread, pork, and syrup.[34]

Although all of the black families studied in the Atlanta University study consumed corn bread and pork, the ubiquitous staples of the southern diet, many also supplemented their diets with a range of other food items. According to the researchers, many of the respondents represented the "higher types of Negro families," a fact that explains the relative diversity of the foods eaten. Those with the highest income levels and those who lived in the city rather than in the country generally had the most varied diets. Some respondents reported consuming a number of additional foods closely identified with southern cooking such as chicken, rice, iced tea, collard greens, cabbage, beans, grits, hominy, squirrel, and possum.[35] Some families also ate items that did not automatically denote southern foodways.[36] These more prosperous families had, it seems, embraced some of the mandates of culinary reform by including expensive, processed, or regionally unspecific food items on their tables, such as beef, store-bought breakfast cereal, and cocoa.[37] The contrast between the foodways of the region's most prosperous black citizens and those of the poorest demonstrates the impact of dietary reformers who saw food choices as a way to exercise one's relative economic privilege. Members of this group enjoyed what Bourdieu regarded as the bourgeois luxury of having a "taste of freedom," which was dependent upon their financial means to go beyond a subsistence diet.[38]

Intraracial Culinary Encounters
IIIIIIIIIIIIIIIIIIIIIIIIIIIIIIIIIIIIIIIIIIIIIIIIIIIIIIIIIIIIIIII

Intraracial culinary encounters across class lines reveal a deep cultural divide between those who enjoyed the "taste of freedom" and those who clung to the "taste of necessity." Bessie Delany, a middle-class black woman, had the unique experience of being forced to give up the diverse diet of uplift and to eat baseline southern poverty meals. In 1911, twenty-year-old Bessie boarded with a working-class family in a small North Carolina town where she worked as a teacher. While living in the household, she ate what she later described as the "worst diet" of her life. In her recollection, her body rebelled against its first prolonged exposure to working-class foods such as fatback, greens, and sweet potatoes. After eating this diet for several months, she returned home for a Christmas visit weighing 153 pounds, a dramatic change for someone who had "always been a slim thing." The family attributed her changed physique to the fact that she had been eating so much pork, a food they regarded with suspicion.[39]

Although Bessie ate what she was served while living with the family, she also endeavored to teach them some principles of nutrition because she was certain that they "didn't know the first thing about vitamins and minerals." She began by allowing the patriarch of the household to sample some of the California grapefruit that her mother had sent in a care package. He soon regretted his open-mindedness, declaring the "ugly-looking fruit" to be sour and unappealing. His preference for the familiar core southern menu items even in the face of Bessie's belief that as a middle-class educated person she had superior knowledge about good nutrition reveals some of the difficulties inherent in the respectability project's attempts to unsettle southern food traditions.

Similarly, in *Not without Laughter*, Langston Hughes's first novel, the author uses food choices to characterize the conflicts between members of the black working class who dined on humble, evocatively southern cuisine and upwardly mobile African American eaters who actively avoided such items. Sandy Rodgers, the youthful protagonist in the novel, observes a wide array of food choices on the tables of members of his own family. His grandmother cooked black-eyed peas and unabashedly "pulled a meat skin through her teeth" while eating, demonstrating a comfort not only with humble food but with displaying table manners that uplift-oriented eaters would have argued reflected poorly on the race.[40] Many of her neighbors in a small Kansas town shared her relish for traditional southern foods and her lack of self-consciousness. The "old women ate pigs' feet and watermelon and drank beer."[41] In contrast, Tempy, Sandy's middle-class aunt, avoided watermelon. Like the Delany family she favored grapefruit, regarding the citrus as a pointed rebuke to white racists who imagined black people consuming watermelons.[42] Instead, Hughes tells his readers, she performatively cooked food designed not to be either racially or regionally specific and cooked in accordance with the latest advances in home economics: "All her meals were models of economical preparation.... No big pots of black-eyed peas or pigtails scented her front hall, either. She got her recipes from the *Ladies' Home Journal*—and she never bought a watermelon."[43]

The meals that Tempy cooked for her nephew were designed to educate him and to elevate him from the southern-inspired meals he ate with his grandmother. To encourage him to exercise restraint and to refute white ideas about black gluttony, Tempy cooked just enough food for those present at the meal, and she did not indulge her nephew with extra dessert. She viewed the dining table as part of the battleground for assimilation, and she wanted Sandy to learn to emulate the foodways she associated with whiteness. "Colored people certainly needed to come up in the world," according to Tempy, "up to the level of white people. . . . Then they would no longer be called 'niggers.'"[44] By monitoring her family's food intake and by cooking recipes from the *Ladies' Home Journal*, Tempy was trying to make her nephew more American. If he ate a performatively middle-class

American diet, forsaking foods associated with poverty, slavery, and the South, perhaps, she hoped, he would be allowed to become a full-fledged citizen.

Regional Conflicts during the Great Migration

Both the culture shock that Bessie Delany described after her first exposure to southern working-class food and the tensions between the fictional Tempy and the rest of her family over what to eat are representative of other interactions among respectable eaters and those whose food habits they thought were in need of reform. These conflicts became the most pronounced in the context of the Great Migration, which took place between 1910 and 1970, when 6 million African Americans left the South for urban centers in other regions.[45] This massive migration dramatically changed the demographics of many of the final destination cities, creating cultural skirmishes throughout the route of the Great Migration as migrants brought regional tastes with them. As the numbers of migrants increased, their food practices were met with increasingly fierce opposition.

Not only did this outmigration lead to cultural clashes between southern migrants and respectable eaters already living in terminus cities, but it also led to a profound and lasting shift in how the cuisine of southern rural African Americans was characterized. Many northern respectable eaters had been born outside of the South and thus did not have the same culinary birthright as the southern migrants. Others had already learned to discard, or perhaps to hide, many of the vestiges of a diet they associated with slavery or with southern poverty in the name of upward mobility and assimilation, and they resented the infusion of unrepentant southern-style eaters. Nonetheless, southern cooking survived transplantation, much to the consternation of those who linked dietary change to racial progress. Furthermore, in spite of the protestations of respectable eaters, who were determined to resist the essentialist implications embedded in the idea of a racial rather than a regional style of eating, southern food slowly became identified as "black" cuisine in these northern urban contexts.[46]

Cultural battles over the fate of southern foodways were particularly pronounced in Chicago, one of the most sought-after destinations for southern migrants during the first half of the twentieth century. In 1890, only 2 percent of the city's population was African American. During World War I, the black population quickly more than doubled, reaching 100,000 people. By 1970, the black presence in the city constituted a third of the total population.[47] This rapid demographic shift inspired class and cultural conflicts between the newcomers and members of the already-established black community who worried not only that new arrivals would provide competition for scarce resources like jobs and housing but also that their allegedly less refined behavior might earn the enmity of the local whites who controlled these resources. Unsurprisingly, given the centrality of food to the project of uplift, these anxieties were frequently manifested in the form of disagreements about what constituted proper food behavior.

A column in the *Chicago Defender* in 1910 encapsulated the heightened state of class tensions in the black community during this era. The unnamed writer complained about "loud talking" at a local theater. Appropriately enough, given the symbolic significance of pork as an iconic southern food, the columnist accused these noisy theatergoers, whom he suspected were "newcomers to our city," of treating the community space as if it were a "hog-pen."[48] Overt prejudices against both southern migrants who behaved "like pigs" and southern-derived eating practices heavy in pork products, especially low-status scraps and offal, were apparent in the pages of the *Chicago Defender*, where columnists paternalistically advised members of the community who allegedly did not know any better against eating the meat-and-carbohydrate-heavy diet associated with southern cooking.[49]

The ongoing southern taste for pork, one of the most reviled symbols of culinary difference in the minds of some assimilationist eaters, was evidenced in the presence of numerous barbecue restaurants and casual "pig ankle joints," which dotted the city's South Side, the area where the black population was concentrated. For the entrepreneurially inclined, setting up a small restaurant generally required less capital and fewer specialized skills than many other kinds of small businesses. Thus food-related businesses—restaurants and small groceries—became the most common variety of black-owned enterprises in Chicago.[50]

The centrality of pork consumption in the life of the community was dramatized when Rogers' Pig Ankle College caught fire in 1911. Workers desperate to salvage the small business's valuable inventory frantically threw pigs' feet, intestines, and mouths onto the city streets, blocking traffic on State Street for an hour.[51] The sight of porcine body parts piled up on a major thoroughfare acted as a visual reminder of the importance of vernacular food culture to an increasingly large proportion of the inhabitants of that section of the city. From the perspective of respectable eaters, the grisly display of animal flesh also served as a metaphor for the unruly lower classes who, in the minds of respectable eaters, opened up their own racialized bodies for public display through their rowdy behavior and by proudly consuming food with negative historical and cultural connotations.

Many members of the black middle class were fearful that their efforts to appear respectable would be overshadowed by what they regarded as the bad behavior of some of the less fortunate members of their race. In a 1939 short story by William H. A. Moore, which was set in Chicago, the author describes some of the characters as "bad eggs." He presents the fact that one man ran a "pig ankle joint and moonshine cellar" as sufficient evidence to substantiate the fact that he had lax morals.[52] Indeed, the consumers and purveyors of less choice scraps of pig flesh were often stigmatized by the elite as being a social embarrassment to the black community. A 1915 article in the *Chicago Defender* described "pig ankle joints" in general as being "unsightly and unsanitary."[53] Furthermore, food reformers were fearful that the poor dietary habits of those of the present generation would have a detrimental impact on their children. The interracial Chicago Commission on Race Relations, which was charged with contextualizing the events of the 1919 race riot in that city, bemoaned poor living conditions in the black community and decried the "ignorance of parents" who allegedly did not know how to feed their children properly, giving them, for example, too many pork products and not enough green vegetables.[54]

Although these anxieties were heightened by the demographic transformations that occurred during the Great Migration, class anxieties about food consumption drew upon preexisting class-based stereotypes. For example, in his 1899 classic sociological study, *The Philadelphia Negro*, Du Bois somberly judged that "in habits of personal cleanliness and taking proper food and exercise, the colored people are woefully deficient."[55] He blamed their current plight on the legacy of slavery and despaired that the poor black people of Philadelphia "waste much money in poor food and in unhealthful methods of cooking."[56] Chief among the food items eaten in black Philadelphia, which Du Bois disapproved of, was "pork fried in grease."[57] Middle-class distaste for working-class food habits was evident in the South as well. In a social anthropological study of 1930s Natchez, Mississippi, a team of researchers led by Allison Davis found that members of the black middle class described the lower classes as "'dirty,' 'filthy,' or 'nasty'" and described "an actual physical revulsion toward proximity with lower-class persons."[58] This sense of disgust was easily transferred either from the individual to the foods he or she consumed or from the foods back to the individual. In a circular fashion, unrespectable eating habits were used to stigmatize members of the working class, and those of the working class were stigmatized because they ate unrespectable foods.

Middle-class ideas about culinary respectability were often used to create and maintain class divisions. Although members of the black middle class feared that improper working-class behavior might damage the prospects of those who failed to embrace the lessons of uplift—for example, by refusing to stop publicly consuming scraps of pork—their lessons in reform were also self-serving. As Evelyn Brooks Higginbotham observes, although uplift enabled black Americans to challenge racism by demonstrating their ability to conform "to the dominant society's norms and manners," it also empowered its adherents to criticize what they regarded as "negative attitudes and practices among their own people."[59] On the one hand, reformers hoped that the working class would heed their advice and behave in a way that would reflect well upon the race. However, on the other hand, they had incentive to hope that their lessons in racial elevation would be ignored because they directly benefited from ongoing class stratification. Without the existence of an allegedly culturally backward working class to serve as their foil, members of the middle class were unable to illustrate the extent of their own accomplishments.

The Program of Food Reform

Conscientious middle-class eaters were also forced to acknowledge that food scarcity, not merely the politics of food preference, was the issue that most plagued many segments of the black community. Though by no means free from financial worry, the Delany family of North Carolina was conscious of their relative privilege. Henry Beard Delany and Nanny Logan Delany, the parents of ten children, served, respectively, as the vice principal and as a teacher at the St. Augustine School. In the late nineteenth and early twentieth centuries, they taught their children that many former slaves "didn't know how to live free" and were to be treated with "the dignity these folks had been denied by others."[60] This proper regard often consisted of making sure that elderly freed people had enough to eat, particularly at Thanksgiving, when the Delany family oversaw the preparation of meals for the needy. They distributed baskets, which contained sweet potato pies, vegetables, and chicken but no turkey, which was considered too luxurious even for the Delany family itself. "Hunger was a big problem for the former slaves," one of the Delany sisters soberly observed. "It always seemed like somebody was knocking on the door looking for food."[61]

Evidence of interclass food charity abounds in the historical record. A 1909 Atlanta University study titled *Efforts for Social Betterment among Negro Americans* reported on a number of efforts to feed needy members of the black community. For example, the Arbutus Club of Minneapolis distributed baskets of food to the poor and planned picnics for hungry children. Members of the Ann Arbor Women's Club boasted that since its founding in 1898, they had given $700, mostly in cash, to the needy. They also gave "clothes, food, fuel, bedding, and flowers to the poor." The Priscilla Brown Mercy Home in Selma, Alabama, claimed to have fed and clothed so many people, including orphans, that "we have not space to place before the public the many needy we have relieved."[62]

The National Urban League, a civil rights organization that was founded in New York in 1910 with the immediate goal of aiding southern migrants as they transitioned to lives in new cities, instituted a number of programs to try to feed the hungry and to help black families weather economic crises. For example, in communities as distant from one another as Atlanta, Georgia, and Columbus, Ohio, the NUL encouraged poor city dwellers to plant gardens and distributed both seeds and advice.[63] In the early years of the Great Depression, the Brooklyn NUL distributed milk and other groceries to needy families and provided childcare, free of charge, for parents "who were unable to buy coal to keep their babies warm nor enough food to keep them alive."[64] Throughout the nation, black self-help organizations banded together to try to meet the needs of the impoverished in their local communities. Members of the minuscule middle class went to great lengths to try to redistribute limited community resources to the neediest people, and charity projects became a persistent part of the uplift agenda.

Ultimately, however, these reformers were faced with the grim reality that they did not have the power to adequately feed every hungry person or to change the structural realities that consigned a disproportionate number of African Americans to poverty. The vastness of the need and the limitations of resources at their disposal encouraged reformers to focus on changing the food behavior of the less fortunate. This emphasis was often predicated upon a willful forgetting of the fact that for many, having enough food to eat was their most pressing issue, not the politics of food selection. This emphasis on improving individual skills and character was, however, in keeping with the politics of uplift, which responded to the seeming impossibility of broad social reform by turning inward and concentrating on personal behavior. Many reformers of this ilk thought that training in modern homemaking methods was one potential solution to both the problem of poverty and the prevalence of unsavory food habits. Theoretically, working-class black people who underwent this training would have improved job prospects, becoming part of a higher-paid class of servants, and the ideas about modern scientific eating that they learned through formal education could positively influence their own food selections.

Students at well-known historically black institutions such as the Hampton Institute, Spelman College, and the Tuskegee Institute could enroll in cooking classes that had well-developed curricula and were taught by formally trained domestic scientists.[65] However, these programs were primarily attended by those who were already amenable to the philosophy of uplift and who were primed to look for ways that changes in their personal behavior could make them, in theory at least, better candidates for first-class U.S. citizenship. Bringing similar lessons to members of the working class who did not have access to these training programs posed the bigger challenge to reform-minded respectable eaters.

Many suggested that churches should play a role in teaching the working class what to eat and how to prepare it. Writing in *The Crisis* in 1911, Mrs. John E. Milholland expressed concern about the difficulties entailed in trying to reach the "masses" with the messages of domestic science and advocated forming "training schools in connection with churches," reasoning that more African American women attended church than institutions of higher learning.[66] A modified version of this proposal was echoed again in the pages of the magazine in a November 1923 column suggesting that churches teach people how to buy food and other necessities and "exercise a powerful influence in checking unwise spending."[67] The Women's Convention, the auxiliary of the National Baptist Convention, took the mandate to address food issues seriously. In 1920, its committee on vital statistics produced a study comparing mortality rates between white and black people that linked different life chances, at least in part, to differences in nutritional intake.[68]

Nannie Helen Burroughs, whose ideas about food reform were briefly discussed in chapter 1, helped convince her fellow black Baptist women to support the establishment of the National Training School for Women and Girls in Washington, D.C. The school attempted to attract working-class students with the hope that if they received training in domestic skills they could command higher wages, earn more respect, and presumably also enhance their own health through their knowledge about proper nutrition.[69] Although the school recruited working-class students and operated on a small budget, Burroughs promised her sisters in the Women's Convention that "we are going to do the best that can be done with what we have. Our table linen will be as white as that used in the Executive Mansion."[70] She also ensured that the school's domestic science curriculum guaranteed her students equal training to that offered at more elite institutions. Her students learned the latest scientific information about food safety, the physiology of digestion, and the nutritional components of individual foods.[71]

Secular organizations such as the National Urban League also looked for ways to indoctrinate working-class eaters on the mandates of food reform and went to great lengths to provide advice and training opportunities related to food preparation and consumption.[72] For example, the Chicago Urban League offered scholarships and job placement assistance to women who wished to attend classes where they would learn about "the chemistry and preparation of foods, dietetics, [and] household administration."[73] In Buffalo, New York, the NUL offered educational classes about proper nutrition. Local members of this upstate New York branch thought that courses in cooking were potentially so transformative that they overlooked the conventional gender norms of the day and offered classes teaching boys how to cook. A report from 1929–30 boasted that the instructors had "thrilled the unmanageable male with the intricacies of lemon pie composition. And, somehow, the difficult behavior traits have disappeared."[74] In this instance, proper food habits were directly correlated with good behavior, and young boys who learned to cook and to eat well earned plaudits for their general respectability.

In Pittsburgh the NUL sponsored homemaking classes where attendees heard lectures about vitamins, feeding children, and making food budgets and watched demonstrations on cooking one-dish meals that satisfied contemporary dietary requirements.[75] The Pittsburgh organization not only offered local African Americans the opportunity to learn modern cooking techniques but also sponsored a food show in 1929 that was attended by representatives of large companies such as H. J. Heinz. Attendees were encouraged to perform a U.S. national identity by acquiring the taste for mass-produced, well-known national brands of food. One community member gushed about the importance of NUL food reform efforts like this one, dramatically claiming that such classes could have an enormous social impact: "I have always thought that delinquency in children and crime in their elders is due to poor nourishment as well as poor surroundings; a demonstration of food preparation ought to be a valuable influence in this district."[76]

In Atlanta, the Neighborhood Union offered working-class southerners who had not been enticed by the promises of migration the opportunity to refine their domestic skills at home. The organization sponsored cooking classes, which were taught by faculty from colleges such as Spelman, Atlanta University, and the Tuskegee Institute, giving even those who did not have the opportunity to enroll in more comprehensive domestic science programs at least some exposure to the latest cooking techniques and scientific ideas about proper diets.[77] Participants in Neighborhood Union cooking classes learned about domestic science–approved meals that emphasized frugality and food purity. They were advised to eat meat no more than once per day and to buy "cheap cuts," which the instructors claimed had "as much food value as those that cost more." Bowing both to local tastes and to the economic realities of most black Atlantans, the cooking school provided students with recipes for "Meat Stew" and "Meat Pie," made with bacon rather than with the more expensive beef favored by most white food reformers. However, students were urged to limit their intake of this southern staple and to augment their diets with domestic science–approved items, which were not typically part of the southern larder. For example, the organization encouraged their students to eat more fish, promoting the food as a nutritious "meal that costs less." However, in keeping with domestic science's infatuation with industrially produced modern foods, the curriculum did not emphasize recipes for preparing fresh-caught local fish but instead called for canned salmon. The cooking teachers working in conjunction with the Neighborhood Union instructed students about how to serve this nonlocal ingredient in the form of a loaf or in a casserole containing mashed potatoes, hard-cooked eggs, and white sauce.[78]

Of all of the lessons offered to the economically disadvantaged students in the program, the inclusion of the recipe for white sauce was likely one of the most symbolically charged. The Neighborhood Union recipe for the white sauce that was to adorn canned, flaked salmon offered a twist on the conventional American recipe that called for butter, flour, and milk: instructors substituted nut butter instead of dairy butter in the dish. The substitution may have been in response to the relative cost of nut butter versus dairy or a way to inject a humble dish with an additional source of inexpensive protein. Regardless, a casserole held together with this modified white sauce referenced one of the core techniques of domestic science as taught at the standard-bearing Boston Cooking School. Laura Shapiro has argued that home economists saw white sauce as a "civilizing influence" on American cooking: "There was virtually no cooked food that at one time or another was not hidden, purified, enriched, or ennobled with white sauce."[79] Domestic scientists, she argued, increasingly favored white foods—white sauces, whipped creams, Crisco shortening, boiled cod, macaroni, and rice. These foods were designed to signal purity—bland, homogeneous, germ-free, modern food.[80] Given the racial politics in an era when the philosophies of eugenics held sway with many progressives and Jim Crow reigned in the South, the allure that allegedly pure white foods may have had for some seems obvious. African American cooking school instructors who taught their students to make dishes covered in white sauce were alluding to a broader food politics that was ultimately assimilationist. In the Neighborhood Union example, the inclusion of nut butter, which inevitably added a colored tinge to the iconic white sauce, is an interesting variation. It could be interpreted either as a critique on the hegemony of culinary whiteness or as a bitter acknowledgment that, pretensions aside, black food reformers knew that African Americans, regardless of what they ate, would not ever be fully assimilated into white society.

The Class Politics of Food Reform

Although the brown-tinged white sauce served in Atlanta might have had some potentially subversive connotations or may have functioned as a culinary commentary about American racism, the cuisine of uplift was almost always assimilationist rather than provocative by design. Furthermore, it was nearly always served alongside a hefty portion of classism. American studies scholar Psyche Williams-Forson is retrospectively critical of the singularity of purpose and the class-based assumptions of food reformers who worked so hard to transform working-class food habits and were unable to see the value of this class's existing food expressions. She argues that by denouncing the "habits and customs" of those who embraced southern foodways, middle-class women "to some extent devalued and disrespected their working-class sisters."[81] A 1911 column in the *Chicago Defender* provides an example of one interaction between an

African American employer and her maid when class concerns became paramount over issues of racial or gender solidarity. No doubt the expectations of many readers were confounded when they realized that a headline referring to a "Hard Problem for Women" was not referring to low wages, sexual exploitation, lack of educational opportunities, or any number of potentially relevant pressing social issues. Instead the column was written in the voice of a young middle-class African American housewife who described "about the hardest problem I have had to solve in my brief housekeeping career." She sought advice about where her household servant, "a good girl," should be allowed to entertain a visiting minister. Not wanting to humiliate the minister by confining him to the kitchen or dining room, spaces where her domestic helper spent most of her time, she allowed Lucy, the servant, to "hold forth" in the higher status parlor. However, she did so with some ambivalence and wrote to seek advice about whether she had solved the etiquette conundrum appropriately.[82] In this scenario, the housewife was primarily concerned with the comfort of the middle-class minister while never considering her servant's own needs and desire to be treated with dignity. Tone-deaf columns such as this one understandably made many members of the working class dubious about the priorities of middle-class reformers.

A pervasive middle-class sense of self-importance is easily discernible in the print culture surrounding food uplift. In an article in the *Chicago Defender* alarmingly headlined "Police! Fire! Murder! Pork Chops! Pigs' Feet!," an unnamed author bemoans the presence of what he or she regards as excessively noisy families residing on Rhodes Avenue. The author complains, "Every one knows we are judged as a race by each individual's actions."[83] The despair that many members of the self-proclaimed "better class" felt about the behavior that they attributed to the less fortunate propelled many in the middle class to offer not only needed assistance to the less well off but also unsolicited advice. In 1918, an annual report for the Chicago Urban League justified taking a heavy-handed approach to imposing uplift values upon the entire community, arguing that "the people who need care and instruction in civics are the last to realize it and never look for it." Since those who allegedly needed uplift-oriented advice were, it was proclaimed, the least likely to seek it, the organization boasted that "the League carries it to them."[84] Reform was depicted as a mandate, and middle-class values were promoted as moral certitudes.

Whether they sought to change black working-class eating habits out of fear of being negatively associated with them in the minds of whites not attuned to class distinctions within the black community or out of true benevolent concern for the health and well-being of people from what they regarded as a lower class that did not know any better, food reform efforts always cast middle-class norms as unambiguously superior to working-class food sensibilities. Although sometimes dependent upon the charity of middle-class food reformers, members of the working class could not have been blind to their condescension and must have been perplexed, at times, by the priorities of those whose philosophies of uplift sometimes seemed geared more toward creating and maintaining class distinctions within the black community than with fighting against racism. Kevin Gaines has charged that the attempts of the black middle class to reform what they regarded as "urban pathology" were always tinged with classist assumptions, which "bestowed on 'better class' blacks an illusory sense of self-importance as it divested poor urban blacks of agency and humanity."[85]

Working-Class Culinary Nationalism

In the realm of food expression, many working-class African Americans were impervious to the machinations of food reformers. Evidence suggests that the disdain that respectable eaters felt for southern food traditions was more than matched by working-class affection for at least some aspects of this cuisine and corresponding annoyance with those who sought to alter these food expressions. The literature of the era captures the keen appreciation many northern urban African Americans had for southern cooking. Jake, the protagonist in Harlem Renaissance writer Claude McKay's *Home to Harlem*, finds comfort in traditional southern African American foods. The sensual pleasure he gets from eating is made clear in a scene where he wishes to consume both a piece of pie and the person who created it: "'All right, I'll try peach,' he said, and, magnetically, his long, shining fingers touched her hand."[86] For him, food is a source of pleasure and not shame, and eating is an emotional action as well as a political one. Food, in his mind, not only conjures up associations with sex but also with motherly love. His favorite place to eat in Harlem is a small restaurant owned by "Aunt Hattie," who speaks in a southern dialect, makes delectable fried chicken, and warmly tells the grateful protagonist, "You jest come heah and eats any time, you wanta whether youse got money or not."[87] When Roy, the protagonist in Langston Hughes's short story "Home," returns to his southern hometown after spending time abroad, his mother welcomes him by offering him what she regards as "real food"—"corn bread and greens and salt pork"—in contrast to what he had eaten on his travels.[88]

Outside of the pages of fiction, too, working-class southerners used their skills in the kitchen to proudly exhibit cultural distinction, not shame. The researchers working on the social anthropological study *Black Metropolis* noted that a black woman named Betty Lou who lacked a permanent home made an arrangement to use the kitchen of a local single man who agreed to grant her access in exchange for a share of her cooking. She was not satisfied with purchasing food made by others but wanted to cook foods associated with her southern childhood home in Alabama. In spite of her poverty and lack of stability, she "took a great deal of pride in her biscuits."[89] Many southern migrants living in northern cities maintained southern food traditions by choice and through great personal effort. In the North, iconic southern foods became, for many, the dishes of both affection and necessity when hard economic times came. One informant told researchers in Chicago that he turned to familiar southern fare when he was short on money: "I had greens last night for supper—I had greens today for lunch—and I had greens tonight for supper! Why? 'Cause I can't afford anything else."[90] Chances are, if the respondent could have afforded a more luxurious diet, southern foods may still have featured prominently in his food selections. A 1914 column in the *Chicago Defender* contained the wry observation that "the store that carries both watermelons and chickens is a hard store for some of our citizens to pass."[91]

Tracy N. Poe speculates that respectable eaters who sought to dissociate themselves from southern food traditions may have actually heightened the appreciation some members of the working class had for this cuisine. She argues, "Faced with seemingly inexplicable opposition from members of their own race, they began thinking of 'down home cooking' as something unique and special."[92] Thus, ironically, in their quest to reform southern regional food habits and to disempower the idea of a racially specific style of eating, black food reformers actually helped create the thing they most feared. An examination of black food expression among predominantly working-class people reveals the beginnings of a proto-culinary nationalism in the early twentieth century. Eaters both north and south who demonstrated an unwavering preference for southern foods preserved and created traditions that decades later were to be labeled as racially specific "soul food." Ignoring the pretensions of middle-class

African American eaters who shunned southern food, proponents of proto–soul food cast those who were unfamiliar with these food traditions as the ones lacking in discernment and taste. In 1895, the *Christian Recorder*, the organ for the African Methodist Episcopal Church, printed an article that criticized the food habits of northerners, arguing that "almost without exception the menu is unsuited to the palates of people who know better."[93] In this formulation, southern regional food, not assimilationist-oriented respectable cuisine, was a sign of superior culture and taste.

In the end, the intraracial conflicts that used foodways as a vehicle for exploring anxieties over social class and differing regional cultures resulted in a hybrid cuisine of compromise. While respectable, assimilationist-oriented cuisine was celebrated in the society columns of black newspapers and touted in domestic science classes offered by various mechanisms of black civil society, southern-inflected cuisine continued to be served on private tables and formed the basis for widespread entrepreneurship in the black community as businesses north and south sought to satisfy widespread cravings for pork, corn, and other common items on the southern table. Although uplift-oriented eaters had deemed these foods unrespectable, the meanings embedded in these items were hardly stable and were slowly and steadily recoded to evoke a set of associations far removed from southern slavery and poverty. Surprisingly, international events brought about by the U.S. entry into Word War I triggered a community-wide culinary reckoning, which encouraged respectable eaters to reconsider their food preferences. As the next chapter reveals, the U.S. Food Administration began urging citizens to eat cornmeal and other foods that had been displaced from the uplift table, events that led to the rebranding of these once-shunned items as the patriotic foods of the American citizenry rather than the foods of a racial or regional other.

World War I, the Great Depression, and the Changing Symbolic Value of Black Food Traditions

Writing in the pages of the National Association for the Advancement of Colored People's organ, *The Crisis*, in 1918, W. E. B. Du Bois urged his fellow African Americans to "forget our special grievances and close our ranks ... with our own white citizens" for the duration of World War I.[1] Although 370,000 black soldiers served in the military during the conflict, most black Americans were destined to respond to Du Bois's call for national unity from the home front. For many, the most frequent reminders they received about the federal government's wartime agenda came in the realm of food selection. Federal propaganda framed food conservation as a war measure, militarizing civilians by equating food behavior with military behavior. Eating in accordance with government guidelines, which called for the conservation of a number of key ingredients in the American diet, was described as a way to actively fight against foreign enemies.

Herbert Hoover, director of the U.S. Food Administration (USFA), continually declared that "food will win the war" in his effort to convince Americans to conserve food for soldiers and U.S. allies abroad. Thus for civic-minded black Americans, food had the potential to win battles fought on two fronts—in the conflagration overseas and in efforts on the home front to ameliorate racism using the strategies of cultural uplift at the table. The 1917 Lever Food and Fuel Control Act gave the president—and by extension his appointee Herbert Hoover—broad authority to regulate the nation's food and fuel supply for the duration of the conflict. Although coveted items like meat, wheat, and sugar were in short supply, Hoover was unwilling to impose domestic rationing and instead launched a propaganda campaign to encourage voluntary conservation at home in order to feed preferred foods to soldiers and allies abroad. The federal government also tasked concerned citizens to increase the nation's food supply by planting gardens and canning surplus fruits and vegetables. Although Americans were asked to be thoughtful about the quantities of food they consumed, the USFA continually assured the public that the government did not expect the populace to go hungry or to damage their health but merely to make substitutions in their diets—to eat, for example, fish instead of beef and cornmeal instead of wheat.[2]

Black Food Reformers Embrace Wartime Conservation

At long last, black food reformers who wished to use their food habits in the campaign to achieve first-class citizenship received official governmental validation for the idea that food choices could be key markers of national belonging. Most respectable eaters agreed with Du Bois's claim that "in the stress of war comes a chance to correct bad habits," and they capitalized on the overseas conflict to emphasize their ongoing agenda.[3] Unsurprisingly, many members of the black working class—who were, as a whole, less optimistic about the idea that good behavior might yield civic rewards—were more ambivalent about the value of supporting the culinary agenda promoted by the apparatus of a racist nation-state. Those in the black working class also had reason to be dubious about the motives and wisdom of their self-proclaimed social betters who not only seized upon the war as one more excuse to proffer unasked-for advice but also used the mandates of war to modify some of the ideas about proper food behavior that they had once dispensed with such confidence.

The scores of governmental dietary recommendations that accompanied mobilization for World War I challenged many of the traditional mandates of respectable eating. While food reformers had previously advocated for elegant food practices and a wholehearted embrace of industrially produced foods, the ethos of wartime conservation called for austerity and culinary self-reliance. Furthermore, the directives of the government-endorsed plan for food economy challenged black middle-class eaters to reevaluate the symbolic significance of foods like beef and wheat. These ingredients, which were once considered emblems of Americanization, were now taboo to consume in great portions due to wartime conservation measures. Ironically, many favorite foods of some members of the black working class, most notably greens or beans flavored with pork scraps and corn bread, which had once been disdained by some middle-class eaters, became reframed as patriotic food choices. In this context, respectable eaters had to reevaluate the meanings they had previously ascribed to various culinary preferences and make rapid and dramatic changes to their notions of an ideal American national diet.

Because the conservation program was both voluntary and limited in scope, Hoover considered the issue of securing broad support from every segment of society to be crucial, and the USFA made numerous outreach efforts aimed at the black community. Most significantly, Hoover created a Negro Press Division with A. U. Craig, a Washington, D.C., schoolteacher, at the helm. Ernest T. Atwell, a Tuskegee Institute faculty member who led the Food Administration's Negro Activities Division and succeeded Craig as the agency's chief African American propagandist shortly before the Armistice, was also influential in the charge to encourage black people to rally around the cause of conservation.[4] Craig concentrated his energies primarily on distributing propaganda to the African American press. The Negro Press Division reached out to nearly 300 black newspapers, a majority of which agreeably printed unedited copy provided to them by USFA staff.[5] Atwell intensified efforts to engage the black community in USFA initiatives by planning public programs such as patriotic pageants and cooking demonstrations, encouraging black theaters to show promotional films, and enlisting volunteers to promote USFA initiatives in each state.[6]

USFA officials asked "leading negroes" throughout the nation to organize food conservation events at Fourth of July celebrations in 1918. Representatives from the Arkansas office hopefully predicted, "We ought to have the negroes of Arkansas on fire with patriotism on that day."[7] The decision to intermingle Independence Day celebrations with the USFA campaign was an obvious way to make adherence to the dictates of food conservation a way of demonstrating fidelity to the U.S. nation-state. Food conservation was linked not only to the ideology of nationalism but also to spiritual issues. Some black ministers throughout the nation preached the message of conservation along with their Sunday sermons. Furthermore, many black business leaders visibly complied with USFA instructions. Some black barbershops adorned their mirrors with USFA slogans, and many black-owned restaurants proudly advertised their support for the program.[8]

Among the most enthusiastic supporters of the campaign were members of the National Association of Colored Women and their local auxiliary organizations who busied themselves distributing propaganda and encouraging citizens in their communities not only to adhere to Hoover's dietary guidelines but also to augment the nation's food supply by planting gardens and canning vegetables.[9] Mary Burnett Talbert, president of the organization from 1916 to 1920, was particularly passionate about the issue of food conservation and pledged to use her office to urge club members to support government efforts, noting that black women had the potential to play "a very important part in this war."[10] Indeed black women throughout the nation enthusiastically offered public support for the initiatives. For example, the South Carolina Federation of Colored Women's Clubs divided the state into seven districts and appointed one club member to work in each area promoting USFA guidelines. The members boasted that collectively they canned 20,790 quarts of fruits and vegetables to augment the national larder.[11]

The support that these conservation efforts garnered was impressive. A columnist writing for the *Kansas City Advocate* boasted that "the best colored men and women" supported the USFA. Their activism in the field of wartime food reform confirmed the author's firm belief that "they are patriotic. They are interested in their country."[12] Seizing upon the potential opportunity for a greater sense of incorporation into the body politic, R. R. White, president of the Georgia State Industrial College for Colored Youths, proclaimed, "I think our people should take a very active part in doing all they can for their Country . . . because in doing so we may be able to win a larger place in the estimation of our fellow citizens."[13]

Working-Class Poverty and the Impossibility of Conservation

Some food reformers, particularly those who had been less involved with the politics of food selection and more engaged with charitable efforts to feed the less fortunate members of the community, understandably believed that the federal organization was out of touch with local efforts that had predated the Great War. They argued that among the working class, the issue of food conservation was hardly a new concern. When A. U. Craig offered to lend the Tuskegee Institute some stereopticon slides about food conservation, administrator Ezra C. Roberts pointedly turned down the offer, reminding him that "our work has been very full in that regard."[14] In their correspondence with the USFA Negro Press Division, others were even more direct in their attempts to point out that this new government advice was redundant. E. A. Long, president of the Christianburg

Industrial Institute, pledged support for the USFA alongside the gentle reminder that we "have always given the question of food conservation special emphasis both in the course of study and in its practical application."[15] Hilda M. Nasmyth, the superintendent of the Adeline M. Smith Industrial Home in Little Rock, Arkansas, expressed overt impatience with government intrusion, telling USFA officials,

Long before we began to practice economy along food lines . . . for the sake of victory over our enemies, in this institution the strictest economy was observed. . . . It has been incumbent upon us . . . to make the dollar go as far as possible, and often-times see a whole dollar in a nickel. In truth, there has been very little the government has hinted at or suggested in order to help our nation in this great struggle that the Negro teachers have not had well in hand and urged upon their people before any special work was done along this line for them.[16]

Both the USFA and the middle-class reformers who supported their initiatives could promote food conservation measures among members of the black community only by assuming a posture of willful ignorance about the economic plight of working-class southerners. Although much USFA propaganda was aimed at personal consumption patterns, Atwell and other government officials also implicitly acknowledged that in the case of black Americans, a different food-related dynamic was often at stake. They were additionally aiming their advice at black domestic servants who, in the words of one "Four Minute Speech" delivered by Committee on Public Information volunteers, "control the food in the homes of a very large proportion of other races."[17] The extent to which patriotic servants could shape the diets of potentially intransigent employers is debatable. What is more certain is the fact that poor black southerners who lived on the "three M's diet" of meat, meal, and molasses already ate in a style that exceeded the demands of the USFA guidelines in terms of its austerity.[18] For starters, the molasses that rounded out the spare diet, which was, according to Marcie Cohen Ferris, actually "the most nutritious member of the infamous three 'm's," had USFA approval as a patriotic substitute for granulated sugar.[19]

Furthermore, poor black southerners already consumed very little meat, one of the primary items USFA officials hoped to conserve. The Food Administration urged Americans to observe meatless meals daily and to abstain from eating meat altogether one day of the week, a feat that did not require much recalibration on the part of poor southerners who ate only small quantities of low-quality, fatty pork.[20] Members of this group rarely, if ever, ate prime cuts of meat and instead often used small pieces of animal protein to flavor their corn bread, greens, or field peas.[21] Their meat consumption did not align with the imaginations of government propagandists who hoped to wrest steaks and pot roasts off of American tables, not the scraps and offal consumed by the poorest Americans. Furthermore, black laborers rarely, if ever, consumed beef, the animal protein most targeted by food conservationists. Their staple of pork was less coveted than beef and consequently not as scarce. Beginning in June 1918, Food Administration officials actually encouraged the substitution of pork for beef as a "direct service to our armies and our allies."[22]

Not only did poor southerners inadvertently comply with USFA recommendations for meat conservation, but the "meal" component of their baseline diet was also in compliance with the dictates of the administration, which urged consumers to eat more corn in order to conserve wheat for the military and for U.S. allies. Corn, a staple in slave rations, continued to be the primary grain consumed by rural southern African Americans after emancipation. The poorest often ate bread made only from cornmeal and water, an unambiguously patriotic choice in the context of the time. Even the growing number of rural southerners who had access to wheat flour used the grain to augment rather than replace their consumption of corn bread. They sometimes added wheat flour to their corn bread and began including flour biscuits on their menus alongside the still ubiquitous staple corn bread. Even when eating wheat alongside corn, rural southerners were still adhering to the USFA regulations that stipulated that merchants selling wheat had to bundle the grain alongside a less desirable flour such as cornmeal, potato flour, oatmeal, or soybean flour in order to minimize wheat consumption.[23]

For these eaters, compliance with the USFA was an accidental fact of southern poverty, not the intentional actions of patriotic eaters. The subsistence southern diet was, in fact, so inadequate that many of the region's poorest inhabitants suffered from a niacin deficiency and a disease known as pellagra.[24] Pellagra causes a variety of adverse health effects ranging from skin lesions to lethargy, diarrhea, dementia, and even death. The illness was common in the South in the early twentieth century. For example, there were 15,381 cases of pellagra and 1,531 deaths from the disease in Mississippi alone in 1915.[25] Among poorer segments of the black community, pellagra and other forms of malnutrition were particularly widespread. A 1921 study of African American preschool-age children in one South Carolina county showed that 28 percent suffered from malnutrition.[26] Black people in this group simply could not afford to conserve.[27]

Given these realities, many members of the working-class population, regardless of racial or ethnic background, dismissed USFA propaganda as irrelevant in their constrained circumstances.[28] Others, particularly those who benefited from wartime labor shortages and received better jobs and higher wages, willfully ignored the government mandates altogether. Harvey Levenstein has noted that although members of the middle and upper classes generally did restrict their intake of the foods regulated by voluntary rationing, among the working classes the consumption of some foods, most notably beef, actually increased during the war.[29] In 1918, a white Arkansas planter complained to the local food administrator that one of his black tenants had stockpiled three barrels of flour in defiance of USFA instructions. Much to the consternation of the planter, the tenant showed no remorse about not cooperating with the program for patriotic eating. He grumbled that even though he "made his negroes grow PLENTY of corn last year, and established a rule before the corn was gathered that any of them who sold any part of their corn would have to move off the place," some of his tenants could not pass up the temptation of flouting USDA guidelines and trying to "get ahead" by hoarding rationed foods.[30] For many among the working classes, the amorphous, psychic rewards of patriotism could not compete with the temptations of the material reality that many could now afford to eat a richer diet than they could before the war.

In their zeal to show support for the federal government, most African American food conservation supporters did not openly acknowledge that USFA mandates were unpopular with those who could afford to buy coveted foods for the first time and irrelevant to those who already consumed relatively little of the wheat, sugar, and meat the government hoped to conserve. In general the USFA's message appealed to members of the middle and upper classes who could afford to be choosy. These individuals could appear virtuous while still eating rich foods, because items such as eggs, cheese, fowl, and seafood were USFA-approved. These foods were, however, often beyond the financial reach of the working poor.[31]

Two months after urging black citizens to "close ranks" and support the war effort, Du Bois gave readers of his editorials in The Crisis some concrete ideas about how they could support the government's mission. He did so without addressing the pressing realities of food scarcity for some members of the black community. Instead Du Bois reported taking comfort in the fact that "war necessities" might teach African Americans at home some "salutary lessons" about food consumption.[32] He proclaimed that although the "Hot Biscuit is a lovely institution . . . it is too costly in work and money and too dangerous to the digestion to come oftener than once a week. The deceitful Pork Chop must be dethroned in the South and yield a part of its sway to vegetables, fruits, and fish."[33] In identifying a choice cut of pork as a key item that African Americans needed to cut down on, Du Bois's advice was in keeping with both USFA recommendations as well as the long-standing leeriness some uplift eaters felt toward pork, a food they associated with slave rations. However, in telling black southerners to cut out premium cuts like "pork chops" when most were actually more likely to eat the less desirable fatback, Du Bois's advice seemed to ignore black economic realities. Furthermore, his instructions to conserve wheat—although in line with the dictates of USFA guidelines—contradicted the dietary program of many respectable eaters who had worked for decades to increase consumption of wheat bread, as opposed to corn bread, among members of the black community. Thus black USFA supporters, like Du Bois, not only had to overlook rural poverty but also had to contend with the fact that although the broad outlines of the USFA's message were consistent with the belief among food-conscious race men and women that food was a political issue, some particular aspects of the government plan conflicted with the racial uplift diet.

The Changing Symbolic Value of Corn

As chapter 2's discussion of Booker T. Washington's food reform efforts at the Tuskegee Institute reveals, wheat was a symbolically important menu item at the uplift table. Most respectable eaters regarded bread made from wheat, the historically preferred grain of both Euro-Americans and western Europeans, as a more wholesome substitute for the slave diet staple of corn bread. Southerners of both races widely consumed locally produced cornmeal during the antebellum era and beyond. However, by the twentieth century, they generally had greater access to national markets and to increasingly inexpensive wheat flour produced by large modern mills.[34] Southerners now had a choice about what kind of bread to consume, and their decision about which to eat quickly became more than a matter of whimsy and taste preference. Breads made with each respective grain took on a different symbolic significance.

White as well as black southerners struggled with the implications of this choice. In a study of early twentieth-century food reform in Appalachia, Elizabeth Engelhardt has demonstrated that corn bread and wheat bread became loaded signifiers in cultural conflicts over class status. Wheat biscuits were used to represent "high culture, modern hygiene and Progressive womanhood." Corn bread brought with it connotations of "ignorance, disease and poverty."[35] Helen Zoe Veit similarly argues that by the early twentieth century, many "biscuit-proud" middle-class southerners throughout the region began to regard consuming corn bread as an embarrassing habit that brought with it connotations of low social standing.[36] For African American eaters, these associations were compounded by the fact that in the black imagination, corn also inspired memories, actual and inherited, of a monotonous and minimal slave diet.

By the twentieth century, wheat thus had become a preferred grain for many uplift-oriented eaters, and corn bread had become a contentious food in the culinary culture wars within the black community. Although it never earned the same enmity from food reformers that pork did, African Americans who seemed to relish corn bread too much were stigmatized as unsophisticated eaters or worse. In language that echoes many of the complaints respectable eaters had made about southern migrants who publicly consumed pork products in Chicago, a writer for the *Washington Bee* complained about migrants to the city whom he described as "loafers who lived on cornbread and hash in other States."[37] The traditional bread was also used as a class marker by middle-class hosts of a "rag-time ball" given in Topeka, Kansas, in 1902. Partygoers celebrated their own good economic fortune by lightheartedly mocking some emblems of poverty. They attended the event, where they were fed a meal of corn bread, milk, and beans, wearing ragged clothes designed to bolster the uncomfortable party theme.[38] In daily life, some respectable eaters regarded being forced to eat corn bread instead of wheat bread as such a hardship that corn bread became a metaphor for general deprivation. A 1905 advice column from the *Baltimore Afro-American* urged farmers not to turn their cattle out to pasture too early in the spring before they could find sufficient food. To illustrate the cruelty of inadequately feeding animals left in their care, the author used the analogy of depriving a person of "biscuits, ham, and egg" in favor of a sparse and undesirable diet of "corn bread and molasses."[39]

In the late nineteenth and early twentieth centuries, African Americans living in urban areas and in the North consumed more wheat than their southern kin.[40] Corn consumption decreased in proportion to local access to affordable wheat, a switch that empowered respectable eaters to proclaim visibly their allegiance to the more coveted grain. Elderly informants to a 1940s government-sponsored survey about African American food habits noted a generational decline in the consumption of corn bread by members of the black community, observing that wheat biscuits had already replaced corn bread and store-bought white bread seemed poised to become more popular than homemade biscuits.[41] In an 1897 column in the *Richmond Dispatch*, an unnamed white author bemoaned the early stages of this transformation, arguing that corn bread, which he said had once been "par excellence 'the' bread of the negro," was becoming less widely consumed, in part because "darkies eschew it where wheat bread is to be obtained." For this cultural observer, fear that corn bread might disappear from southern tables was linked to anxiety over the social and economic elevation of former slaves. Manifesting nostalgia for a bygone era, he claimed, "The high toned colored damsels who are turned out by our public schools are not the adepts that our old Aunt Dinahs and Aunt Peggys were."[42] Unlike the respectable eaters who celebrated wheat as a sign of racial progress, the writer for the *Richmond Dispatch* identified wheat bread as a negative symbol of social change. However, both agreed that corn was the grain of the antebellum past, while the bread of the present and the future was made out of wheat.

In the corn bread conflicts within the black community, reformers were frequently more likely to elevate or reframe rather than replace the traditional food. A 1907 recipe in the *Washington Bee* borrowed one of the era's code words for fussy, elegant middle-class food to describe corn bread; the author of the recipe sought to make the old-fashioned dish "dainty" by steaming rather than baking it.[43] A series of early twentieth-century recipes in the *Baltimore Afro-American* likewise tried to rescue cornmeal from its southern connotations. Readers who wished to eat products made from the grain while also casting aside associations with slavery could elect to make New England Johnny Cake, Indian Pudding, or even a peculiar "Chinese Bread" made from eggs, butter, cornmeal, wheat flour, and rice instead of a nominally southern rendition of the staple.[44] For status-conscious eaters hungry for cornmeal, these recipes were designed to make a humble food tied uncomfortably to the historical memory of slavery seem cosmopolitan.

Prior to World War I, respectable eaters knew that the association of corn bread and other iconic southern foods with slavery and poverty had to compete with nostalgia over fond memories of menu items widely served at family dinners and community gatherings. A 1914 editorial in the *Indianapolis Freeman* contravened the work of respectable eaters who promoted an assimilationist diet that eschewed pork and corn. The author instead declared that dishes like hog jowls, greens, and corn bread "belong to the colored people." This corn bread partisan even went so far as to frame his favorite foods as black national dishes, remarking that "every nation has its dish . . . just . . . as every nation has its flag."[45] Because corn bread was so widely and affectionately consumed, most reformers were content merely to add higher-status breads made from wheat flour to the collective breadbasket. In 1896, another article in the *Indianapolis Freeman* somewhat comically encapsulated the passions that conversations over wheat bread versus corn bread inspired, claiming, "Cornbread and biscuit are, seemingly, very small and insignificant articles, but they caused the demolition of several chairs and pitchers, and filled a home with sadness. Moral: Always cook two kinds of bread."[46]

The motto "Always cook two kinds of bread" was a guideline followed by many in the black community. Corn bread and either wheat rolls or biscuits were served side by side at many casual community dining events, and recipe columns in black newspapers give instructions for seemingly endless variations of bread made from both grains.[47] Corn bread, however, was seldom served at formal meals where the culinary stakes were considered the highest. Society columns reported that wheat breads alone graced the menus of many important social events, including birthday celebrations and engagement parties thought notable enough to be covered by the press as well as at the meetings of prominent charitable and fraternal organizations.[48]

The USFA's mandate to conserve wheat meant that uplift eaters who had long busied themselves baking Parker House rolls and water crackers were asked to reverse course and revisit corn bread. The USFA program challenged Americans to change the symbolic significance they had long given to wheat, which was now subject to voluntary rationing initiatives, and to shift their allegiance back to corn, which was not subject to the conservation guidelines. Respectable eaters who had faith in the government program linking food choices to citizenship had to reimagine corn bread as a patriotic American food.

Many food reformers valiantly tried to reverse their previous activism and to rebrand corn bread. Mrs. K. Bertha Hurst, the wife of an African Methodist Episcopal bishop, gave a lecture tour in Florida in 1918 where she tried to convince black audiences to let go of their preference for wheat. She urged her audiences to "get back to grits and gravy, milk and mush."[49] A USFA press release specifically created for black newspapers similarly described corn bread as an emblem of patriotism. The article tried to change the symbolic connotations of cornmeal, but it did so while also acknowledging that the grain had once served as a painful symbol, remembering, "Corn, once upon a time, was always on the table either as cereal, bread, vegetable or desert [sic], but when wheat came in corn went out. Again corn is king. As a child we remember the humiliation we felt at having to eat corn bread, but how times have changed!! In the exclusive tea rooms which formerly served wheat bread, pastries, etc., we find large demand for corn bread, corn griddle cakes, mush, etc. and little or no call for pastry made of wheat, or wheat bread."[50]

USFA supporters who urged the race to reclaim and rebrand corn as a symbol of nationalism and not of slavery were faced with the conundrum that although they embraced government food regulations as a ritual of citizenship, they could not immediately erase long-standing negative associations of African Americans with corn. Helen Zoe Veit has demonstrated that in the 1910s, most white Americans associated corn with southern African Americans, regarding corn bread as a quaint, backwards regional staple.[51] In a 1918 book review for a reprinted edition of Minnie C. Fox's *The Blue Grass Cook Book* (1904), a writer for the *New Orleans Times-Picayune* celebrated the wartime timeliness of the reprint due to the inclusion of a number of recipes involving cornmeal. Despite the fact that Fox explicitly printed recipes contributed by both black and white women, the reviewer gave exclusive credit to black cooks who were "famous for their dishes in which corn meal is the principal ingredient."[52] During the war years, black food conservationists dressed in the garb of "Mammy" imparted their allegedly innate racial knowledge about how to utilize cornmeal to rapt white audiences.[53] Capitalizing on the persistent stereotype that black women were born cooks, Portia Smiley, a secondary school teacher, donned nineteenth-century garb and toured New England giving demonstrations to largely white crowds about how to cook cornmeal.[54] The dilemma of respectable eaters who wished to dissociate themselves from the cuisine of slavery while also patriotically following USFA guidelines was painfully embodied in the figure of these bandanna-wearing southern mammy impersonators. Respectable eaters who wished to promote corn consumption found themselves in the uncomfortable position of being forced to grapple publicly with the legacy of slavery for the benefit of white consumers who ate up "moonlight and magnolia" fantasies with far greater enthusiasm than their government endorsed cornmeal.

These painful stereotypes aside, conscientious wartime eaters were surrounded by visuals created by government propagandists who churned out posters declaring that corn was "the food of the nation."[55] Framed in those terms, it was impossible for respectable eaters to reject corn as a negative symbol without also spurning their quest for fuller national incorporation. In the context of wartime, the cuisine of uplift inadvertently merged with the unreformed food habits of many working-class black southerners and southern migrants who had never fallen prey to the belief that good food behavior offered a pathway to citizenship. Not only did USFA guidelines sanction corn as a patriotic grain, but other items on the southern poverty menu also met the Food Administration standards for patriotic dishes. Reah Jeannette Lynch's *"Win the War" Cookbook*, which was sponsored by the National Council of Defense, gave readers numerous cornmeal recipes, and it also offered an endorsement of the timeworn southern cooking method of using salt pork to season greens and legumes, including the regional staple cowpeas.[56] Similar advice appeared everywhere. The cuisine of southern poverty, which respectable eaters had shunned in favor of dainty and elegant repasts, was now—at least temporarily—being hailed as the food of U.S. national pride.

The symbolic reordering that wartime food conservation dictated diffused some of the anxiety that respectable eaters felt toward the humble foods of the black working class and led to a culinary reconciliation of sorts. When it came to the battleground of the culinary culture wars in the black community, many had indeed decided to "close ranks" as respectable eaters embraced foods common in black working-class diets, which they had once spurned. Respectable eaters could now link an austere diet to patriotism and willing sacrifice rather than to the forced deprivations of slavery.

The importance that some adherents to the philosophy of uplift had once assigned to food selection choices began to seem even less significant during the lean years of the Great Depression. During the economic downturn, Du Bois no longer used the pages of *The Crisis* to urge African Americans to set aside racial grievances in the name of patriotism as he had done during the Great War. Instead, in a January 1934 editorial titled "Segregation," he urged the black community to turn inward and to focus on collective advancement through economic cooperation. Du Bois chal-

U.S. Food Administration poster promoting corn as a patriotic food choice, 1918. (Lithograph by Lloyd Harrison; Library of Congress LC-USZC4–10124)

lenged the sensibilities of assimilationist supporters of the NAACP when he argued that "it is the race-conscious black man cooperating together in his own institutions who will eventually emancipate the colored race, and the great step ahead today is for the American Negro to accomplish his economic emancipation through voluntary determined cooperative effort."[57] He realized that middle-class devotion to the politics of cultural uplift had not yielded full citizenship rights any more than had black patriotism during the First World War. Increasingly, Du Bois cast off the petty class warfare that had become embedded in the respectability project and became more cynical about the ability of an interracial, middle-class organization like the NAACP to adequately address the dire financial situation of the black community during the Great Depression. He had became convinced that the organization had been too quick to work condescendingly "for the black masses but not with them" and was too attuned to fighting against segregation and discrimination at the expense of aiding working-class African Americans in their struggle for economic justice.[58] These concerns led to conflict among the leadership of the organization, which encouraged Du Bois to resign from the NAACP, give up his editorial pulpit at *The Crisis*, and resume his struggle against white supremacy from his post at Atlanta University. Historian Jacqueline N. Moore finds some irony embedded in Du Bois's about-face, claiming that he "now attacked the very talented tenth he had championed in the past and advocated the separate black economic advancement that Booker T. Washington had cultivated."[59]

Du Bois and Washington's Culinary Rapprochement

At the turn of the twentieth century, both Washington and Du Bois had embraced the respectable eater's certainty that individual food choices mattered. Both men believed that by eating properly, African Americans sent symbolic messages to the white community about black equality. As chapter 3 reveals, Du Bois's earliest activities in the realm of food politics consisted of practicing a strict personal regiment; distributing dietary advice to his daughter, Yolande, and to other potential members of the talented tenth whom he counted on to become race leaders; and criticizing the food habits of the black working class, whose behavior he deemed backward and unhealthful. Du Bois hoped that by eating low-calorie foods, especially vegetables, he could ensure his physical health and serve as an embodied refutation of white attempts to denigrate black bodies.

Using himself as an exhibit of black physical equality, he could educate white Americans and lead less fortunate African Americans by his bodily example.

Washington also believed that individual food choices mattered. He insisted on the right of Tuskegee students to enjoy high-status foods like beef and wheat bread, which he labeled as culinary symbols of assimilation. As he grew older, he increasingly began to share Du Bois's interest in the relationship between diet and physical well-being. Food, he realized, could function as a medication as well as a symbol. The dyspepsia that Du Bois feared might afflict him if he let down his guard while he was a young man at Harvard became the bane of Washington's existence in middle age. Washington ordered "Bell's Papayan tablets," which were designed to alleviate indigestion, by the hundreds.[60] Like Du Bois, Washington sought advice from well-known health advocates of the day, including, most notably, John Harvey Kellogg. Washington traveled to Battle Creek Sanitarium, where he partook of the high-fiber, vegetarian regimen, which was touted as a cure-all. He also hosted ambassadors from Battle Creek at Tuskegee, where they not only supervised Washington's own eating habits but also encouraged other members of the local community to consume more vegetables and eschew meat.[61]

Despite their famed disagreements, it is clear that Washington and Du Bois believed in the necessity of both individual and race-wide bodily reform. Good food behavior, they earnestly hoped, might prove to be a tool for assimilation if used to deflate contemporary ideas about the inferiority of black bodies or as a way to improve the health of the black community if fuller incorporation was denied. Even if white society was unyielding, they believed that food choices were still important because a proper diet could preserve individual black lives.

For Washington, the politics of food consumption were always linked to what he regarded as the potentially even more important issue of food production. He saw food reform not only as a means of uplifting the race by promoting the consumption of healthful, high-status foods but also as a way to bolster black economic independence. He urged black farmers to strive for food self-sufficiency and to use their ability to support themselves as a buffer against white supremacy. He advised African Americans to limit, as much as possible, dependency upon wages paid by white employers or goods purchased at white-controlled stores and to produce as much of their own food as they possibly could. In his small realm of Tuskegee, Washington strove for self-sufficiency as he encouraged those in the campus community to produce and preserve their own food and thus limit their dependence upon the benevolence of white donors to the institution. Although Washington never lived to see his fabled rival's culinary and philosophical evolution, Du Bois clearly recognized the wisdom of seeking greater economic autonomy as the black community began to suffer from the ravages of the Great Depression.

As Du Bois's political thought tilted further in the direction of socialism, this reorientation necessitated a growing understanding of food behavior as less a matter of individual predilection and more an issue of communal concern. In the context of the Great Depression, the matter of what one should eat paled in importance alongside the issue of having enough to eat. Rather than continuing to prioritize full social and economic entry into a white-dominated U.S. nation-state, Du Bois began to entertain a form of economic black nationalism reminiscent of Washington's. In 1937, Du Bois charged the talented tenth with using their educational training to assume leadership roles in the "economic development of the Negro race in America." They could do this by helping African Americans collectively harness their power as both consumers and producers of goods.[62]

Although the Great Depression was the catalyst that inspired Du Bois to use his pulpit at *The Crisis* to endorse economic self-segregation, he had been interested in exploring the possibility of cooperative black economic enterprises for almost three decades. He first wrote publicly about the issue in the 1907 study *Economic Co-operation among Negro Americans*, sponsored by Atlanta University. This 184-page publication detailed the long-standing efforts of African American organizations such as burial societies, banks, insurance companies, and cooperative grocery stores to provide "mutual aid in earning a living."[63] Du Bois was, in fact, well versed enough in the details about cooperative economics that in 1918 he was able to give African American banker B. M. Roddy detailed advice about how to start a cooperative grocery store in Memphis, including his suggestion that shares in the business should be sold in relatively affordable increments of five, ten, or twenty-five dollars.[64] His interest in the possibility of black economic cooperation accelerated as his faith in the possibility of black integration into the wider national economy diminished. In a 1936 column in the *Pittsburgh Courier*, he proclaimed, "We would make a big mistake if we did not try in every legal way to co-operate with surrounding civilization and integrate ourselves with it." However, even as he endorsed the idea of full economic integration, he discounted it as a viable possibility. He warned the black community not to "forget the value of our own selves and our own race and our own contributions" because "acceptance of colored people by white people in the United States is always more or less partial." Instead, African Americans needed to channel the majority of their energy inward and to "co-operate as Negroes in order to employ ourselves and give ourselves decent incomes."[65]

Economic and Culinary Cooperation in the 1930s

Du Bois was hardly alone in his belief that consumer cooperation offered the black community its best chance at surviving the ravages of the Great Depression.[66] The 1930s saw an upsurge of interest in cooperatives, and many of these initiatives revolved around the most fundamental of concerns: how to best feed the community. During the 1930s, black culture wars over what to eat faded in importance alongside concerted collective efforts to make sure that everyone had something to eat. For many—like Du Bois—separatist economic nation-building began to seem like a more viable strategy than the quest for full U.S. national incorporation.

Black satirist and journalist George Schuyler responded to the growing economic desperation in the black community by founding the Young Negroes' Cooperative League (YNCL) in 1930. He served as president of the organization and recruited community organizer Ella Baker to assist as the national director. His incendiary recruitment rhetoric proclaimed that "the old Negroes have failed." He admonished "young Negroes" to "take up the burden of leadership," telling them, "You must succeed where the oldsters have failed. . . . Put your faith in individual effort and perish, put it in co-operative effort and prosper."[67] Schuyler's belief that a new generation should be installed as the leaders of economic progress was so adamant that he insisted that YNCL members had to be thirty-five years or younger despite the fact that he was thirty-five years old himself when he founded the organization.[68] Schuyler regarded the older generation of race leaders as "hopelessly bourgeois."[69] Although he did not specifically critique the foodways of uplift that emphasized elegant dining habits and carefully selected, domestic scientist–approved menu items, the new focus on consumer cooperation provided an implicit rebuttal to those erstwhile concerns. For many, crushing economic necessity made the issue of the symbolic significance of particular food choices fade in significance alongside the activist impulse of the black cooperative movement, which by its very nature emphasized group solidarity and sought to minimize class distinctions.

Schuyler's YNCL had hoped to operate as an umbrella organization, linking the buying clubs and cooperative businesses that it expected would spring up throughout the nation.[70] Initial interest in the group's activities seemed promising. By 1931, the organization had 400 members and had inspired the formation of consumer education study groups in a number of states.[71] However, despite this initial burst of enthusiasm and efforts to encourage widespread, moderate financial support for the organization via Ella Baker's "A Penny a Day for Economic Security" program, the underfunded national office closed in 1932.[72] The organization did not immediately disappear altogether, though. Baker continued her role in promoting cooperation long after the YNCL stopped paying her modest salary. Her commitment to consumer cooperation, which she deemed to be a "revolutionary" activity, was ongoing.[73] After the efforts of the YNCL eventually fizzled, Baker worked as an educator giving classes on consumer issues for the Worker's Education Program, sponsored by one of Franklin D. Roosevelt's most ambitious New Deal programs, the Works Progress Administration.[74] Her pragmatic ability to move from an organization founded by and designed to work for the black community to a program funded by the federal government was representative of the elasticity of many race leaders who were willing to explore the possibility of black economic advancement through a variety of channels. For many, it was possible to identify both with the idea of full incorporation into the U.S. nation-state and with the idea of a separate black economy. Either model was appealing if it provided a means for group-wide subsistence. The goal of maximizing the health and well-being of as many members of the black community as possible proved to be a tenacious match for abstract ideological discussions about national loyalties.

Baker's core belief in the potential of economic cooperation was echoed by many African Americans. The state of race relations was such that most talk about economic cooperation was inward-looking with a focus on how members of the black community could combine their scarce resources for the mutual benefit of all. A 1936 editorial in the *Philadelphia Tribune* bemoaned the fact that "colored people" in Philadelphia "spend more for eggs than the proprietors of the Negro operated food stores receive during a year for all commodities." Although the writer regretted that only a small portion of the race's buying power was channeled toward black businesses, the central claim of the editorial was much larger: black consumers did not appreciate their own economic power. If small amounts of capital—such as the funds allocated for items like eggs—were pooled, the shared resources would be enough to form a consumer-owned store that would save the members money on their groceries while also wresting economic power away from white business owners.[75]

African Americans in various locations responded positively to this challenge to redirect a small portion of their resources to form joint enterprises. Collectively owned grocery stores and food buying clubs were frequently the most common and the most successful of these initiatives. Black-run cooperative groceries opened throughout the nation in places as far-flung as Harlem, New York; Birmingham, Alabama; Philadelphia, Pennsylvania; Washington, D.C.; Richmond, Virginia; and Gary, Indiana.[76] Harlem's Own Cooperative, of which Ella Baker was an officer and an enthusiastic member, began by distributing low-cost milk to members residing at the cooperatively owned Dunbar apartment complex. This initial experiment in collective buying led to the eventual creation of a larger grocery business.[77] Members could buy shares in the co-op for $5 each, and on Friday and Saturday nights they could shop for a wide variety of packaged goods, including canned soups, meats, and vegetables, at the organization's 149th Street store.[78] At a cooperative grocery store founded by 400 black consumers in Buffalo, New York, in 1931 and staffed entirely by African Americans, consumers boasted taking in $3,200 in the first week of business.[79] Inspired by the idea of collectivism on a different scale, the owners of various black grocery stores throughout the U.S. joined together to form a "voluntary chain" sponsored by the Colored Merchants Association. The headquarters of this umbrella group organized joint advertising and collective buying programs designed to help these vulnerable small businesses weather the economic downturn.[80] Interest in black-owned grocery stores—whether owned jointly by black consumers or individually by black entrepreneurs—became so pronounced during the Depression years that the Atlanta Daily World wryly remarked that "it is becoming almost a fad to open a grocery store."[81]

Even those who could not claim an ownership stake in a cooperatively owned grocery store could find other opportunities to collaborate in the struggle for subsistence through buying clubs. For example, in 1932 a YNCL-sponsored buying club in Philadelphia organized to purchase collectively the weekly groceries for fifty families.[82] Similarly, black housewives in Detroit came together to jointly purchase wholesale vegetables from growers in Florida, while ambitious members of Chicago's Thrift Consumers Cooperative formed a buying club that eventually evolved into a full-fledged grocery store.[83] Even black farmers from the rural South, who were among the nation's most exploited workers and most intense victims of racial violence, experimented with the cooperative purchasing of food supplies. In 1930 a group of African American farmers in Mississippi pooled their meager resources to buy a train car full of food and agricultural supplies at wholesale, a venture that they estimated saved them 42 percent of the retail cost.[84]

As impressive as these cooperative efforts were, collective buying programs could not stave off the economic ravages of the Great Depression. As J. Todd Moye points out, "No voluntary purchasing program was a match for the realities of double-digit unemployment, a collapsed banking system, and a cratered manufacturing sector, especially if it depended on the earning power of wage workers from a marginalized racial minority."[85] Nonetheless, the cooperative movement proved to be an important training ground for black activists, including, most notably, Ella Baker, who took the lessons about grassroots organizing that she learned while working in the YNCL and used them throughout her long, influential career as a civil rights activist affiliated with the National Association for the Advancement of Colored People, the Southern Christian Leadership Conference, and, most notably, the Student Nonviolent Coordinating Committee.[86] Furthermore, the cooperative grocery stores and food buying clubs constituted an important exercise in culinary nation-building. The rhetorical importance of food cooperatives had much greater cultural reach than the actual on-the-ground initiatives, which typically had little staying power in spite of the enthusiasm of core members. Nonetheless, the idea of cooperative buying became perhaps the biggest food-related topic in African American public discourse during the 1930s. Where and how to get food became a far more pressing issue than the question of what to eat, which had preoccupied turn-of-the-twentieth-century respectable eaters embarked on a program of cultural uplift.

As had been the case during World War I, food issues continued to be framed as political ones by the black press and by numerous race leaders during the economic downturn. While during the First World War, participation in USFA-sponsored voluntary food conservation had been viewed by many as a way to demonstrate patriotic loyalty to the United States, during the Great Depression African American food-buying cooperatives were a manifestation of a potent strain of economic black nationalism. For reformers of this ilk, food became, at least theoretically, a means for constructing a separate black nation that operated as independently as possible from the whims of white supremacy. Furthermore, the idea of black culinary separatism that Washington had nurtured at Tuskegee, which became more pronounced during the lean years of the Great Depression, was to gather momentum during the coming decades. However, during the early years of the classical phase of the civil rights movement, a resurgent optimism that America might, at long last, embrace African Americans as equal citizens temporarily reanimated the tenacious idea that food practices could serve as a vehicle of U.S. national incorporation. Ultimately, though, as the next chapter will reveal, these vain hopes were no match for the emergence of a full-fledged culinary black nationalism exemplified by the emergence of the concept of "soul food" in the 1960s.

The Civil Rights Movement and the Ascendency of the Idea of a Racial Style of Eating

In 1948, food columnist Freda DeKnight railed against "a fallacy, long dis-proved, that Negro cooks, chefs, and caterers can adapt themselves only to the standard Southern dishes, such as fried chicken, greens, corn pone, hot breads, and so forth." She used the platform of her influential cookbook, *A Date with a Dish: A Cook Book of American Negro Recipes*, to argue that "like other Americans," black cooks "have naturally shown a desire to branch in all directions."[1] Because DeKnight's cookbook first appeared shortly before the advent of the classical phase of the civil rights movement, activists and cultural observers intent on integration were likely sympathetic to her emphasis upon the democratic range of the black culinary imagination.[2] However, despite her adamant stance in favor of the essential Americanness of black food expression, she simultaneously grappled with another idea about African American food habits that threatened to unsettle her core belief. DeKnight's strong assertion of black gustatory belonging to the U.S. nation-state was tinged with a culinary essentialism that labeled black cooks and eaters as "other" at the same time that she argued for their U.S. national incorporation. Although DeKnight rebelled against a reductive and singular idea about African American food expression, she also contended that the racial positionality of the cook influences the taste of any given dish. She claimed, "There are no set rules for dishes created by most Negroes. They just seem to have a 'way' of taking a plain, ordinary everyday dish and improvising it into a creation that is a gourmet's delight. Whether acquired or inherent, this love for food has given them the desire to make their dishes different, well-seasoned, and eye-appealing."[3]

In DeKnight's mind, what transformed a recipe into a "Negro dish" was not a specific set of ingredients or a culinary history that could be traced to the plantation South or to Africa but rather the identity of the person doing the cooking. Black cooks, she asserted, made black food regardless of what they were preparing. Her cheerful endorsement of the stereotype of an innately talented black cook stood in defiance to the core principles of the respectability project that had influenced most African American food writers who predated DeKnight. In raising the question about whether black culinary skill was "acquired or inherent," she refused to pay obeisance to the reigning social scientific proclamations that race was a cultural and not a biological category while also anticipating future attempts of cultural nationalists to exploit the flawed idea of racial essentialism to support their nation-building agenda. Her suggestion that the assigned racial categorization of the cook was what made a dish tasty and authentic anticipated the emergence of a new food politics that would ultimately overpower the voices of culinary assimilationists.

By the mid-1960s, many black activists, including some who had become disillusioned by the unfilled promises of the movement, began to contemplate more fully the implications of the claim that talented black cooks made dishes that were "different" and thus perhaps not quite so typically "American" after all. Although culinary reformers of this variety embraced DeKnight's ideas about black culinary distinctiveness, they also reified the association of blackness with southern cooking, an idea that *A Date with a Dish* had worked so hard to shatter. These food reformers celebrated the concept of what they labeled as "soul food," a style of eating based upon the plantation staples of corn and fatty pork that had made up the backbone of the southern plantation diet.[4]

DeKnight's twin impulses to celebrate a uniquely African American way of cooking while also advocating for the essentially "American" character of black food practices can be followed back, in some form, to the period of emancipation. Although the idea of black food as undifferentiated from other American food was predominant until the second half of the twentieth century, earlier hints of the idea of culinary distinctiveness are evident as well. The intellectual history of the idea of "soul food" can be traced for at least a century before the concept was fully articulated. Shortly after the end of the Civil War, African American food writers began looking for ways to define their relationship to southern food traditions.

The Ascendency of the Idea of a Racial Style of Eating

The Food Imaginary in Early African American Cookbooks

Cookbooks frequently reveal more about aspirational food habits than actual daily practices, and African American cookbooks from the late nineteenth and early twentieth centuries yield valuable insights into the meanings assigned to certain food items. The earliest published African American recipe collections generally do not endorse the idea of an essential, cohesive form of black food expression. Untutored in the later politics of soul food, which celebrated southern food as an emblem of black resiliency and as community intellectual property, the vision promulgated in early black food writing is generally more cosmopolitan than proprietary. Yet, because the majority of the nation's black population lived in the South and actually ate many of the foods associated with that region, these early food writers had no choice but to grapple with the meaning of southern food traditions. In so doing they laid the groundwork for the ultimate rhetorical transformation of a regional style of eating into a racial one.

Malinda Russell's *Domestic Cook Book: Containing a Careful Selection of Useful Recipes for the Kitchen*—the earliest extant cookbook written by a black author, published in 1866—is not a compilation of recipes documenting southern vernacular cooking. Russell, a free woman of color prior to emancipation, was a native southerner who made her living as a cook in Virginia and later as the proprietor of a boardinghouse and a pastry shop in Tennessee. She learned to cook in what she describes as the "plan of 'the Virginia housewife,'" referencing Mary Randolph's 1824 cookbook *The Virginia Housewife*.[5] By tracing her culinary lineage to Randolph, who was related to Thomas Jefferson by marriage, Russell endorsed the idea of an interracial and jointly American culinary tradition. Rather than emphasizing the improvisation and innovation of the illiterate enslaved cooks who played an enormous role in creating the food knowledge encapsulated in Randolph's foundational text, Russell privileged the idea of the written codified knowledge represented by a cookbook. In doing so, she was not rejecting the cultural contributions of her ancestors as much as she was carving out a place for herself as a skilled professional. She had to contend with the persistent stereotype that, in the words of writer and politician Charles Gayarré, "negroes are born cooks."[6] To counter the idea that her kitchen know-how was an innate racial trait rather than the outgrowth of training and experience, Russell framed cooking as intellectual task.

Russell designed her cookbook to earn money after her life savings were stolen during the chaos of the Civil War; thus, she likely chose to document her most popular recipes in order to attract the largest possible book-buying audience. The recipes she recorded were disproportionately for dessert items. Although some dishes such as "Sweet Potato Baked Pudding" and "Sweet Potato Slice Pie" reference common southern ingredients, most dishes lack even that much regional specificity.[7] The titles of many recipes, in fact, point to origins, either real or imagined, far from the American South. Dishes such as "Queen's Party Cake," "Dover Cake," "Carvies' Plum Pudding," "French Tea Biscuit," "Irish Potato Custard," and "French Lady Cake" proclaim direct European antecedents.[8] Due to the diversity of Russell's recipes, food writer Toni Tipton-Martin has labeled her text as an "Emancipation Proclamation for black cooks." The book, Tipton-Martin argues, clearly "dispels the notion of a universal African American food experience."[9] Russell's recipes are not designed to perform either a specific racial or a regional identity, and her imagined audience is correspondingly limitless. She published her recipes because "they are valuable" and "every family has use for them."[10] Although she can be seen as the progenitor of a long and distinguished tradition of African American food writing, she believed that her dishes held general appeal and were not the distinctive product of a black or southern imagination.

Another early African American cookbook, *What Mrs. Fisher Knows about Old Southern Cooking*, is—as the title indicates—more overtly wedded to the idea of a distinctly southern, but not yet distinctly African American, style of eating. Abby Fisher, a San Francisco caterer who was likely born into slavery in South Carolina, may have been able to capitalize on local ideas about exotic southern cuisine in order to distinguish her skill set from that of other cooks on the West Coast.[11] Fisher's definition of what constitutes southern food is elastic and expansive, transcending the corn and pork tropes commonly used to describe southern food. She includes such recipes as "Milanese Sauce," "Yorkshire Pudding," and "Charlotte Russe," which nod directly toward Europe, and "Cranberry Jelly," which references New England. Other items like her recipe for beef bouillon or fish chowder would have gained the endorsement of the most ardent proponent of the bland cuisine of Americanization promoted by turn-of-the-twentieth-century domestic scientists. The upwardly mobile "dainty" eaters of the era could enjoy her recipe for "Ladies' Custard," a dish named to indicate that it was best suited for a delicate and refined palate.[12]

Although her vision of southern cuisine does not consist entirely of a narrow list of canonized ingredients and preparations, she does record recipes for "Plantation Corn Bread or Hoe Cake," two kinds of gumbo, and "Creole Chow Chow," dishes that are clearly meant to unabashedly evoke typical southern fare.[13] Furthermore, Fisher promotes herself as an authority on these dishes not only by virtue of her regional background but because of her racial heritage as well. For example, she vouches for the authenticity and efficacy of her recipe for "Blackberry Syrup—For Dysentery in Children" because it is "an old Southern plantation remedy among colored people."[14] In so doing, she laid some preliminary ground-work for the culinary nationalism that was to emerge in full force a hundred years after emancipation.

Somewhat similarly, Rufus Estes, whose *Good Things to Eat* appeared three decades later, combines recipes that are quintessentially south-ern with those that reflect a more cosmopolitan palate. In contrast to the recipes recorded by Russell and Fisher, Estes, a chef for the U.S. Steel Corporation who had been born into slavery in 1857, does not record only dishes widely considered suitable for entertaining or for fancy feasts. Rather, he includes recipes for humble dishes like "Pig's Feet," but even his renderings of preparations of unwanted animal scraps are presented with international flair, as is the case in his recipe for "Pigs Ears, Lyonaise." The ears, which are simmered with onion and garnished with lemon and a slice of bread, are presented as a dish associated with French rather than African American peasant cooking.[15] Throughout the book, he references both southern regional and global antecedents. He instructs his readers both on how to stuff a "'possum," an animal associated with the cuisine of southern poverty, with sausage and rice and how to stuff a more elegant turkey with truffles and bacon.[16] His recipe titles range from "Dressing for Italian Ravioli" to "Japanese or Chinese Rice" (a somewhat confusing dish flavored with tomato juice, paprika, and cheese) to "Southern Corncakes."[17]

While not disavowing his southern regional food heritage, Estes did not hold a narrow vision of his culinary range or birthright. Although not ashamed of food associated with southern poverty, Estes refused to limit himself to those dishes and certainly did not frame them, as another gen-eration of black cooks would, as part of his racial heritage. He felt free to borrow from various culinary traditions and created a compilation of reci-pes that reflected both the vernacular food traditions of his humble child-hood and the more self-consciously sophisticated foods he learned to pre-pare throughout his long career working as a chef.

Other printed African American recipes from the era promoted a greater rhetorical distance from the foodways of the South while not completely severing the association of African American ways of eating with southern food practices. The *Montana Federation of Negro Women's Clubs Cook Book* included recipes for only two dishes that the authors explicitly labeled as "southern." They identified the same number of recipes as "Mexican."[18] Contemporary newspapers often featured cooking columns that boasted an equally catholic vision of what constituted black cuisine. Early twentieth-century readers of the *Baltimore Afro-American* were tutored on how to make both watercress tea sandwiches and corn pone, foods that evoked both the drawing room and the plantation.[19] Although some recipes paid homage to southern foods, regional recipes were generally outnumbered by dishes with more worldly connotations.

Cooking columnists writing for black newspapers knew that their audience consisted largely of African American uplift-oriented eaters. They realized that this small but outspoken group regarded the quotidian decision about what to eat as a significant part of the politics of racial representation. As previous chapters of this book establish, respectable eaters sometimes eschewed iconic southern foods as a means of separating themselves from both a painful history and working-class eaters they imagined to be less discriminating. However, evidence suggests that to some extent these class anxieties may have been based upon skewed stereotypes and unfounded generalizations about the food habits of the poor. Even working-class southerners did not necessarily always celebrate or eat what later became known as a classic soul food diet. Although the intellectual antecedents of soul can be traced back to the nineteenth century, the concept was one that both respectable eaters and working-class southerners ultimately had to learn.

Actual Food Habits

In the late nineteenth and early twentieth centuries, researchers sponsored by the U.S. Department of Agriculture conducted a number of dietary studies that collected information about what African Americans ate in locations ranging from the rural South to the urban North.[20] Together these findings offer important clues about the daily food habits of average African Americans. When analyzing information about "ordinary" people that was acquired by representatives of an "official" organization, it is important to be mindful of the uneven power dynamics between those who were interviewed and those who were extracting information. We cannot know how diligent interviewers were about crafting questions, making observations, or listening to respondents. Nor can we be certain that the people they studied were willing to share accurate information about their private habits, particularly when they were speaking to a member of a different racial group. Furthermore, we cannot be sure about how representative these studies, which relied on relatively small sample sets of data, were of most African American diets. Yet in the absence of unmediated access to the pantries of people long deceased, these surveys offer one of the most detailed, even if flawed, glimpses we have into the diets of early twentieth-century African Americans.

In 2001, anthropologist Robert T. Dirks and librarian Nancy Duran conducted a comparative analysis of these data sets and found that many of the items commonly associated with the soul food menu today were consumed at best infrequently by many turn-of-the-twentieth-century African Americans.[21] These studies reveal that the purported southern staples of "hog and hominy" were indeed commonly eaten, particularly in the Deep South; however, these became proportionately less important as consumers were confronted with greater food options.[22] Items that by the 1960s would be considered staples on the iconic African American dinner table, such as black-eyed peas, rice, and chicken, were consumed intermittently in earlier decades. Their frequent absence from the table may have been due in part to issues of affordability and seasonality, but preference may have played a role too. For example, rural Alabamians and Virginians reportedly ate dark leafy greens at certain times of the year, yet greens, which are now a soul food staple, were never identified as a core menu item. Furthermore, despite contemporary associations of fried chicken with soul food, chicken, which was a relatively expensive form of animal protein until the 1930s, was identified as a secondary or, more frequently, a peripheral food choice in each of the areas studied.[23]

Among the items commonly associated with southern, or more specifically African American, foodways by the late twentieth century, the sweet potato was the food most consistently featured on the dinner tables of African Americans throughout the nation. While contemporary studies of white eating habits documented the presence of sweet potatoes on only 24 percent of white dinner tables, the food item was consumed in 47 percent of black homes. Interestingly, sweet potatoes were eaten in 40 percent of white southern households, a fact that seems to indicate that black consumers of sweet potatoes were as likely evoking a regional preference as they were a self-consciously racial food sensibility.[24]

The food habits of African American migrants offer particularly important information as we seek to discern whether foods that were to become part of a culturally resonant "soul food" menu in the 1960s were equally

A sharecropper and his daughter planting sweet potatoes in North Carolina, 1939.
(Photo by Dorothea Lange; Library of Congress LC-USF34–019910-E)

significant to earlier generations of black eaters. As chapter 4 reveals, some
southern migrants were intent on maintaining regional food preferences
after leaving the South. When members of this group proudly and publicly consumed, for example, pork scraps or offal, they offended the sensibilities of middle-class African Americans living in terminus cities of
the Great Migration who had a different set of ideas about proper food
behavior. Although these performatively "southern" eaters raised the ire
of conscientious eaters with a different sensibility, evidence suggests that
not all southern migrants were reluctant to make dietary changes or resistant to the uplift-oriented vision of food reform. Some southern African
Americans were willing, even eager, to eat different foods when they had

The Ascendency of the Idea of a Racial Style of Eating

the ability to do so. Specifically, many preferred to eat beef and wheat rather than the soul food staples of pork and cornmeal when they could.[25] In aggregate, these dietary studies indicate that many African Americans ate eclectically and widely, choosing among the options available to them rather than adhering to a limited, southern regional menu. For example, studies of working-class black residents of Philadelphia and Washington, D.C., near the turn of the twentieth century show that the respondents ate more mutton than fatback, more oatmeal than cornmeal, and more apples than turnips.[26]

Additional government-sponsored research about African American eating habits in the 1940s provides valuable information not only about what people were eating but also about contemporary African American perceptions concerning their diet. At the urging of federal officials who wished to secure widespread compliance with a mandatory wartime food-rationing program, the National Research Council established a Committee on Food Habits under the leadership of anthropologists Carl E. Guthre and Margaret Mead. The committee was charged with conducting extensive studies about American eating habits that paid attention to variations along regional, ethnic, and socioeconomic lines. Among other things, researchers wanted to find out if there was a separate and identifiably African American cuisine, and they set out to answer this question in part by asking black respondents what they ate in comparison with other members of their local communities.

Fieldwork conducted by researchers affiliated with the project revealed that black respondents recognized at least some racial differences in consumption patterns. In the study of the diets of African Americans living in an unspecified community in the upper South, researchers noted that local African Americans generally agreed on these statements:

> Whites eat more Irish potatoes.
> Whites eat more salads.
> Whites eat less cabbage because they dislike the smell.
> Whites like onion and garlic more.
> Whites eat more white bread; Negroes have biscuits three times
>   a day.
> Negroes eat more bacon and have less fresh meat.
> Poor whites eat more like Negroes.
> Whites can eat many things Negroes can't afford.[27]

Interestingly, these observations about different food practices are geared more toward comparing the alleged quantities of foods consumed by black and white members of the community than toward comparing the specific foods eaten. The implication seems to be that both black and white people ate ingredients such as Irish potatoes, onions, and bacon but in different quantities. Some of these noted differences, if they are to be given credence, could be explained in terms of not only preference but also ease of access. Bacon, which was allegedly consumed in greater quantities by black people than by white people, would have been far less expensive than the fresh meat purportedly favored by whites, who were generally financially better off than their black counterparts.

When summarizing the differences between the two groups, black respondents ultimately pointed to the issue of economic disparity as the primary marker of difference with the claim that "whites can eat many things Negroes can't afford." The researchers ultimately concluded that "Negroes do not on the whole regard their diet as inferior in quality to that of whites, but do regard it as inferior in quantity." However, not all of the African Americans whom they interviewed thought that white people were better off than they were. Researchers noted, for example, that middle-class African Americans were sometimes disdainful of the diets of poor whites, who, according to one observer, "hardly ever eat salads or soups."[28] This observation contextualizes the earlier claims that "whites eat more salads" and "poor whites eat more like Negroes" if we presume, as seems to be the case, that salad was regarded as a high-status food in this community. Thus this study indicates that even when typical class roles were reversed, dietary differences between white and black members of the community were often understood primarily in socioeconomic rather than racial terms.

In the 1943 report of all the research conducted by the Committee on Food Habits that year, members of the organization presented their blunt overall finding that "there are no American Negro food habits." Instead they argued that the "rural Negro in the South eats substantially the same as does his White neighbor of similar economic circumstances, while the Negro school teacher or physician reared in the North eats the same food as his white counterpart serves."[29] Thus in their estimation, class markers and regional affiliations proved to be better predictors of dietary choices than racial identification. The Committee on Food Habits' findings seem to indicate that many African Americans ate foods similar to that of whites from a similar social class, and few regarded dietary choices as a means of performing a separate racial identity. However, at the same time that some black Americans were emphasizing their culinary similarity with their white neighbors, others—particularly African Americans with southern origins who lived outside of the region—were beginning the process of reframing their style of eating as a racially specific one.

Langston Hughes memorably encapsulated a growing racialized enthusiasm for southern food items in the 1940s using the vehicle of his fictional character Jesse B. Semple (often referred to as "Simple"), a southern transplant living in Harlem. In a 1945 short story, Simple bemoans the fact that opossum, a favorite food of his southern childhood, is not available in Harlem to serve on his Christmas table. In exasperation Simple proclaims, "As many Negroes as there are in Harlem, there ought to be at least one 'possum around." Ultimately, however, he believes that his desires are thwarted by a white culinary hegemony so extensive that even Santa Claus is implicated. Simple is certain that if the status quo were reversed and if Santa Claus were colored, he would be willing to deliver a possum directly to the black residents of urban New York City.[30]

In a story written four years later, Hughes's character is still complaining about the conflict between his own taste sensibilities and those enshrined in American holiday traditions. He bristles against the predominance of the turkey on the American Thanksgiving menu, remarking, "Those pilgrims did not know how to scarf." Simple prefers to eat pork, extolling the versatility of an animal that when slaughtered could be divided into a number of dishes that he found equally delectable. He includes pork chops, spareribs, hams, snouts, pig's feet, pig's tail, pig ears, jowls, hog maw, pig's knuckles, and chitterlings in his catalog of favorite pig parts. Subversively Africanizing the ritual feast by inserting a black presence into the mythology of the so-called 1621 "First Thanksgiving," Simple proclaims, "Had I lived amongst them Pilgrims . . . I would have found me a hog in them woods."[31]

For some, the idea of a distinctly black way of eating became a means of integrating southern transplants, like the fictive Simple, with other members of the northern black community and to create a sense of racial, rather than regional, culinary belonging. However, for black southerners, the racialization of regional cooking styles happened more slowly. In fact, ideas about the essential similarity of black and white tastes and food habits undergirded the assumptions of many of the activists who were to participate in the direct action campaigns of the civil rights movement.

The Civil Rights Movement and the Symbolic Significance of American Foods

Iconic American foods became important symbols in the direct action protests that emerged on a heretofore unimaginably large scale in the 1960s when student protesters staged waves of sit-ins at the segregated lunch counters of the South, seeking equal access to foods like tuna sandwiches and french fries that served as emblems of a bland, American style of eating.

Stalwart civil rights activist Ella Baker famously reminded movement observers that the youthful protesters who participated in sit-ins aimed at the desegregation of southern restaurants acted out of much loftier goals than the desire for a "hamburger or even a giant-sized Coke."[32] Instead, she proclaimed that the students who organized these protests were concerned with nothing less than the "moral implications of racial discrimination for the 'whole world' and the 'Human Race'" and not merely with their inability to conveniently fill their stomachs with an iconic food and beverage.[33] Nonetheless, that act of being denied equal access to these symbolic American food items, which often could be purchased only alongside humiliations such as being served through the back door, functioned as a powerful and ongoing reminder of second-class citizenship. For a time, southern public spaces such as regional outposts of Woolworths and McDonald's could be interpreted not merely as dispensers of mediocre food, like the hamburgers and Cokes referred to in Baker's often-quoted statement, but also as battlefields in a revolutionary struggle.

Even though Baker's point—that the movement was about far more than the ability to access the fat, carbohydrates, and sugar packaged in the form of the seemingly ubiquitous burger and Coke—was irrefutable, the symbols she chose to illustrate her point were carefully chosen and thus worthy of additional consideration. Coca-Cola and the hamburger have been widely utilized to symbolize American culture both at home and abroad. Given the reach of these foods as signifiers, to be denied access to these items became a pointed reminder of the politics of American racism and exclusion. At the same time that young civil rights activists were agitating for the right to consume Coke, or whatever other items they desired, with dignity and under equal terms at dining establishments throughout the South, artist Andy Warhol was both commenting upon and solidifying the semiotic power of the iconic glass Coke bottle as a U.S. national symbol through work such as his 1962 silkscreen *Green Coca-Cola Bottles*,

The Ascendency of the Idea of a Racial Style of Eating

Coca-Cola for sale in Natchez, Mississippi, 1940. (Photo by Marion Post Wolcott; Library of Congress LC-DIG-fsac-1a34333)

which depicts multiple silhouettes of the bottle arranged in neat rows. Ironically, given the historical context of the sit-ins, Warhol interpreted the beverage as a democratic, cultural leveler, claiming, "A Coke is a Coke, and no amount of money can get you a better Coke than the one the bum on the corner is drinking."[34] Although the activists and the pop artist differed in their interpretations of Coke as a symbol of exclusion or of access, they agreed about its essential Americanness and thus could not deny its cultural power.

Today, Coca-Cola is the most widely distributed product in the world, and its ascendency was well under way when Baker referred to it in her famous essay.[35] During the Second World War, the company gave GIs inexpensive access to the beverage wherever they were stationed overseas, a policy that both encouraged the idea that Coke was a patriotic American beverage and fueled appetites for the sugary drink overseas as the concoction gained international exposure.[36] In the wake of the war, the Coca-Cola company continued its concerted campaign of global expansion, the success of which was epitomized in the classic 1971 commercial "I'd Like to Buy the World a Coke," which features a multiracial cast of Coke enthusiasts wearing various national and ethnic costumes and proclaiming their fidelity to the drink.[37] Although today the soft drink inspires kaleidoscopic connotations ranging from ideas of American freedom and prosperity to critiques of consumerism and imperial overreach, the beverage has always been interpreted as being closely linked to the nation where it originated.

Similarly, Josh Ozersky has argued that the hamburger has "a special semiotic power." Throughout the globe, the combination of a patty of ground beef served on a soft, split roll conjures up associations of the United States, a linkage made more notable by the fact that in the fractured history of American cooking, there have been so few emblematic foods.[38] The symbolic significance of the dish was taken to even greater heights when it was served, as was the case in Freda DeKnight's rendition, with "American" cheese.[39] It is unsurprising that Warhol eventually seized upon the hamburger too as part of his artistic quest to isolate and comment upon American icons. *Hamburger, 1985–1986* both thematically and visually references his 1960s commemoration of Coca-Cola. His decision to place the burger in his canon of representative American food images was further solidified when he appeared in Danish director Jørgen Leth's film *66 Scenes from America, 1982*. Performing a quotidian Americanness, Warhol agreed to be filmed slowly eating a Burger King Whopper, which he slowly and deliberately dips into a puddle of Heinz ketchup.[40]

Consciously or not, the idea that eating a hamburger was a quintessentially American action resonated with many civil rights activists who, like Warhol, came of age appreciating the reach of the symbol. In 1961, as the sit-ins continued to unfold, Ray Kroc, owner of the McDonald's franchise, created "Hamburger University" to train franchisees in the rapidly proliferating chain that could boast of having 710 restaurants in forty-four states by 1965.[41] The young adults at the vanguard of the direct action campaigns of the civil rights movement lived in a built environment that continually reinforced the cultural importance of Cokes and hamburgers through the rapid growth of the number of public spaces where these items were advertised and consumed.

For the youthful activists who participated in the sit-ins, being deprived of their right to consume symbolic food items alongside their fellow Americans was directly allegorical to their second-class citizenship status. Most did not yet seek consolation or empowerment in the new set of symbols that were in the process of being branded as soul food. Instead they sought access to the means—both material and symbolic—of equal citizenship. James Farmer, one of the founders of the Congress of Racial Equality, recalled that Coca-Cola indirectly fueled his future activism. As a young child living in Mississippi, he remembered being confused and

The Ascendency of the Idea of a Racial Style of Eating

frustrated when his mother would not allow her thirsty son to purchase a Coke using his own nickel after he watched a young white boy buying a drink at a local drugstore that would not serve black customers. Her unsatisfying explanation for the fact that young Farmer would have to wait until he got home to quench his thirst was, "He's white . . . you're colored." Temporarily crushed by the pain of having to explain segregation to her still-innocent child, Farmer's mother collapsed in tears on her bed after the pair returned home. Years later, after Farmer was incarcerated for participating in the Freedom Rides, he wondered, "Would the man have been in a cell in Parchman in 1961, if the child had not been denied his soft drink in Holly Springs thirty-eight years before?"[42]

Many other African Americans made similar connections between the right to consume symbolic American foods and citizenship being awarded or denied. Boxer Muhammad Ali recalled winning an Olympic gold medal in Rome in 1960 and returning to his hometown of Louisville, Kentucky, only to be refused the right to eat iconic American foods like hot dogs and hamburgers. He was enraged by the irony that the United States was willing to confer the status of citizenship selectively and partially:

Yeah, I'm defeating America's so-called threats or enemies. And the flag is going *don-ton-ton-ton-tonnn, don-ton-ton-ton-ton*—I'm standing so proud—*don-ton-tonnn, ton-ton-tonnn*—because I done whooped the world for America—*don-ton-ton-ton-ton-tonnn*. I took my gold medal, thought I'd invented something. I said, "Man, I know I'm going to get my people freedom now. I'm the champion of the whole world, the Olympic champion. I know I can eat downtown now."

And I went downtown that day, had my big old medal on and went in a restaurant. See, at that time, like, things weren't integrated; black folks couldn't eat downtown. And I went downtown, I sat down, and I said, "You know, a cup of coffee, a hot dog." He said—the lady said, "We don't serve Negroes." I was so mad, I said, "I don't eat them, either. Just give me a cup of coffee and a hamburger."[43]

Former Student Nonviolent Coordinating Committee chairman John Lewis similarly made a direct linkage between citizenship and the consumption of American foods. On a road trip through Alabama in the 1990s, he marveled that a local Hardee's restaurant in a predominantly black area invited people to go inside both to register to vote and to eat a burger. He recalled, "It seems like only yesterday that people of my color were spat on and beaten if we even stepped into a restaurant like that. As for registering to vote, well, you were taking your life into your hands if you tried to do that back then. Who would have dreamed that one day we would be able to do both, at the same time in the same place?"[44] In the recollections of Ali and Lewis, eating a hamburger was an important rite of citizenship, on par with casting a ballot or, even more spectacularly, representing one's nation at the Olympics.

The Civil Rights Act of 1964, which forbade discrimination in public accommodations, guaranteed the right of African Americans to perform these rituals of Americanization at integrated lunch counters. After protesters won the desegregation of Nashville lunch counters in 1960, a widely circulated photo of Diane Nash and three other student activists eating at a newly desegregated lunch counter at a Greyhound bus terminal shows the demonstrators sitting with labeled glasses of Coca-Cola in front of them, the beverage clearly functioning as a signifier of citizenship. Even Colin Powell, a soldier in the U.S. Army rather than a member of the advance guard of the civil rights movement, recalled how significant the passage of the Civil Rights Act of 1964 and subsequent desegregation of southern dining was to his sense of dignity. In the aftermath of the landmark legislation, he returned to a restaurant in Fort Benning, Georgia, where he had once been denied service and pointedly ate a hamburger.[45] Student Nonviolent Coordinating Committee member Martha Prescod Norman Noonan recalled being heckled by white diners at a newly integrated Holiday Inn in Selma, Alabama, in 1965. Noonan calmly defended her right to be there by calling the local director of public safety, who sent two squad cars to discourage any potential conflict. She stood her ground, recalling, "I think I ate two entrees—my food and the food of one of my companions who was too nervous to eat."[46] The performative eating in each of these scenarios demonstrates that transgressing the Jim Crow boundary of the segregated restaurant was a post-1964 rite of passage of political and personal consequence to many.

Although Noonan persisted in the symbolically significant action of cleaning her plate, in the aftermath of that milestone she observed that "there was so much tension that evening that I decided for the rest of my time in Alabama I would confine most of my socializing to the black community."[47] No longer legally denied access to these spaces, she declared voluntary retreat. Prior to 1964, Student Nonviolent Coordinating Committee activist Stokely Carmichael had already reached a similar conclusion and viewed integrated dining as fundamentally unappealing, rejecting the

The Ascendency of the Idea of a Racial Style of Eating

interracial consumption of foods like hamburgers and Cokes as a meaning-ful symbolic rite. At a sit-in in Aberdeen, Maryland, he broke nonviolent dis-cipline by responding to an angry white woman who raged at the protesters for not being content to "stay with your own kind." He informed her, "Lady, believe me, we aren't here 'cause we think the food is good, or because your company is attractive, okay? We here for one simple reason and one reason only. *You*, collectively, do not have the right, none of you, to tell us where we can go or cannot go. . . . It's a matter of principle. Once we establish that principle, I guarantee you'll never see my face in this place again."[48]

Noonan and Carmichael were not alone in their decision to reject some of the opportunities that their organizing had created and to search for a new culinary politics. Not only did African American activists increas-ingly shun integrated dining opportunities when they were offered, but many took their crusade a step further by rejecting the kinds of foods being served at lunch counters and cafeterias throughout the United States. Some African Americans began to carve out a distinctive cultural nationalist identity at the table. In 1974, blues musician Taj Mahal labeled a hamburger "a serious vulgarity," a stance that took Baker's earlier asser-tion that mainstream American food was beside the point to a different level.[49] Through the culinary lens of Taj Mahal and others, acquiring access to once-forbidden sites of public consumption was not a desired privilege now open to the southern black community but instead a potential com-munal liability.

The sentiments voiced by Carmichael when he claimed that sit-ins were staged on principle, not out of a desire for meaningful integration, were increasingly shared by many protesters who emerged from the civil rights struggle with a new critique of American culture and a changed understanding of the goals of the struggle. Disillusionment came when the victorious activists learned that legislative changes could not remedy long-standing structural inequalities overnight. Many also felt betrayed by white allies who sought to control rather than to assist in demonstra-tions and organizational activities. And others, their consciousness raised, found an increasing number of reasons to question the morality not just of entrenched southern racists but also of a federal government that was at best tepid in its desire to remedy past wrongs. Many looked to regions outside of the South where the tangible gains of the movement—an end to segregation and southern disenfranchisement—were less transformative and began to formulate a more expansive activist agenda to address socio-economic inequalities across the entire nation.[50]

One response to the shared disenchantment was to turn inward and to further concentrate on strengthening the black community rather than to wait for redemption to come from the outside. Now that the legal, if not the structural, barriers to full inclusion into U.S. society were crushed, black nationalists were free to contemplate the benefits of such exclusion. Many argued that forced marginalization had led to the creation and preservation of a distinctive black culture, and some activists channeled the energy that had been used in civil rights demonstrations in the direction of celebration as they extolled the virtues of a unique cultural aesthetic in music, fine arts, literature, fashion, and food. During that era, the modifier "soul" was frequently attached to different forms of black cultural expression and used to describe what historian William L. Van Deburg has called the "essence of the separate black culture" and "in-group cultural cachet."[51] One of the most significant areas where this cultural nation-building took place was in the construction of the concept of soul food as a unique black cultural creation and as a unifying cuisine.

The Birth of the Concept of Soul Food
||||||||||||||||||||||||||||||||||||||||||||||||||||||||||||||||||||||

Beginning in the nineteenth century, African American ministers sometimes utilized the expression "soul food" metaphorically to describe positive inputs, such as prayer or religious instruction, that they hoped would nurture the spiritual life of their congregants.[52] Beginning in the 1960s, the phrase was employed to describe actual foodstuffs that would purportedly feed both the body and the spirit. A canonized set of totemic soul foods promised to connect spiritually the cook and eater to the larger black community and to the entire scope of African American culture and history.

The widespread adoption of the term "soul" to refer to a specific set of menu items rather than to a set of uplifting religious practices seems to coincide roughly with the midpoint of the classical phase of the civil rights movement in 1960 and 1961. The phrase began appearing occasionally in the black press, generally in quotation marks, to describe rural southern food as it was prepared and enjoyed by African Americans. In a 1961 interview with the *Pittsburgh Courier*, rhythm and blues singer Hank Ballard felt obliged to define "soul food" after admitting to having an affinity for the cuisine, which he said consisted of foods like chitterlings, barbecued ribs, chicken, black-eyed peas, rice, and collard greens.[53] A 1960 gossip column in the *Los Angeles Sentinel* printed local mixologist Bill Davis's confession that he subsisted on peaches and cottage cheese and could not digest "soul food," which he felt obliged to describe for the uninitiated as consisting of foods such as ham or grits.[54] Although Davis recognized the concept of soul food, he did not yet feel any pressure to declare his culinary allegiance to the foods associated with the idea. The following year, journalist J. Gillison, who had not yet been fully tutored on the tradition of soul food, expressed weariness and befuddlement about the concept of soul, "a word that really gets batted about these days."[55]

Given the obviously uneven diffusion of the phrase throughout the black community, ambassadors for the cuisine set out to offer lessons designed to help solidify the concept and amplify its cultural significance. Writing in the *Philadelphia Tribune* on March 25, 1961, Masco Young shamed his readers, charging that each should "CONSIDER YOURSELF A SQUARE if you don't know what 'soul food' is." He then offered what he clearly regarded as a much-needed tutorial, explaining, "It includes such down-home delicacies as stewed chicken and rice, fried chicken, rice, gravy, and greens, and ham hocks and black-eyed peas."[56] Apparently aware of the fact that his soul food primer captured the material particulars but not the ideological essence of a phrase referring to a racially proprietary and historically significant style of eating, Young offered a more detailed lesson in the *Cleveland Call and Post* the following month. In an invented conversation between characters he names "Cool Breeze" and "Johnny Treetop," he divulges that soul "is a spiritual something." Johnny recalled his surprise at encountering a restaurant in New York City selling smothered fried chicken, barbecued chicken with gravy, chicken and dumplings, pork chops, chitterlings, ham hocks, turnip greens, and collard greens under the label "soul food." In response, Cool remarked that "we've been eating soul food all our lives. . . . It's just that the other folks just now catching on to how good this jive is." To these fictional characters, black southern foods had always offered a means of transcendence, and the only thing notable about the emergence of the descriptor "soul food" on restaurant signage was the fact that these traditional foods were now being celebrated publicly and far from the region where they originated.[57]

These foundational discussions about soul food, which were designed in part to shame and in part to tutor the uninitiated, were relatively short-lived, and the phrase was soon used widely both inside and outside the black community to refer to a uniquely black culinary tradition characterized by a set of canonical dishes and food items with origins in southern regional cooking. By the late 1960s, the ascendency of soul was so complete that it was even proclaimed in the pages of the *New York Times* by restaurant critic Craig Claiborne, a white southerner, who praised the cuisine while willingly ceding intellectual property rights to both soul food and to southern regional cooking—concepts that he conflates—to the black community, arguing, "Inasmuch as the vast majority of all the cooks in the South have been Negro, it may be said that soul food includes all dishes that are traditionally Southern."[58]

In a highly influential 1962 essay titled "Soul Food," poet, playwright, and cultural critic Amiri Baraka (then known as LeRoi Jones) worked to unsettle Freda DeKnight's earlier claims of African American culinary similarity to the food of other Americans. Baraka bristled at the idea that African Americans did not enjoy a unique and identifiable food culture. In his soul food manifesto, Baraka poetically praised the pleasures of foods such as "maws" that "ofays seldom get to peck," fried chicken, greens, and black-eyed peas.[59] Although his articulation of the concept of "soul food" may have served as a necessary primer for some, the kinds of food Baraka was extolling had already been discovered or rediscovered by many middle-class northern African Americans such as the "prominent lawyers, medics, politicians, and businessmen" whom a reporter for the *Philadelphia Tribune* spotted eating "down home food" at a local restaurant in 1960. According to the *Tribune*, although this style of food had once been "frowned upon by the masses of the so-called 'elite' Negro society," now members of this group could not get enough of this "fashionable" country cooking.[60] Southern vernacular cooking traditions, which had once been a source of anxiety and shame for many members of the black middle class, had suddenly become respectable. A 1969 article in *Sepia* declared with no small degree of wonder that "soul food moves downtown," noting that chitterlings, once a "badge of poverty," had been transformed seemingly overnight into a "badge of soul."[61]

The popularization of soul food was accompanied by an intense sense of liberation for some. Cookie, a columnist for the *Sacramento Observer* who migrated to California in 1962, relished the fact that the cherished food items of her childhood were gaining a wider audience in her newly adopted state. In the past, she recalled having been "ostracized for bringing a watermelon . . . to a picnic," but now she declared that southern food enthusiasts could finally relish their preferred foods and "stop buying those spray cans to rid your home of the collard greens aroma."[62] Within the South, too, the black culinary pride of the era was often palpable. In his memoir about his childhood in West Virginia, Henry Louis Gates Jr.—who was often derided for his alleged racial militancy by older relatives who referred to him as "Stokely" or "Malcolm"—recalled that some members of his family were befuddled by the widespread attempts of civil rights protesters to integrate white lunch counters and restaurants. In the minds of these homegrown culinary nationalists, these actions made little sense because, in contrast to African American cooking, "the food wasn't any good anyway."[63]

In his 1961 short story "Bones, Bombs, and Chicken Necks," Langston Hughes memorably captures the ebullient mood of soul food proponents in contrast to the ambivalence of those who had not been swept up in the excitement of the politicized reframing of black culinary expression. Hughes describes a conflict between his recurrent character Simple and his wife, Joyce, who disagree about proper decorum. Seized by the sense of cultural liberation associated with the advent of soul food, Simple insists on gnawing on a pork chop bone in front of the open window of their home, a practice that Joyce criticizes as "most inelegant." Simple responds by listing a number of atrocities committed by white people, claiming, "I think white people would do better to set in front of their windows and gnaw bones. . . . When I gnaw on my bone or suck my chicken neck, I am not hurting a soul."[64] Not only is Simple certain he is not doing harm by publicly and enthusiastically eating his favorite foods, but he considers doing so a matter of racial pride and a practice that is worth emulation by white people. Simple's culinary nationalism is so strongly felt that he criticizes a black woman for asking a grocery store clerk to wrap up a watermelon so that no one would see her carry it home, claiming, "I would eat one before the Queen of England." In his mind it was wrong for people to "pass for non-chitterling eaters if they are chitterling eaters."[65] Using another food metaphor, he urges his fellow African Americans to embrace a racialized food identity, saying, "If you're corn-bread, don't try to be an angel food cake."[66]

The complicated food politics that Simple tried to untangle using the metaphors of corn bread and angel food cake were initially the most visible outside of the South, where items from the soul food menu were still generally served without fanfare or without reference to any kind of identity politics outside of regionalism. The concept of "soul food" was first popularized in northern and western contexts and was applied only retroactively to food eaten by African Americans in the South. According to Paul Freedman, in the aftermath of the Great Migration, "urban blacks who had grown up in the North gradually came to identify with what had previously been dismissed as 'country' [food]." Freedman argues that the term "soul food" served the function of "denoting a common possession even for those who had not grown up on a farm in the South."[67] The experiences of Carol Barnett, a restaurateur who was born in Queens in 1950, exemplify the process Freedman describes. Barnett claimed that she could not speak definitively about southern food culture "because I didn't grow up in the South," but she nonetheless maintained a clear idea about what constituted soul food, saying, "That's what we know how to cook best. It's like Chinese people, you have all these Chinese restaurants cropping up and they sell Chinese food because that's what they know how to make. . . . As long as you have Black people you're going to have soul food. This is our food. Just like as long as you have Italian people you're going to have spaghetti and lasagna and all that stuff."[68] Barnett, who came of age after the concept of soul food had transformed the conversation about black food culture outside of the South, took the idea of "soul food" for granted. However, previous generations had to learn the concept and sometimes even some of the food traditions that were to become associated with soul.

The Invention of Tradition

The ubiquitous references to soul food that sprang up in the 1960s collectively worked to naturalize the concept and to obscure its complex origins.[69] Borrowing Eric Hobsbawm's concept of an "invented tradition," Katharina Vester argues that "soul food is, strictly speaking, an invented tradition, as it presents a strategically simplified narrative of African American cooking that served the goal of unifying diverse and numerous communities into a political (and cultural) whole, evoking a sense of pride and achievement in its members."[70] According to Hobsbawm, the work of "inventing traditions . . . is essentially a process of formalization and ritualization."[71] Hobsbawm's idea that traditions emerge as part of a self-conscious process is certainly applicable, though perhaps unevenly so, to the idea of soul food. The formalization of the concept took place during a discrete, identifiable historical moment, but members of the African American community had different learning curves when it came to absorbing the rituals of soul food. For some, the phrase described food traditions that were already dear and familiar, becoming a way to ideologically reframe current habits. For others, the emergence of the idea encouraged the revival of practices

The Ascendency of the Idea of a Racial Style of Eating

once discarded. For yet others, the tradition of soul food was something that had to be learned.

Hobsbawm's attempt to differentiate a "tradition" from a "custom" provides useful insights into the fact that the branding of soul food happened, for the most part, in regions outside of the South where the celebrated food customs were initially created. According to Hobsbawm, customs ("southern cooking" in this case) do not "preclude innovation and change up to a point," while traditions are characterized by "invariance."[72] As the earliest attempts to define soul food reveal, the inventors of the concept traditionally explained the phrase by reciting its constituent recipes and ingredients. Although there were certainly variations in how the soul food menu was described, the key elements became commonly enough agreed upon that self-styled "soul food scholar" Adrian Miller was recently able to identify fried chicken, catfish, chitterlings, greens, black-eyed peas, macaroni and cheese, sweet potatoes, corn bread, and red drinks (such as Kool-Aid) as the core foods that "devoted soul foodies . . . are most likely to have for lunch or dinner."[73] In contrast, renowned African American cook and cookbook author Edna Lewis famously rebelled against the strictures of the invented tradition of soul food. Lewis was a proponent of what she regarded as the living custom of southern food, regarding soul food as "hard-times in Harlem—not true Southern food." Instead Lewis emphasized the diversity of the cuisine of her southern childhood, saying, "We ate bountiful foods—vegetables, fruits, grains, beans, and more fish than meat."[74] For Lewis, soul food constituted a limited and static rendition of the southern food of her childhood, but soul food initiates who first encountered the cuisine in the North or the West lacked the same regional frame of reference.

While southerners routinely ate the dishes that were part of the soul food repertoire without much fanfare in the late 1960s, African Americans in the Bay Area of California lived in a region with an eclectic and cosmopolitan dining culture where soul food was hardly the default cuisine. For many southern transplants or other local residents with strong ties of family or friendship to the South, items on the soul food menu were familiar even if the newly heightened cultural valence attached to these foods was not. In this environment, choosing to eat soul food publicly was a way simultaneously to nourish one's body and to demonstrate black cultural consciousness. For many, the practice of soul food was a deliberate exercise and an intellectual one that had to be learned. As late as 1968, an columnist writing for the *Oakland Post* still felt obliged to define the term for the newspaper's black readership, drawing upon a definition from *The Negro Almanac* to do so. "So called 'soul food,'" the article proclaimed, was "the traditional food of southern Negroes."[75] Local residents interested in learning more about the cuisine could seek it out at a wide variety of educational and cultural events. For example, politically conscious and culturally curious Bay Area residents could sample soul food at the 1969 "Black Spectacular" sponsored by the Marin County co-op or eat "chicken, ribs, and 'chitlins'" at the 1970 Black Culture Day in Oakland. Serious students of the cuisine could even enroll in soul food cooking classes held at the local YWCA.[76] More casual observers could receive a soul food tutorial at home by watching Sarah Rawls, a Fresno area resident with Texan and Georgian roots, prepare imaginative dishes such as "Grandpa's Wild Deer with Raisin and Cornbread Stuffing" on *Sarah's Southern Gourmet*, which aired on Bay Cablevision.[77]

During the height of enthusiasm for soul food, Bay Area students could even learn to prepare classic dishes for course credit. In 1969 Alphea Gipson, a student at Berkeley High School, East Campus, startled her mother, who did not realize that her daughter knew how to prepare southern food, when she skillfully cooked chitterlings, mustard greens, sweet potatoes, and corn bread and served the meal to her mother, her aunt, a high school counselor, and two teachers as part of a course assignment.[78] Soul food education began at the primary school level too. In 1971 students at the community's Longfellow Elementary School enjoyed the soul food that was served during a celebration of the "Young Black Experience." The interracial crowd dined on chitterlings, black-eyed peas, greens, and corn bread that had been donated by parents and teachers intent upon tutoring area residents on the rudiments of rural southern cooking in its newly branded incarnation as a black, rather than a regional, way of eating.[79]

Due to the efforts of these soul food educators and activists, the young people of Berkeley even saw soul foods added to their school menus. In 1968 the Berkeley Board of Education agreed to enlarge the cafeteria's lunch offerings to include items such as collard greens, barbecued ribs, and sweet potato pie. The board stopped short of the Black Student Union's request that the school hire new black staff members to prepare the food, emphasizing the fact that the kitchen already employed two black workers, who could—it was implied—bring requisite soul to the task.[80] In fact, for some local residents it was the identity of the cook rather than the peculiarities of his or her techniques and recipes that gave a dish its racially tinged soul. A 1971 food column in the *Oakland Observer* toyed with various meanings of soul food, seeing the term as a potential signifier for "freedom" or of the "nostalgia of home and fireside." However, the writer's soul food catalog included not only typical items like sweet potatoes and pork but also hamburgers, pot roasts, and banana splits, foods more often associated with a generically American style of eating. According to this expansive definition, even these iconic U.S. national foods could be transformed into soul food when prepared by and eaten by black people.[81]

Changing Definitions of Soul Food

Increasingly, soul food was described not only in terms of actual ingredients and recipes rooted in southern plantation cooking but also as having an ineffable quality that transcended the particularities of its components. Sometimes the ability to cook soul food was linked to having had a distinctive kind of historical experience. For example, home economics students at Rufus King High School in Milwaukee self-published a collection of soul food recipes in 1968. They traced the origins of the recipes that they included for items such as "Catfish Head Soup" and "Chitterlings Curley-Cue" to the era of slavery, claiming that it was the "soul" of enslaved cooks, and by extension of those who inherited the tradition, that "caused the special taste to be created."[82] Similarly, a 1966 position paper written by members of the Student Nonviolent Coordinating Committee who came to believe that black empowerment necessitated the expulsion of white members from their civil rights organization argued that white people "cannot relate to chitterlings, hog's head cheese, pig feet, ham hocks, and cannot relate to slavery, because these things are not a part of their experience."[83] In this formulation, soul food was seen as a metaphor for the subjective experience of being black in America with its attendant forms of knowledge that could be gained only experientially.

Other times, the mysterious quality that purportedly transformed southern food into soul food was not a concrete set of historical experiences but instead the innate racial essence of the cook. Throughout the early 1970s, authors of soul food cookbooks expanded upon and amplified the claim that Freda DeKnight had made in *A Date with a Dish* more than two decades before that the racial identify of the cook influenced both the taste and the meaning of particular dishes. In 1971's *The Integrated Cookbook: Or, the Soul of Good Cooking*, Mary Jackson and Lelia Wishart urged their readers not to confuse "so-called Southern cooking, often a thin, white man's parody," with soul. Since the ingredients in the southern larder, white and black, are often indistinguishable, Jackson and Wishart differentiated between these styles of cooking by pointing to "a certain vagueness, an illusive [sic] quality," that separated black from white cuisine.[84] Princess Pamela, the proprietor of a soul food restaurant on East Tenth Street in Manhattan, positively contrasted the "loving art" of soul with the soulless and implicitly white food of the domestic science movement.[85] In 1970 Mother Waddles claimed that all a soul food cook needed to create a dish that belonged to the genre was "imagination and a gospel song to sing."[86] Writing in the pages of *McCall's* magazine in 1970, Vertamae Smart-Grosvenor articulated a definition of soul food that transcended literal plantation roots and encompassed everything from chicken feet to couscous to vanilla wafers. Even more than a set of food practices, she argued that "soul cooking is a feeling."[87] The practices inside the soul kitchen could be defined either narrowly to refer to southern cooking or broadly to include nearly anything prepared or eaten by a "soul person." Actual material food was significant, but specific ingredients and techniques did not themselves create "soul." The primary marker of authenticity inevitably became the racial identity of the cook or the eater, or both. Grosvenor proclaimed, "Soul food is eating with the right people."[88]

The Basis for Critique

The ascendency of soul food represented the triumph of culinary black nationalism over the efforts of black food reformers in the first half of the twentieth century to use the table as a space to debunk ideas about inherent racial differences. These self-consciously respectable eaters had embraced a democratic and inclusive concept of American cuisine rather than the idea of a shared, cohesive racial food heritage. For this group, food expression had been a means of demonstrating physiological equality and of refuting stereotypical ideas about a peculiarly black appetite. They saw iconic American foods as symbols of status, which they had an equal right to consume. Along the way, some rejected the southern food heritage that proponents of soul food would later label as their racial birthright. Others, particularly those who had grown up in the South, continued to eat traditional southern foods, but before the advent of the idea of soul food most

The Ascendency of the Idea of a Racial Style of Eating

did not regard this style of eating as a distinctively racial cultural production or regard fidelity to soul as a political litmus test.

Soul food constituted a radical, and in some ways an ironic, departure from most of the post-emancipation history of African American food politics. The concept of soul food, although ideologically rooted in particular narratives of African American history, tended to ahistorically downplay the hybridity of southern cuisine.[89] The idea of a solely black proprietorship of soul food necessarily minimized the contributions of culinary knowledge made by Europeans. Given the legacy of white supremacy and the general state of American culinary amnesia about black cultural contributions, this exclusion surely seemed politically and morally understandable. However, perhaps even more significantly, given the political climate of the day, this way of framing soul food overlooked the foundational Native American impact on not just southern regional but all American cooking.[90] Furthermore, the increasingly common idea that soul food had an intangible quality that had nothing to do with the particular dishes in the canon, as well as the position that soul food could be created only by black people, reified the idea of essential racial attributes that many race leaders had traditionally worked to unsettle. In this formulation, the items on the soul food menu were not the contextualized products of a set of historical exchanges and processes; they were instead the materialization of an innate blackness.[91] Even though the ability to create soul food was described as a positive essential racial attribute, the implications of the idea that soul people invariably ate soul food proved to be unsettling to some.

Promoters of this essentially black style of eating often disseminated these ideas at the expense of other culinary memories. The idea of soul food did not adequately take into account the food sensibilities of upwardly mobile African American southerners who had discarded many of the benchmarks of southern food as soon as they had the financial means to do so. The idea of soul food also excluded those who continued to eat foods in line with turn-of-the-twentieth-century respectable eaters, who had turned to domestic science cookbooks and industrial food producers to create a cuisine that they believed signified middle-class sensibilities and culinary assimilation. As Adrian Miller points out, "Early soul food boosters glossed over the rich and varied culinary traditions within the black community," including an understanding that southern cooking varied not only by socioeconomic status but also by subregion. "Soul,"

Miller argues, "does not adequately account for cooking styles from the Chesapeake Bay, the Lowcountry, and the Lower Mississippi Valley."[92] Furthermore, the concept of soul food did not have space for the hungry civil rights activists who saw iconic American foods as symbols of citizenship, which they demanded the right to consume.

Soul food supporters also had to contend with the ironic juxtaposition of the overflowing buffet lines and loaded plates at new temples of soul such as Sylvia's restaurant in Harlem, founded in 1962, with the cuisine's heritage as the food of deprivation.[93] As Ann Yentsch astutely points out, many African American cookbooks, including those self-consciously marketed as being part of the soul food tradition, engaged in culinary mythmaking rather than culinary history. She notes, for example, that a profusion of decadent dessert recipes serves as a misleading testimony about a past of material abundance that did not exist for the majority of rural black people, who rarely could have afforded to eat expensive sweets.[94] Thus the newly incarnated soul food cuisine departed in significant ways from its purported historical antecedents.

Others found the association of soul food with the diet of slavery problematic, regarding this relationship as an obstacle to their ability to embrace uncritically the concept. Still others worried that the cuisine was unhealthful and as such was a poor choice as the basis for culinary black nation-building. From almost the moment of its inception, the idea of soul food was met with a vociferous criticism that sought to, once again, emphasize the diversity of black people and of black food expressions. In the late 1960s, many culinary black nationalists agreed with the idea that African American food habits constituted an important facet of the project of cultural nation-building, but new groups of food reformers modified or rejected the soul food model to better fit their particular visions of that nationalist future.

The Ascendency of the Idea of a Racial Style of Eating

Culinary Nationalism beyond Soul Food

By the late 1960s, some black nationalists had become alienated by the very fashionableness of soul food. In some areas, local residents complained that demand for the food had led to higher prices for the ingredients needed to make recipes that had been traditionally prepared by people living in poverty.[1] Writing in the pages of the *Sacramento Observer* in 1969, one soul food cook grumbled that when she first moved to Sacramento in 1962 she had trouble finding chitterlings, but now, she quipped, "I can find chitterlings; but I can't afford them."[2] Black Panther Eldridge Cleaver regarded the idea of "soul food" as a "mocking slogan," employed by members of the black bourgeoisie who were "going slumming." He claimed that the poor people who regularly consumed the foods associated with the southern poverty diet did so out of necessity while wishing in vain they could afford to eat more luxurious foods like steak. Thus Cleaver quickly grew impatient with the sudden middle-class discovery of foods like chitterlings, regarding the newfound fascination with soul food as a trivialization of the experience of living in poverty. He snidely remarked that he wished newly minted culinary nationalists "really *did* have to make it on Soul Food" alone.[3]

For many, the concept of soul food was at best a temporary ideological resting place on a journey toward greater culinary radicalism. Some activists began to push aside items on the soul food menu due to cynicism about either the symbolic value or the nutritional value of this style of eating. By the late 1960s, an increasing number of cultural nationalists were inspired to create a set of dietary practices outside the soul food paradigm. They did so for various but often interrelated reasons. Some ate particular foods as a means of performing a Pan-African—in contrast to a narrower African American—sense of identity. A large number of African Americans shunned certain foods associated with the soul food menu, most frequently pork, for religious reasons. Others rejected traditional southern foods in order to separate themselves from the painful past of slavery or to distinguish themselves from white people. Still others avoided soul food due to health concerns.

Diasporic Soul Food

IIIIIIIIIIIIIIIIIIIIIIIIIIIIIIIIIIIIIII

Some critics began their process of rejecting soul food by reframing it as a broadly diasporic cultural invention rather than a distinctly southern one. The formulation of a Pan-African idea of soul appealed to some cultural nationalists who wished to reject the aspects of the soul food performance that appealed to white diners like *New York Times* food critic Craig Claiborne—who had publicly embraced the concept in 1968—and to culinary adventurers like the white and Asian diners who visited Barbara's Soul Kitchen in Sacramento in the late 1960s, pleasing and amusing the proprietor with their sudden interest in the style of cooking she brought west from Indianola, Mississippi.[4] For food reformers critical of these trends, the idea of soul food had become simultaneously too mainstream and too provincial.

Increasingly, cultural nationalists conceptualized the diasporic people of African descent as members of a stateless, borderless nation that could be unified, in part, through common cultural connections. Kwasi Konadu explains the nationalist emphasis on culture by saying, "In the African diaspora, peoples of African descent do not have a state structure, so they root notions of nationalism in people and culture."[5] The culinary nationalists who wished to incorporate a cultural citizenry that extended beyond the United States had to construct ideas of a shared food culture that was not rooted exclusively in the geographic space of the American South.

Helen Mendes, author of the pioneering *African Heritage Cookbook*, proclaimed in 1971, "Soul food unites African-Americans not only to their people's history, but with their contemporary Black brothers and sisters around the world."[6] That same year, critic Dorothy Johnson announced that Ellen Gibbs Wilson's *West African Cookbook* offered "authentic and meaningful data" that was particularly useful to the growing number of African Americans whose primary interest in soul food was dictated by "identification with Africa."[7] Vertamae Smart-Grosvenor's own concept of soul food was transformed as she discovered transatlantic culinary connections firsthand. In her landmark *Vibration Cooking: Or the Travel Notes of a Geechee Girl*, Grosvenor recalled the excitement of exchanging recipes with a Senegalese woman she met in a Paris market. She was astonished to find similarities in dishes cooked on both sides of the Atlantic. This realization inspired her to look for African antecedents to familiar southern dishes like sweet potato pie.[8] Others experienced similar epiphanies that shaped their understanding of the black culinary tradition. One African American traveler to West Africa in 1970 reported that eating "real soul food" on the continent "made us realize that our efforts at cooking here in America are very meager."[9]

The menu at a "Black Solidarity Day Celebration" in Boston in 1970 similarly emphasized a transnational understanding of soul food, one laden with a critique of internal colonialism. Organizers promised a menu consisting of "African and colonized African (soul) food."[10] Presumably, the "African" food served at the festival could be enjoyed freely, but those who opted for "colonized African" foods would—the description implies—also be consuming a troubled history. It is unsurprising, then, that the acknowledgment of African origins often had the impact of displacing traditional southern foods from the black nationalist table. Increasingly a new kind of food activist pushed traditional soul food items aside in favor of food imprecisely described as "African."[11] For example, a recipe vaguely labeled "Ghana Stew," which appeared in the *Oakland Post* in 1972, was accompanied by the prophecy that readers who made the recipe—which consisted of beef flavored with tomatoes and nutmeg and served with cornmeal dumplings—"may never go back to neckbones and chitterlings."[12] Those who were unwilling to shun the food traditions of their youth altogether often chose to augment traditional foods with a new sense of African-inspired culinary cosmopolitanism. For example, in 1967 some 300 African Americans gathered at the Blue Hill Christian Center in Boston to observe the American rite of a Thanksgiving feast "Afro-American style." Attendees ate not only "American soul food" but also "delectable dishes from the countries of Kenya, Mozambique, Nigeria, Tanzania, the Sudan, Uganda, Brazil, and Jamaica."[13]

The culinary black nationalists who consumed African-inflected soul food were influenced by and participated in the self-conscious work of cultural construction. Dietary concerns melded easily with the objectives of black nationalists who honed a distinct set of cultural practices, ostensibly of African origin, that would unite people of African descent across the globe. The food celebrated as southern soul food was clearly part of the cultural heritage of the descendants of enslaved Africans living in the United States. However, many of the dishes inspired by contemporary African menus that began appearing at black cultural festivals in the late 1960s were culinary newcomers in the quest to create the idea of a racially distinctive style of eating. For black food radicals, the invention of a diasporic food tradition was designed to meet present-day needs that demanded a degree of distance from slavery and more self-conscious ties with black people throughout the globe. Diasporic soul food could help fulfill these ideological needs and help create a new kind of black identity.

Maulena Karenga, one of the cofounders of US Organization, a cultural nationalist group founded in California in 1965, was at the forefront of this movement of cultural creation. New African American attitudes about food habits were present in the first observances of Kwanzaa, an annual holiday that Karenga created in 1966, claiming that the antecedents of the celebration were African harvest festivals.[14] Following his instructions, observers of Kwanzaa lit candles, gave gifts, and honored ancestors between December 26 and January 1. Each aspect of the holiday was carefully orchestrated. Observers greeted each other in Swahili and assembled ceremonial items such as a candleholder containing seven candles, each representing one of the *Nguzo Saba*, or "seven principles," of the holiday. These principles guided the black community toward shared values such as unity and faith. Houses were to be decorated in red, black, and green, the colors of the African nation, and adorned with meaningful items like corn, designed to represent offspring.[15]

Early adherents of Kwanzaa were encouraged to fast from sunup to sundown to purify their bodies. Observers were instructed to think about the ritual significance of both consuming and abstaining from food. The fast was to be broken at sunset with only fruits, vegetables, and nuts. The period of abstention ended on December 31 with the *karamu*, or feast, which was to include a meal in "the traditional manner," consisting of "foods in the African style, and eaten without European utensils."[16] Despite Karenga's justification of the necessity of the holiday and his instructions about many details of its observance, relatively little was written about the nature of the food to be served beyond the recommendation that it be "African" in origin. At the first Kwanzaa observance held in Los Angeles, attendees ate chicken, rice, black-eyed peas, and West African greens called *jama jama* as part of a menu that conjured up associations with southern-style African American cooking while also heralding a more diasporic understanding of black cuisine.[17]

Culinary Nationalism beyond Soul Food

The earliest Kwanzaa observers operated under the assumption that food behavior was an important factor in identity construction, but their prescriptions for proper eating habits were more vague than the rigid codes developed by culinary nationalists elsewhere. Increasingly, the table was used for the dual purposes of acting out a Pan-African food identity and promoting beliefs about healthful living. In many nationalist circles, the idea of consuming "healthful" food became even more significant than the mandate to consume "African" food.

The Rejection of Soul Food

A group of culinary critics, whom Frederick Douglass Opie labels "food rebels," consciously rejected the idea of soul food, whether defined as a southern or as a more diasporic style of eating, altogether. This group characterized American food culture as unhealthful and corrupting, often dismissing "soul food" as a pernicious rebranding of "slave food."[18] For example, in the early 1970s, members of the New Orleans Pan African collective, Ahdiania, viewed soul food as "a degrading indulgence," in the words of historian Russell Rickford.[19] The group's 1973 *A Food Guide for Afrikan People* claims that although soul food tastes good and that "there is nothing else in the world like it," eating it was detrimental to the health of people who consumed it "as a substitute to satisfy . . . otherwise frustrated lives."[20] Increasingly, many black nationalists urged African Americans to adopt a mostly vegetarian, whole-foods diet as a way to signal their rejection of the American values embedded in a painful past and as a means to improve the physical and financial health of the people they increasingly conceptualized as members of an oppressed, stateless black nation.

As discussed in chapter 6, prior to 1964, civil rights activists fighting to desegregate southern restaurants and lunch counters sometimes interpreted iconic food and drink like hamburgers and Coca-Cola as symbols of American citizenship. Later on, some "food rebels" argued that the meat that went into making the iconic hamburger was served alongside connotations of domination and violence and that sugary Coca-Colas should be linked to bad health.[21] If hamburgers and Coca-Colas had—during the era of the sit-ins—been interpreted as symbols of citizenship denied, the renunciation of these items was often later understood as citizenship rejected.

For some of the radical food reformers of the era, the expanded access to forbidden sites of public consumption that followed the passage of the

Civil Rights Act of 1964 was not thought of as a desired privilege now open to the southern black community but instead as a potential communal liability.[22] The right to participate on equal terms in American consumer capitalism soon began to seem less desirable to many who began to question the value of what Sarah Banet-Weiser has referred to as "consumer citizenship."[23] Furthermore, not only was the right to shop side by side with white Americans construed to be of dubious value, but the goods for sale in the American marketplace had also become a source of anxiety.

Dietary health soon became a pressing concern for many involved with the task of nation-building. However, as Clovis Semmes has demonstrated, the scholarly literature has not yet adequately explored this aspect of the black consciousness movement.[24] Semmes argues that shared "naturalistic health beliefs" helped promote "group cohesion by providing a distinctive lifestyle, shared sacred beliefs, and a common moral order."[25] The increasing concern about the health value of foods that made some quintessentially American items suspect rendered many dishes on the soul food menu of dubious value as well.

The Nation of Islam's Soul Food Critique

Elijah Muhammad, leader of the Nation of Islam (NOI), was an early and ardent proponent of a regimented, cultural nationalist diet that did not follow the soul food tradition. Muhammad declared himself the "messenger of Allah" and dispensed the divine wisdom he claimed to receive on a variety of subjects, including proper eating habits, beginning in the 1930s. His advice about healthful living found new audiences among those interested in the product of cultural nation-building in the late 1960s. Soon sympathizers could turn to his two-volume series *How to Eat to Live*, published in 1967 and 1972, to learn about the NOI's strict food consumption guidelines. He also circulated his dietary teachings through the organization's newspaper, *Muhammad Speaks*, which had a weekly circulation of at least 70,000 and likely reached even more readers through informal channels of exchange.[26]

Although Elijah Muhammad did not use the term "soul food," Doris Witt has noted that he "intensified his condemnation of traditional southern black dietary practices as the popularity of soul food began to peak."[27] Unwilling to consider plantation foods a legitimate source of race pride, Muhammad urged his followers to cast off the "slave diet," which the NOI

Culinary Nationalism beyond Soul Food

believed was deleterious to the physical and mental health of the black nation. Following the convictions of orthodox Muslims, the NOI forbade the consumption of pork, which was labeled "a grafted animal . . . grafted from rat, cat, and dog."[28] However, NOI dietary restrictions went beyond the mandates of traditional Islamic dietary law and included many items associated with the southern diet, including collard and turnip greens, corn bread, sweet potatoes, and black-eyed peas. The NOI deemed these foodstuffs unfit for human consumption.[29] To improve their health and to free themselves from the legacy of slavery, NOI members were ordered to shun foods associated with that traumatic past. Dietary transformations, Elijah Muhammad implied, were linked to spiritual ones. Edward E. Curtis IV argues that the NOI saw the body as "the main battleground for the souls of black folk." The organization closely regulated the habits of its members to bring about the "reformation of the black body."[30] By maintaining harmful food practices, the NOI warned, black Americans were allowing their bodies—and by extension, their minds—to be colonized by the forces of white oppression.

Although the Nation of Islam had only about 20,000 members in 1966, the membership rolls alone do not capture the outsized influence the organization had on the black community. Most of the culinary nationalists of the era were heavily influenced by NOI teachings.[31] No single intellectual figure had a stronger galvanizing impact on the Black Power movement in general than NOI minister Malcolm X, whose teachings were widely reported upon and discussed among politically aware African Americans. In 1964 Malcolm X traced what he regarded as the long-standing superiority of black food practices back to the beginning of civilization. He argued that Africans had always been more advanced than their European counterparts, and he urged African Americans to embrace racial culinary differences:

> They didn't cook their food in Europe. Even they themselves will show you when they were living up there in caves, they were knocking animals in the head and eating the raw meat. They were eating raw meat, raw food. They still like it raw today. You watch them go in a restaurant, they say, "Give me a steak rare, with the blood dripping in it." And then you run in and say, "Give me one rare, with the blood dripping in it." You don't do it because that's the way you like it; you're just imitating them, you're copying, you're trying to be like that man. But when you act like yourself, you say, "Make mine well done." You like cooked

food, because you've been cooking a long time; but they haven't been cooking so long—it wasn't too long ago that they knew what fire was. This is true.[32]

Like Malcolm X, Elijah Muhammad also used meat consumption to differentiate black from white culture. He wished to separate the eating habits of his NOI followers from those of Christians, a category that presumably included not only white people but also black people who ignored his teachings. Christians, he claimed, were brutal and unenlightened in their methods of livestock slaughter, cooking, and food consumption. He argued that sufficient care was not taken to protect slaughtered animals from fear, evidence that they "actually murder the animals they eat."[33] Malcolm X agreed, claiming, "They're blood-thirsty, they love blood. . . . I've watched them; when I was a little boy, I lived on a farm with white folks. When they shoot something, they just go crazy, you know, like they were really getting their kicks."[34]

In light of the association of meat-eating with whiteness and brutality, it is unsurprising that Muhammad's prescribed diet advised abstention from pork, a staple of the southern diet. Increasingly, he discouraged all meat consumption. Muhammad proclaimed that although eating other forms of animal flesh was not necessarily sinful, meat should be avoided for its lack of nutritional value. A vegetarian diet was deemed the most healthful and most virtuous way to eat.[35] Because he believed that white men were the original carnivores, he encouraged vegetarianism as a nationalistic decision. In the eschatology of the NOI, the white race would eventually die out, and meat eating would vanish with it.[36]

For Nation of Islam followers, food practices were also an aspect of their program of economic nationalism. The organization urged members to pursue land ownership and to cultivate their own food. In 1971 a series of pen-and-ink drawings appeared in each issue of *Muhammad Speaks*, which depicted African American men and women producing their own food. "Get Behind Muhammad's Program," a two-page spread that appeared in multiple issues, showed a large photograph of Elijah Muhammad against a landscape covered by orchards and populated with farm animals. Nearby were a factory that processed eggs and a black-owned cannery. "Muhammad's Program" urged NOI members to pursue independent black foodways at the level of production, ensuring gastronomic separatism in every aspect of the food system.[37] The NOI actively pursued black nutritional self-sufficiency. Members founded Muslim-owned restaurants and grocery stores, purchased farmland, and even established a fish-importing business.[38] Muhammad urged his followers to opt out of American consumer culture in favor of the creation of a separate black economy.[39]

Dick Gregory's Radical Vegetarianism

IIIIIIIIIIIIIIIIIIIIIIIIIIIIIIIIIIIIIIIIIIIIIIIIIIIIIIIIIIIIIIIIIIIIIIIIIIII

Well-known comedian and civil rights activist Dick Gregory, like some members of the NOI, also emphasized the brutality of carnivorousness and questioned his relationship to American consumer capitalism. Gregory had been involved in the southern sit-in movement, and in 1964 he was arrested and jailed for participating in a sit-in at the Truckers' Inn in Pine Bluff, Arkansas.[40] That same year, both he and his wife, Lillian Gregory, were arrested while sitting in at a Dobbs House restaurant in Atlanta. Gregory confounded the management by announcing (truthfully) that he had purchased stock in the publicly traded company and arguing that he could not be evicted from a restaurant he partially owned.[41] Thanks in part to his efforts, African American residents of the city were eventually granted equal access not only to the symbolically charged hamburger but also to dishes like "Mammy's Fried Chicken," a meal that even more directly raised questions about the desirability of eating in racist dining establishments.[42]

For Gregory the issue of food access conjured up associations beyond the immediate task of fighting for the right to enter places of public accommodation on equal terms. The physical space of a restaurant also revived old anxieties about not having enough to eat. Even after Gregory became a successful comedian, memories of an impoverished childhood still plagued him, and he embarked on what he called his "Steak Career" of voracious omnivorism. He would go into a restaurant—such as the ones he helped integrate—and order "three, four, five, or six dinners—lobster, steak, chicken, pork chops and barbecued ribs in a single serving."[43]

By the mid-1960s, participation in the civil rights movement extinguished Gregory's appetite for animal flesh. His commitment to nonviolence as a tactic of protest and a value system encouraged him to identify a linkage between violence against humans and violence against nonhuman animals. He noted, "Animals and humans suffer and die alike." From 1965 onward, he "refused to accept that I had to stoop to the lowliness of *killing* something to get my dinner."[44] Similarly, Nick Fiddes has observed that historically, meat consumption has been interpreted as a symbol of dominance and potency, as "the ultimate authentication of human superiority over the rest of nature."[45] By associating the unequal power relationships embedded in American racism with the system of animal slaughter, Gregory connected his critique of meat consumption and his attempts to dismantle the existing power structure. His evolving system of food ethics led him to believe that by eating meat, he was actually bolstering the forces of domination and oppression.

Eventually Gregory's dietary reform initiatives became entangled in not only ethical but also corporeal concerns. What began as an answer to a moral question about whether nonviolent social protest and meat-eating could be integrated into a consistent belief system expanded into a quest for a healthier way of living. He modified his initial attempt to follow a vegetarian diet after his weight jumped from 167 pounds as a carnivore to 288 pounds as a vegetarian who would "go into a soul food restaurant and wipe out the yams, greens, black-eyed peas, macaroni and cheese, corn bread, squash, dressing."[46] He soon came to believe that far from being a source of racial pride, "soul food," with or without an animal flesh component, could be deadly. He argued that "the quickest way to wipe out a group of people is to put them on a soul food diet. One of the tragedies is that the very folks in the black community who are the most sophisticated in terms of the political realities in this country are nonetheless advocates of 'soul food.' They will lay down a heavy rap on genocide in America with regard to black folks, then walk into a soul food restaurant and help the genocide along."[47]

Convinced that African Americans who ate soul food inadvertently collaborated with white supremacist attempts to degrade black bodies, Gregory evolved toward a fruitarian, raw foods diet. He committed to eating "only fruit, direct from plants and trees, in a natural state, fully 'cooked' by Mother Nature's outdoor oven," and to rejecting industrially produced, processed foods.[48] He and his wife, Lillian, raised their ten children following these dietary guidelines, and Gregory punctuated his eating program with periodic cleansing fasts.[49] African American naturopath Alvenia M. Fulton guided him on his journey, claiming, "If we human beings are children of nature, then it is to nature we must look for our health, welfare, and survival."[50] Like Gregory, Fulton worried that bad habits were deleterious to health, proclaiming that "man's tastes are so molded by his culture that they are useless to him as guideposts in nutrition. He must be taught what and how to eat."[51] Fulton and Gregory interpreted their culinary obligation to the community as a mission to change the idea that all forms of

Culinary Nationalism beyond Soul Food

black expressive culture should be treated with reverence. Soul food was not a communal asset but a liability.

Gregory enthusiastically promoted Fulton's dietetics as an extension of his civil rights activism, believing that bad diets bolstered the forces of white supremacy by weakening or killing black bodies. Although Gregory's strict fruitarianism inspired few wholesale converts, his commitment to maintaining the physical health of the black community was widespread in nationalist circles in the late 1960s and early 1970s.

Building a New Culinary Nation

Writer Amiri Baraka, one of the most influential activists of the era, has been frequently portrayed as a supporter of traditional southern African American foodways in the wake of his passionate 1962 essay titled "Soul Food." Baraka hinted at what he regarded as the metaphysical properties of soul food when he answered a question about whether sweet potato pies tasted anything like pumpkin by saying, "They taste more like memory."[52] His poetic tribute to foods like hog maws, okra, and hoecakes has immortalized him as a defender of that diet, leading food studies scholar Doris Witt to label Baraka a "proponent" of black regional southern cooking in opposition to "detractors" such as Elijah Muhammad and Dick Gregory.[53] Similarly, historian Frederick Douglass Opie contrasts Baraka and Muhammad, portraying them both as advocates for race pride who nonetheless had different concepts about proper food habits. Opie claims that Baraka "advocated soul food as black folk's cuisine" in contrast to NOI "food rebels" who eschewed pork and other southern staples such as black-eyed peas.[54] These generalizations—although true at a certain historical moment—obscure Baraka's own culinary evolution throughout the 1960s.

By the end of the decade, Baraka and the other members of his Newark circle "did not eat meat, only fish, and otherwise were vegetarians."[55] Baraka, no stranger to personal evolutions, transformed himself from the Beatnik poet LeRoi Jones to Amiri Baraka, a central figure of the Black Arts Movement. He also evolved from soul food proponent to the leader of an organization that rejected traditional southern food practices as harmful to communal health. Baraka went from praising soul food as "good filling grease" in 1962 to an asceticism that led him to give up alcohol and tobacco and to reassess his relationship to traditional African American cooking.[56] His earlier embrace of soul food not only reflected pride in black cultural productions but also allowed room for the hedonistic pleasure of taste sensations. However, his new stance on dietary matters encouraged him to consider food choices as primarily a matter of self-discipline. Baraka believed that communal dietary decisions should be made by leaders like himself who could help free the black community from the shadow of the slave diet that had been regulated by white oppressors. He did not reject the premise of hierarchy as much as he resented the fact that black dietaries had historically been as influenced by the white power structure as by black culinary volition. Baraka's dietary turn sought to institute a new order and a new system of national culinary allegiances.

Although his ideological journey eventually shifted him out of the orbit of a narrower form of cultural nationalism into a race-conscious Marxist sensibility, in the late 1960s Baraka took inspiration from Karenga's emphasis on cultural nation-building. Under the auspices of the Committee for Unified Newark (CFUN), Baraka joined Karenga in self-consciously creating cultural traditions that he hoped would foster a shared sense of identity. Theorists of the movement analyzed the relationship of the black community to the fine arts, to modern technology, and to various religious, educational, and political institutions.[57] In a number of position papers, Baraka and his collaborators made specific programmatic recommendations about how the black community should be organized, beginning with the family unit. Their patriarchal concept of the family emphasized male-dominated heterosexual relationships and called for the performance of rituals to celebrate the creation of black families. Milestones such as marriage, the birth of a child, and death were to be commemorated in culturally specific ways, which included attention to the kind of foods served at these events.

To teach these principles, Baraka led a "Political School of Kawaida" in Newark. Drawn from a Swahili word meaning "customs" or "systems," *kawaida* referred to cultural nationalist values and rituals, which included ideas about food consumption. Baraka urged cooperative buying as a means to channel economic power and cooperative eating as an important ritual used to encourage group solidarity. The ideal *chakula* (food) that was to be served at family or community gatherings consisted of vegetables, fruits, grains, fish, and milk.[58]

CFUN sympathizers were to be careful about what they ate but were simultaneously instructed to avoid being perceived as too interested in dietary practices. They were told, "We are not fanatical about food but the national liberation of our people."[59] The message about food fanaticism

Culinary Nationalism beyond Soul Food

may have been designed to distinguish Baraka's followers from the members of the NOI, whose famously rigid dietary rules were well known in the black community, but the confusing admonishment was also undermined by the number of mandates about food behavior included in the literature describing the group's rituals. CFUN members were urged to train their bodies to reflect their internalized sense of cultural difference. Members who bent their bodies (often literally) to the will of the organization knew that their actions would be scrutinized not only by group members looking for an external litmus test of ideological fidelity but also by outsiders. As sociologist Randolph Hohle argues, cultural nationalists who deliberately embodied a separatist political ethos by, for example, wearing African-inspired garb or repudiating pork or other foods inspired increased police scrutiny as well as more generalized white resistance to the black liberation struggle. Hohle maintains that American liberalism set limits on "acceptable levels on the embodied racial self while struggling for racial and civic inclusion."[60] Members of CFUN and likeminded groups deliberately tried to unsettle both white and politically moderate black expectations for bodily comportment by creating disciplined black bodies that followed an elaborate set of rules.

Rites of passage and special holidays were all to be commemorated with specific food practices. On "Leo Baraka," a community celebration of Amiri Baraka's birthday, adherents were required to consume only fruit and fruit juice in observance of the day. Watermelon was to be served at the birth of a child, and at the *kuziliwa karamu* (birthday feast), fruit was again served along with "natural cakes."[61] By avoiding sugar, the group followed advice similar to that offered by black nutrition guru Alvenia M. Fulton, who condemned white sugar as unwholesome and forbade its use under all circumstances in favor of sweeteners such as honey.[62] The stigmatization of sugar should also be examined in relationship to what Harvey Levenstein has labeled the widespread "sucrophobia" of the 1960s and 1970s. This rejection of sugar was fueled by scientific research and hearings held by the U.S. Senate Select Committee on Nutrition and Human Needs. These studies linked sugar consumption to a variety of health ills, including heart disease and hyperactivity in children.[63] The cultural nationalists who spurned sugar did so in order to protect their bodies and those of the next generation.

Following the lead established by US, Baraka's adherents maintained a strict gender hierarchy, and the women in the organization bore the responsibility for cooking and serving food. They performed their tasks under a specific protocol, which stated that men should be fed before women "because respect and appreciation should be given to providers."[64] The CFUN charged women with the task of studying nutrition in order to feed, but not overfeed, their families. The organization's literature instructed them to prepare meals that were largely vegetarian but could include fish. Nationalist women were warned against encouraging gluttony in their children, being told that overfeeding a child could lead to the creation of a "greedy, selfish person." Character flaws like these could not be tolerated because the "Nationalist baby has a purpose."[65] Since the health and strength of black children was a shared national asset, members saw the proper feeding of children as a relevant issue for the entire black community. Unsurprisingly, even outside the domestic sphere women continued to focus their work, at least in part, on food consumption. CFUN leaders instructed nationalist women to pressure school lunch programs to stop serving pork and sugarcoated cereals and to explore the possibility of cooperative food buying within the black community.[66]

The ideas that the CFUN institutionalized in Newark were similar to those shared by a group of cultural nationalists living in neighboring New York. The East, a community institution founded in Brooklyn in 1969, included an independent school, a performance space, cooperative businesses, and a newspaper, among other initiatives. Group members were generally in sympathy with the critiques of traditional food habits that had emerged in Newark.[67] They rejected the paradigm of southern soul food and created a whole-foods diet that referenced the black diaspora with Swahili expressions. Instructions for feeding children given to the staff of the independent school, Uhura Sasa Shule (Freedom Now School), give clues as to the nature of the shared dietary rules of The East family. Staff members fed the children meals consisting of whole grains, fruits, and vegetables and forbade them from eating meat, dairy, or sugary foods.[68] Adults too had ample opportunity to eat nationalist cuisine. The "Black Experience in Sound" hosted musical performances in an alcohol-free space where patrons could dine on dishes such as Kuumba rice or East punch from the popular East kitchen.[69] Kawaida rice, a popular vegetarian dish of brown rice, broccoli, mushrooms, and red and green peppers, drew its name from the term used to describe a distinctive black value system.[70]

Sales of its popular food served an important function in keeping The East financially afloat, and the success of the health-conscious cuisine inspired offshoot ventures, including a catering company. A community-owned bakery showed that although both CFUN and The East were cautious about sugar intake, occasional indulgences were allowed. It served bean pie, a perennial NOI favorite, indicating ties of dietary sympathy between the organizations. However, the inclusion of sweet potato pie on the menu, an item condemned by Elijah Muhammad, signifies the limitations of this culinary convergence and illustrates that most partakers at the cultural nationalist table brought a broad range of dietary influences with them.[71] For both the NOI and the members of The East, however, black foods were to be served by and for the black community. The Tamu Sweet–East bakery served food at "black prices," endeavoring to make culinary manifestations of black culture affordable to the less prosperous in the community and freeing public food consumption from the taint of the capitalistic marketplace.[72]

Members of The East, who referred to themselves as "family," created a web of interlocking institutions and pledged themselves to mutual cooperation. Like CFUN, they adhered to Kawaida, a value system that adherents described as a "faith."[73] This belief system was buoyed by many of the mechanisms associated with organized religion, including holidays like Kwanzaa and various written creeds. Male members of The East pledged to abide by the "Brotherhood Code," which expressed a respect for Kawaida and mental, physical, and spiritual solidarity with the movement. Physical obligations included the vow to "observe dietary rules so that our functions are not hampered by illness." Eating a whole-foods, vegetarian diet was important to maintain individual wellness and to ensure the strength of the entire community. "When we are weak, the Nation shares our weakness," the code stated.[74] For culinary nationalists, food decisions were a matter of community concern. Healthy black bodies belonged to the nation, they believed, and the failure to obey dietary rules could be seen as a form of community betrayal.

Similar dietary advice circulated regularly through cultural nationalist circles. In his classic *The Destruction of Black Civilization*, Chancellor James Williams justified the focus on food as a significant issue for the black nation to address. He argued, "There is nothing mystical about the reasons why one group of people can easily become physically and mentally strong while another becomes physically weak and less mentally alert. An abundance of nutritious food and pure drinking water may spell the difference between advance and decay."[75] Johari M. Amini, a Chicago writer associated with the Black Arts Movement, was inspired by this observation and concurred that proper food habits were essential to the health of the black nation. In her pamphlet *Commonsense Approach to Eating: The Need to Become a Vegetarian*, she proclaimed, "Our survival as Afrikan people demands work. . . . We must do more than merely 'survive.' We have been doing that since we were brought to the western hemisphere. We must begin to live."[76] According to Amini, soul food had enabled the black community merely to stay alive, while a more ethical and healthful vegetarian diet could enable the stateless black nation to thrive.

In 1970, when more than 4,000 people from around the United States gathered in Atlanta for the founding meeting of the Congress of African People (CAP)—a nationwide organization inspired by CFUN and organized under the intellectual leadership of Baraka—attendees discussed food reform in the black community as a key part of the post–civil rights political and cultural agenda.[77] Declaring that it was "nation time," CAP sought to focus disparate calls for black self-determination around a unified program and shared ideas about black culture. At the meeting, Reverend James Cone and Reverend Bill Land ran a workshop that explored religion in the nationalist movement. They articulated a theology that "teaches us no matter what we call ourselves (Baptist, Muslim, Hebrew, etc.) we are Black first, and all those other things next."[78]

Cone and Land urged members of the black nation to follow their dietary pronouncements, which included an indictment against foods similar to those eaten by enslaved people, a diet they labeled "garbage." Although they gave a "wise Black woman" credit for making "hog guts" and other aspects of the southern poverty diet palatable, they called for new food practices for a new era.[79] The ministers did not advocate for vegetarianism, but they did join the NOI in prohibiting the consumption of pork, shellfish, and catfish. They also condemned the consumption of animal blood and fat, deeming the increasingly maligned American hamburger dangerous due to the high fat concentration in ground meat.[80] Cone and Land urged periodic fasting, both as an antidote to weight gain and as an opportunity to cleanse the body and to condition the mind. They warned that revolutionaries might face situations when they would have to go without food and urged CAP supporters to practice the discipline of denial in anticipation of potential future hardships.[81] Food practices were to be centered on discipline, not on gustatory pleasure.

Never intellectually intransigent or afraid to evolve ideologically, Baraka announced in 1974 that CAP would now embrace Marxism and reject Kawaida as an organizing principle.[82] This change led to a less chauvinistic attitude toward the women in the organization and to the relinquishment of many of the ritualistic aspects of Kawaida that Baraka and others

Culinary Nationalism beyond Soul Food

had so painstakingly created.[83] For Baraka, who had begun entertaining doubts about the importance of the new dogma about dietary practices, this change enabled him to justify easing those restrictions.

This ideological transformation inspired the immediate resignation of Jitu Weusi, director of The East, and of Haki Madhubuti, director of Chicago's Institute for Positive Education, from CAP. Baraka viewed their unwillingness to evolve as a betrayal, and he spurned Madhubuti for his insistence on clinging to cultural nationalistic eating practices. Although Baraka had a strong role in creating the dietary rules that came to be associated with Kawaida, those values became less important as he continued his political evolution. He accused Madhubuti of practicing a form of nationalism that "involves mysticism, e.g. the fanatical concern with the diet."[84] In addition, Baraka argued that it was hypocritical for Madhubuti to object to the philosophies of white people such as Marx and Lenin while he recommended dietary books written by J. I. Rodale and others Baraka considered to be "bohemians," "food faddists," and "petit bourgeois American whites."[85] Although Baraka still applauded the shared cultural nationalist impulse to give up pork as a means of "breaking down the slave culture that engulfed us," he now argued that "dressing up Afrikan and drinking distilled water and eating raw vegetables is not a revolutionary program."[86]

For Madhubuti, food concerns remained at the heart of his conception of activism, and he continued to maintain that poor diets could be linked to various health problems in the black community. Although Baraka accused Madhubuti of hypocrisy because he had utilized books written by white health food advocates, Madhubuti's shift toward vegetarianism happened within the context of black nationalism. Malcolm X's decision to give up pork led Madhubuti to denounce all meat consumption.[87] He decried meat-eating as unhealthful and argued, "The North Vietnamese are winning a war and their major diet consists of organically grown rice and organically grown vegetables."[88] Madhubuti declared that an unhealthy diet was counterrevolutionary. He argued that an obese African person demonstrated a failure of self-control and lacked the energy needed to be an ally in the struggle to build a strong black nation.[89] Suitable for the racially charged subtext of the indictment, Madhubuti urged cultural nationalists to "stay away from anything that is white: there are *no* natural foods in nature that are white. Any food that is white is a mutation of the natural. Foods like white flour, white milk, white sugar, white corn meal and white eggs are dead food."[90]

Vegetarianism Becomes Mainstream

These culinary activists did not operate in cultural isolation within the black community. They were aware of, and indeed contributed to, ongoing conversations about both meat-eating and problems with the industrial food system circulating among conscientious eaters outside of the black community during the 1970s. A 1975 article in the *New York Times* titled "Vegetarianism: Growing Way of Life, Especially among the Young" noted that the ascendency of vegetarianism was visible in the proliferation of vegetarian restaurants, a growing number of vegetarian foods available in grocery stores, and the increasing availability of meat-free options in college cafeterias. The article reported that the predominantly white vegetarians featured gave up meat due to religious concerns and revulsion at violence and killing, ideas that they held in common with many black culinary nationalists.[91]

Despite some ideological similarities, black and white vegetarians often turned to different dietary role models. While black culinary nationalists who advocated for less meat-intensive diets pointed first to the teachings of Elijah Muhammad, the activism of Dick Gregory, or the dietary recommendations made by the Congress of African People, white people who adopted a similar stance were more likely to call attention to Frances Moore Lappé's 1971 book, *Diet for a Small Planet*, which linked global food scarcities to the disproportionate amount of resources used for meat production.[92] Many vegetarians inspired by Lappé wished to reverse changes in the food system caused by newer forms of intensive agriculture and to reclaim what they saw as a simpler, more pastoral way of life that had been displaced by technology. Historian Warren Belasco argues that for this group, "brown rice became the icon of antimodernity."[93] They believed that "mass-produced, processed food encouraged alienation from nature, society, one's own body."[94]

Both black nationalist and white countercultural eaters used food practices as a way to demonstrate their disaffection with American culture, but they generally differed in their prescriptions for better alternatives. Proponents of what Belasco labels "countercuisine" developed a set of unconventional food practices as a way to establish identities on the margins of mainstream culture and to reject domination by a centralized power structure, but white countercultural eaters did not propose an alternative national identity. In contrast, black nationalist eaters wanted to create a black nation that operated in lockstep, unified by ideological and cultural goals and to use ideas about food as a means of opting out of white U.S. culture and into a black cultural nation.

African Americans who changed their cultural regimes in response to the influence of culinary nationalist thinking often expressed frustration at those who had not undergone the same kind of transformation. For example, in 1970 a black man identifying himself as Melvin wrote to an advice columnist for the *Chicago Defender* expressing despair at the fact that although he wore an Afro, dressed in non-Western attire, and ate a vegetarian diet, his wife of eleven years was unwilling to change. He worried that their marriage could not survive in the face of these significant cultural and philosophical differences.[95] Like Melvin's intransigent wife, most African Americans did not make radical culinary changes in keeping with the mandates of the new culinary nationalism.

Most African Americans in the 1960s were likely unaware of Baraka and Madhubuti's dietary dispute, had not read Amini's defense of vegetarianism, and were more likely intrigued than convinced by Gregory's radical food politics. Nonetheless, critiques of mainstream food culture articulated by these and other black nationalist eaters helped inspire concerns about healthful eating even among African Americans who did not consider themselves to be either cultural nationalists or engaged political activists. Cultural nationalist prohibitions against eating pork, a belief that was common among nearly all black radical eaters, had a tremendous influence on many segments of the black community. In 1970 Vertamae Smart-Grosvenor recalled making black-eyed peas and rice "with beef neck bones instead of swine since so many brothers and sisters have given up swine."[96] A 1969 *Ebony* article, which conflated the food traditions of NOI members and orthodox Muslims throughout the Middle East, noted that "even black non-Muslims caught up in the current revolutionary mood are rejecting 'the pig,' either because it was the main meat served to slaves or because it is believed unhealthy."[97] A 1979 study that compared the food habits of black and white southerners noted a high degree of similarity between the two groups' consumption habits but observed that black respondents were more likely than whites to label pork an unhealthful food.[98] The idea that soul food was suspect affected even those not self-consciously involved in the cultural nationalist project.

African American collegians were particularly open to new ways of thinking about dietary practices. In the October 1972 issue of *Black Ink*, the black student newspaper at the University of North Carolina, Gwen

P. Harvey urged black students to quit eating the "greasy hamburger and french fries heaped on our plates with a mere shrug of the shoulder" and to scrutinize more carefully what they ate.[99] In the December 1980/January 1981 issue of the *Black Collegian*, Ralph Johnson and Patricia Reed, students at the State University of New York at Old Westbury, echoed the teachings of Elijah Muhammad when they complained, "Black Americans are under the illusion that their cultural food is soul food," which they described as unhealthful slave food.[100] Frederick Douglass Opie estimates that by the late 1970s, about 1 percent of African American college students were vegetarians, and many more gave up pork or certain highly processed foods.[101]

Alternative food ideas influenced middle-class adults as well. In 1974 *Ebony* magazine declared "Farewell to Chitterlings" and profiled a number of African Americans who had given up meat, mostly for health reasons. The article noted that, ironically, "some American blacks who can now afford filet have elected instead to dine on raw carrots and cabbage juice."[102] Florence Somerville, the food editor for the *Chicago Defender*, frequently printed vegetarian recipes in her column between 1972 and 1974. Her pronouncement that "vegetarian diets are exciting" was accompanied by a drawing of an anthropomorphized carrot scolding a sheepish pig. The carrot, depicted at one point as muscle-bound and lifting weights while standing next to a diminutive pig, appeared in her column several times as an ambassador for vegetarianism. Somerville's recipes for curried spinach soup, eggplant pizza, and "Oriental eggs" did not directly reference the soul food diet. Her recipe for "beefy green beans" calls for beef broth or bouillon. While not vegetarian, it did offer an alternative to traditional methods of seasoning vegetables with pork.[103]

African American soul food proponents who wished to explore meatless options without spurning the idea of shared black culinary traditions could turn to Mary Keyes Burgess's *Soul to Soul: A Soul Food Vegetarian Cookbook*, which appeared in 1976. Burgess became a vegetarian for health reasons as well as for biblical ones after she learned about religious criticisms of pork consumption.[104] She offered her readers the chance to have it both ways, to consume soul food while also embracing some of the dietary changes that were part of the new cultural nationalist project. Burgess's cookbook provided meat-free recipes for classic soul food items such as crackling bread made with artificial bacon and "fried chicken" made from processed soybeans. Her definition of "soul" offered a path of reconciliation for those who wished to celebrate the cultural ingenuity of southern food habits while maintaining a veneer of vegetarian, moral nutritional superiority.

Burgess's endorsement of industrially produced meat substitutes such as Worthington Stripples, Veja-Links, and Skallops encouraged would-be conscientious eaters to combine their food ethics with a more concerted degree of participation in consumer capitalism. By the late 1970s, corporate America was exploiting the concerns of conscientious eaters by marketing processed foods labeled "healthy" or "natural" to lure back consumers who had attempted to withdraw from the conventional food system.[105] The proliferation of mass-marketed vegetarian foods changed the foodscape to such an extent that declaring culinary independence from the U.S. nation-state had become more challenging than ever for alternative eaters who were now left to ponder the ethical implications of not only the hamburger but the soy burger as well.[106] The corporatization of alternative styles of eating made it more challenging than ever for dietary critics to opt out of participating in a food system that they found morally problematic. Furthermore, the critiques of the "food rebels" were ultimately no match for the tenacious concept of soul food that ultimately subsumed competing visions of black food practices along with their complex, variegated history.

Conclusion

On April 22, 1971, supporters of the Bay Area Urban League hosted a dinner to celebrate the group's twenty-fifth anniversary. Diners entered the Grand Ballroom of the luxurious Fairmont Hotel in San Francisco to find tables elaborately set with china and silver. To the surprise of many, each table was also adorned with a bottle of Louisiana Hot Sauce and a pitcher of Kool-Aid. These deviations from the usual style of meal served at the Fairmont were designated to serve as markers that a "soul food" dinner was to follow. While previous generations of Urban League activists had worked to displace southern working-class foods from black dining tables, at this late twentieth-century meal, race leaders publicly ate braised oxtails, rice, corn bread, beans, and collard greens in a luxurious dining room in one of the nation's most cosmopolitan cities.

This remarkable and symbolically significant meal was served and eaten with a strong degree of group self-awareness. Sturdy cards placed at each table acknowledged, with some degree of wonder, that "this food style is currently enjoying a popularity among people from all socio-economic backgrounds." However, the organizers of the feast wanted to make sure that the trendiness of the food did not allow diners to "forget the bitter origins that produced these dishes." The soul food on display that evening was designed to do the cultural work of unifying the diners into one cohesive social, cultural, and culinary group and to remind them of their shared connection to a "vicious cycle of racism and poverty."[1]

For the irrepressible California assemblyman Willie L. Brown, who was in attendance that night, the weight of the historical context did not diminish his joy in eating the meal. In a deliberate effort to establish his credentials as a soul food insider, Brown protested in faux indignation that the beans should have been red rather than white and jokingly claimed that he was pained to see so many members of the high-toned crowd attempting to eat oxtails with a knife and fork. Regardless of the mechanics of how these homey dishes were consumed in this very public setting, this dinner, and others like it, represented the ultimate failure of the respectability project to make the case for the essential Americanness of black food expression. Furthermore, the meal demonstrated that the critiques of "food rebels" like Dick Gregory and the members of the Nation of Islam that had unsettled some members of the black community had ultimately been unable to stop the ascendency of soul food, which was now the predominant way of framing the politics of black food expression. As members of the Urban League consumed these "cheap, filling . . . good" dishes, they were also performing a shared, transcendent black national culinary identity.[2]

Food habits, such as those exemplified at this Urban League soul food dinner, are markers of identity that can be decoded to reveal much about the social, political, and cultural worlds of individuals and of groups. As this book demonstrates, generations of African American conscientious eaters used mealtime as an opportunity to construct and perform complex, shifting ideas about national belonging. Food choices, one of the most quotidian manifestations of culture, provide a revealing glimpse into the felt experiences of both assimilationist eaters and independent nation-builders who used eating practices as a powerful, yet frequently overlooked, way of demonstrating physiological loyalty either to the U.S. nation-state or to an independent black nation or, in varying degrees, to both.

Successive generations of activists used the processes of food procurement, consumption, and digestion in their quest to protect themselves and their communities from the potentially devastating impact of the system of white supremacy. Near the turn of the twentieth century, respectable eaters like Mary Church Terrell endeavored to eat diets that were "pure," technologically advanced, culturally sophisticated, and free from the taint of association with the foodways of slavery. Conscientious eaters such as W. E. B. Du Bois and Booker T. Washington argued that African Americans had the right, and indeed the obligation, to eat symbolically significant and healthful foods as a means of performing their bodily equality. These race leaders steadfastly taught the mandates of food reform to their students, to their children, and to other members of the race who looked to them for wisdom and guidance. However, the symbolic values of many key foods of the African American and American diet were far from stable. Over the decades, reformers argued over the desirability and meaning of consuming beef or pork, corn bread or wheat bread. Intraracial culinary clashes between middle-class respectable eaters and working-class southern migrants during the Great Migration reveal that the appeal of self-conscious dietary reform was not universal. Refusing to modify one's diet, whether in defiance of middle-class norms or in deference to the demands of culinary desire, was every bit as much a political act as adopting foods designed to help the consumer perform particular ideas about citizenship and status.

During the classical phase of the civil rights movement, some food reformers held onto the Progressive Era belief that eating symbolically resonant "American" foods was one way of claiming the rights of citizenship. However, in the aftermath of the movement, the once-predominant idea that food practices could be used as a democratic leveler was replaced by newly assertive ideas about black cultural and culinary distinctiveness. Proponents of "soul food" used food habits to reimagine a distinctly black corporeality by rejecting the idea of an assimilationist table and ingesting the cuisine of a separate black cultural nation. The ascendency of the idea of a culturally unifying, aesthetically black practice of "soul food" was so powerful that this way of framing food expression overshadowed most earlier culinary impulses and memories. However, even this seductive vision, though predominant, was not totalizing. Critics of soul food soon argued that the concept bore the taint of the system of white supremacy that it initially sought to unsettle. In the late 1960s, a new group of food reformers rejected soul food due to either its association with the slave diet or its perceived poor nutritional value or because of concerns over the violence embedded in the practice of meat consumption.

Throughout the twentieth century, conscientious eaters of whatever ideological persuasion maintained the shared hope that individuals had the power to transform themselves and their communities through everyday actions. Because white society systematically built and rebuilt mechanisms to exploit or devalue black bodies, culinary nationalists of whatever ilk hoped that eating well—however it was defined—could help to fortify black bodies against the forces that wished to degrade them. The doggedness with which each group of reformers endeavored to practice what they preached demonstrates the shared conviction that race politics were not merely the product of thought but also the amalgamation of bodily experiences that could be felt.

NOTES

ABBREVIATIONS

BAA   *Baltimore Afro-American*
CD   *Chicago Defender*
DBP   W. E. B. Du Bois Papers, 1868–1963, Special Collections and
             University Archives, University of Massachusetts Library, Amherst
BTWP   *Booker T. Washington Papers*, ed. Louis R. Harlan, vols. 3–4
             (Urbana: University of Illinois Press, 1974–75); ed. Louis R. Harlan
             and Raymond W. Smock, vols. 5–6, 9–13 (Urbana: University of Illinois
             Press, 1976–77, 1980, 1981–84)
BTWP-LOC   Booker T. Washington Papers, Manuscript Division, Library of Congress
BTWP-TA   Booker T. Washington Papers, Tuskegee University Archives
NHBP   Nannie Helen Burroughs Papers, Manuscript Division, Library of
             Congress
NULP   National Urban League Papers, Manuscript Division, Library of Congress
USFA-NPS   U.S. Food Administration Records, Negro Press Section,
             National Archives, Kansas City, Mo.

INTRODUCTION

1. Lester Walton to Du Bois, September 19, 1924, DBP, mums312-b169-i088. Du Bois also acknowledged the sensual pleasure of eating when he proposed a January 1948 lunch date, arguing "that food after the holidays would taste just as good as before." See Du Bois to Walton, January 5, 1948, DBP, mums312-b123-i015.

2. Walton to Du Bois, November 7, 1925, DBP, mums312-b031-i308.

3. Du Bois to Walton, May 10, 1946, DBP, mums312-b112-i254.

4. Du Bois to Walton, November 25, 1946, DBP, mums312-b112-i258.

5. Du Bois to Walton, January 30, 1930, DBP, mums312-b057-i013.

6. Aberjhani and West, *Encyclopedia*, 63–64; Lewis, *Harlem*.

7. Du Bois to Walton, February 4, 1927, DBP, mums312-b041-i350.

8. Walton to Du Bois, April 27, 1942, DBP, mums312-b099-i156; Frank J. Prial, "Luchow's Symbol of the Good Old Days," March 24, 1982, *New York Times*, 3.

9. Winter, *Boardwalk Empire*. This episode is the source of the information in the next several paragraphs.

10. Social scientists St. Clair Drake and Horace R. Cayton documented a historical analog to the well-drawn, fictional White in their landmark study of 1930s Chicago— "upper shadies," whose social aspirations were reflected on their dining tables, with "wild duck and pheasant in season, chicken and turkey in season and out." Drake and Cayton, *Black Metropolis*, 547–48.

11. C. Fisher, "Food," 275.

12. Washington, *Up from Slavery*, 16.

13. Washington, 58.

14. Washington, 53, 58. For a vivid description of the time period after emancipation, see Litwack, *Been in the Storm So Long*.

15. Washington, *Up from Slavery*, 58.

16. Washington, 162.

17. Harlan, *Making of a Black Leader*; Harlan, *Wizard of Tuskegee*; Norrell, *Up from History*.

18. See also C. M. Brown, "Politics of Industrial Education"; Coclanis, "Wash(ington)"; Spivey, *Schooling for the New Slavery*; Bresnahan, "Implied Readers"; and Wells, "Up from Savagery," 53–74.

19. Peterson, "Colonialism and Education," 151.

20. Coclanis, "Wash(ington)," 90.

21. Heneghan, *Whitewashing*, 161.

22. Elias, *Civilizing Process*, 105.

23. Elias, xiii.

24. A. Smith, "National Cuisines," 446. See also Appardurai, "National Cuisine."

25. Slocum, "Race," 305.

26. Gerstle, *American Crucible*, 4.

27. Bracey, Meier, and Rudwick, *Black Nationalism*, xvii.

28. Van Deburg, *Modern Black Nationalism*, 2.

29. Robinson, *Black Nationalism*, 2. Wilson Jeremiah Moses also advocates for a stricter definition, arguing that "classical black nationalism . . . may be defined as the effort of African Americans to create a sovereign nation-state and formulate an ideological basis for a concept of national culture." See Moses, *Classical Black Nationalism*, 2.

30. Robinson, *Black Nationalism*, 2.

31. B. Anderson, *Imagined Communities*, 6.

32. Tompkins, *Racial Indigestion*, 1.

33. For a thoughtful discussion of food as performance see Szanto, Wong, and Brady, "Stirring the Pot."

34. Goffman, *Presentation of Self*, 15.

35. Bourdieu, *Distinction*, 188.

36. Brillat-Savarin, *Physiology*, 3.

37. Du Bois, *Souls of Black Folk*, 3.

38. Bracey, Meier, and Rudwick, *Black Nationalism*, xxix.

39. Robinson, *Black Nationalism*, 5.

40. Du Bois, *Souls of Black Folk*, 3.

41. For a discussion of how food studies is contributing to our understanding of embodied historical experiences, see Pilcher, "Embodied Imagination." For a challenge to the idea of mind-body duality, see Lakoff and Johnson, *Philosophy in the Flesh*.

42. Ingold, *Perception*, 4–5.

43. B. Turner, "Turn of the Body," 9.

44. B. Turner, 10. Maxine Leeds Craig concurs, arguing that although "actions of states and social movements may explain racial formation, the body is the ultimate target of a state's action; it is where material inequality is experienced, and where discourse is naturalized or resisted." See Leeds, "Racialized Bodies," 323.

45. Porter, "History of the Body," 224.

46. For a study of various attempts to "eat right" in the United States, see Biltekoff, *Eating Right*.

47. Warnes, *Hunger Overcome*, 7.

CHAPTER 1

1. Harley, "For the Good of Family and Race," 343–44; Terrell, *Colored Woman*, 235.

2. Terrell, *Colored Woman*, 120.

3. Terrell, 124.

4. Terrell, 121.

5. It is unclear precisely when Terrell started learning to cook. She recalls that for the first several years of her marriage in 1891 the couple lived in a small apartment. Her descriptions of learning to cook take place later, after the couple purchased a home. Crisco, a significant ingredient in the holiday menu she describes, was not invented until 1911. See Terrell, 113–26.

6. Sarah Tyson Rorer's version of the "Queen of All Puddings" contained shortening; see Lincoln et al., *Home Helps*, 66.

7. Coombs and Batchelor, *We Are What We Sell*, 152.

8. Terrell, *Colored Woman*, 125.

9. Terrell, 122.

10. Terrell, 123.

11. For more insights into the politics of racial uplift, see Meier, *Negro Thought*; Higginbotham, *Righteous Discontent*; and Gaines, *Uplifting the Race*.

12. Higginbotham used the phrase "politics of respectability" to describe the work of middle-class churchwomen who "equated public behavior with individual self-respect and with the advancement of African-Americans as a group." Higginbotham, *Righteous Discontent*, 14.

13. Brundage, "Introduction," 20.

14. For a more extensive discussion about culinary racial stereotypes, see Wallach, *How America Eats*, 185–91; Manring, *Slave in a Box*; Williams-Forson, "Chickens and Chains," 127–28; Wallach, "Food and Race"; Goings, *Mammy and Uncle Mose*; and P. Turner, *Ceramic Uncles*.

15. For more information about the limits of southern progressivism, see Woodward, *Origins of the New South*; and Gilmore, *Gender and Jim Crow*.

16. Shapiro, *Perfection Salad*.

17. Riis, *How the Other Half Lives* and *Battle with the Slum*, 401.

18. Quoted in Levenstein, *Revolution at the Table*, 99.

19. Addams, *Twenty Years*, 286.

20. Ellis, *Americanization*.

21. Addams, *Twenty Years*, 167.

22. For more information about the New England Kitchen, see Biltekoff, *Eating Right*, 24; Levenstein, *Revolution at the Table*, 44–59; and Shapiro, *Perfection Salad*, 139–54.

23. Veit, *Modern Food*, 79.

24. Wallach, *How America Eats*, 129–30; Shapiro, *Perfection Salad*; Elias, *Stir It Up*; and Levenstein, *Revolution at the Table*.

25. Levenstein, *Revolution at the Table*, 60–71. Although training servants was posited as a solution to the problem, these educational programs generally were not popular with those they were intended to serve. See Salmon, *Domestic Service*, 183.

26. Women's Educational and Industrial Trade Union, *Bulletin of the Domestic Reform League*; "A School of Housekeeping," *Cambridge Tribune*, June 23, 1900; Women's Educational and Industrial Union Papers, box 1, folder 5, Schlesinger Library, Cambridge, Mass.

27. Vapnek, *Working Women*, 118, 124.

28. Lasch-Quinn, *Black Neighbors*, 6.

29. "Tuskegee Culls Ideas for Chefs, Cooks from White House," *New York Amsterdam News*, August 9, 1936, 13.

30. H. Williams, *Self Taught*; J. Anderson, *Education of Blacks*.

31. S. Cohen, "Industrial Education Movement."

32. S. Cohen, 99.

33. Engs, *Educating the Disfranchised*.

34. Enck, "Tuskegee Institute."

35. Du Bois, *Philadelphia Negro*, 139; May, "'Obtaining a Decent Livelihood.'" For a profile of black domestic workers in the first decades of the twentieth century, see Haynes, "Negroes in Domestic Service."

36. For more information about the stereotype of African Americans as instinctive cooks, see Witt, "Intersections of Literary and Culinary Studies," 107; Veit, *Modern Food*, 116–17; Cooley, *To Live and Dine in Dixie*, 82; and Sharpless, *Cooking in Other Women's Kitchens*.

37. Sharpless is careful to point out that cooking was a skill that had to be painstakingly learned. See Sharpless, *Cooking in Other Women's Kitchens*, 11–31.

38. Shapiro, *Perfection Salad*, 186; Wallach, *How America Eats*, 108–9.

39. Hamilton, "Twentieth Century"; Shapiro, *Perfection Salad*, 186; Strasser, *Satisfaction Guaranteed*.

40. Bobrow-Strain, *White Bread*, 20.

41. Work, *Negro Yearbook*, 321.

42. Williams-Forson, *Building Houses*, 98–99. See, for example, the following from the *Chicago Defender*: "Man Should Eat Food Raw," July 8, 1911, 6; "Plain Food, Good Cooks and Hard Work Will Save Doctor Bills," October 30, 1915, 8; "Concerning the Appetite: Timely Advice—How and What to Eat," October 19, 1912, 3; and "Individual Drinking Cups Favored by Uncle Sam: The Dangers of the Germ-Laden Cup," November 16, 1912, 8.

43. Editorial, *CD*, March 26, 1910, 2.

44. Washington, "Twenty-Five Years of Tuskegee."

45. Bruce, "Tuskegee Institute," 104, 110. For useful guidance in analyzing early twentieth-century representations of black female bodies, see Purkiss, "Beauty Secrets," 14–37.

46. Cooley, *To Live and Dine in Dixie*, 35.

47. Richards, *Euthenics*, viii.

48. Richards, 19.

49. Mitchell, *Righteous Propagation*, 147–48; Parker, "'Picture of Health,'" 173.

50. Richards, *Euthenics*, 135.

51. Du Bois, *Quest of the Silver Fleece*, 176.

52. F. Fletcher, "The Housekeeper," *CD*, March 6, 1915.

53. Gilmore, *Gender and Jim Crow*, 12–13.

54. Williams-Forson, *Building Houses*, 93.

55. Williams-Forson, 94–95.

56. F. Farmer, *Boston Cooking-School Cook Book*, 382; C. H. Brown, *"Mammy,"* 18.

57. C. H. Brown, *"Mammy,"* 16–21.

58. Delany and Delany, *Having Our Say*, 132–33.

59. Shapiro, *Perfection Salad*, 41.

60. "Dainty Potatoes," *Washington Bee*, March 21, 1908, 3. For examples of other "dainty dishes," see "Some Table Dainties," *CD*, June 1, 1912, 8; and "Christmas Little Cakes," *Philadelphia Tribune*, December 18, 1915.

61. F. Farmer, *Boston Cooking-School Cook Book*.

62. Williams-Forson, "Chickens and Chains," 127–28.

63. "Mrs. Rosa Richardson Entertains Supreme Representatives," *BAA*, September 2, 1911, 4.

64. "A Stay-at-Home Fourth Calls for Fried Chicken," *BAA*, July 4, 1931, 16.

65. For an analysis of both the symbolic and the material significance of chicken, see Williams-Forson *Building Houses*.

66. McKay, *Home to Harlem*, 161–62.

67. "Poor Diet Causes High Death Rate: Pork, Greasy Foods, Cornbread, Peas Constitute Faulty Diet," *BAA*, April 21, 1928, 5.

68. "Making Your Community Christian," 25, NHBP, box 46, folder 16.

69. "Meals," NHBP, box 312, folder 4.

70. 1929 Annual for the National Training School for Women and Girls, "Sunday School before Breakfast," NHBP, box 312, folder "School Programs for Student Activities."

71. "Meals," NHBP, box 312, folder "Miscellany."

72. "Physiology First Preparatory" and "Domestic Science," NHBP, box 311, folder "National Trade and Professional School Curricula and Teaching Procedures." Psyche Williams-Forson argues that Nannie Helen Burroughs was a proponent of southern foods such as fried chicken, turnips, and candied sweet potatoes. On that basis, one could speculate that for Burroughs the manner in which food was consumed was more significant than the particular foods selected. See Williams-Forson, *Building Houses*, 96–97.

73. "Chance to Prolong Life—Be Modest in All Things," *CD*, November 12, 1915, 5.

74. Delany and Delany, *Having Our Say*, 17.

75. Shaw, *What a Woman Ought to Be*, 43; Ritterhouse, *Growing Up Jim Crow*, 84–85.

76. Gaines, *Uplifting the Race*, xv.

77. For another analysis of the role of food in West's novel, see Williams-Forson, *Building Houses*, 105–9.

78. West, *Living Is Easy*, 251–52.

79. "Com. Fortune Dined," *Colored American*, July 4, 1903, 1.

CHAPTER 2

1. "The Students Had Today," April 25, 1901, BTWP-LOC, reel 438.

2. Washington, "An Address before the Alabama State Teachers' Association," June 8, 1892, *BTWP*, 3:234–35.

3. "Fannie Merritt Farmer to Washington," June 2, 1896, *BTWP*, 4:176; "Washington to John Harvey Kellogg," April 3, 1912, *BTWP*, 11:510; "Washington to Edward Atkinson," November 7, 1897, *BTWP*, 4:337–38; "Wilber Olin Atwater to Washington," April 17, 1895, *BTWP*, 3:546; "Washington to Jabaz Lamar Monroe Curry," September 21, 1894, *BTWP*, 3:460–70.

4. Levenstein, *Revolution at the Table*, 45–54.

5. New England Cotton Manufacturers' Association, *Transactions*, 203.

6. E. Atkinson, *Science of Nutrition*, 215–23.

7. Tuskegee Institute, *Tuskegee Normal and Industrial Institute Catalogue*, 76.

8. Levenstein, *Revolution at the Table*, 54.

9. J. R. Lewis to Washington, April 25, 1895, BTWP-TA, box 2, folder 12; Edward Atkinson to Washington, April 26, 1895, BTWP-TA, box 1, folder 2.

10. *Hardware: A Review of the American Hardware Market*, April 10, 1895, 22.

11. "Jabez Lamar Monroe Curry to Washington," April 17, 1894, *BTWP*, 3:403–4.

12. *BTWP*, 5:454; Norrell, *Up from History*, 102–3.

13. *BTWP*, 3:467.

14. "Washington to Alice J. Kaine," September 5, 1894, *BTWP*, 3:466–67; "Washington to Elizabeth J. Scott," December 28, 1894, *BTWP*, 3:494.

15. Alice J. Kaine to Washington, January 8, 1895, BTWP-TA, box 2, folder 57.

16. "Alice J. Kaine to Washington," September 12, 1894, *BTWP*, 3:467.

17. In comments on this chapter, Anthony Stanonis noted that the presence of a white domestic scientist on campus also offered an inversion of stereotypes claiming that black women were natural cooks.

18. E. Atkinson, *Science of Nutrition*, 218.

19. Biltekoff, *Eating Right*, 24; Levenstein, *Revolution at the Table*, 44–59; Shapiro, *Perfection Salad*, 139–54.

20. Shapiro, *Perfection Salad*, 145; Levenstein, *Revolution at the Table*, 48–59. For some of the recipes served, see Abel, *Practical Sanitary and Economic Cooking*.

21. A. Atkinson, "Atlanta University."

22. Wallach, *How America Eats*, 12–14; Wright, *History of English Food*; Spencer, *British Food*.

23. Whitwell, "Axioms," 204.

24. "A Sunday Evening Talk," October 6, 1907, *BTWP*, 9:368.

25. "A Sunday Evening Talk," December 10, 1911, *BTWP*, 11:409.

26. Harlan, *Wizard of Tuskegee*, 144.

27. "Washington to Warren Logan," November 23, 1899, *BTWP*, 5:270.

28. "P. G. Parks to Washington," September 18, 1906, BTWP-LOC, reel 452; "E. T. Atwell to P. G.. Parks," April 17, 1906, BTWP-LOC, reel 452.

29. Atwater and Woods, *Dietary Studies*, 20. Researchers at Tuskegee collaborated with the USDA in collecting the data for this study.

30. Horowitz, *Putting Meat on the American Table*, 13.

31. Atwater and Woods, *Dietary Studies*, 20.

32. Atwater and Woods, 16.

33. Atwater and Woods, 20.

34. C. Wilson, "Cornbread," 152–54. The symbolism of cornmeal versus wheat is discussed in greater detail in chapter 5.

35. Wallach, *How America Eats*, 13.

36. Washington to Mr. Saffold, September 14, 1898, BTWP-TA, box 001.002, folder 1898.

37. Washington to Mr. Saffold, October 22, 1898, BTWP-TA, box 001.002, folder 1898.

38. Washington to Mr. Saffold, October 22, 1898, BTWP-TA, box 2, folder 15.

39. For sample Tuskegee menus, see BTWP-LOC, reel 438.

40. Washington to Mr. Saffold, September 28, 1898, BTWP-TA, box 001.002, folder 1898.

41. Tuskegee Institute, *Tuskegee Normal and Industrial Institute Catalogue, 1909–1910*, 75–76.

42. There are literally hundreds of everyday Tuskegee menus preserved in the Booker T. Washington Papers housed at the Library of Congress. One sample menu was published in Washington, *Working with the Hands*, 50.

43. Margaret Murray Washington Notebook, December 2, 1898, Tuskegee University Archives.

44. Washington, *Up from Slavery*, 66.

45. Campbell, *Moveable School*, 47.

46. Campbell, 47, 49.

47. Ross, "Aggressive Mobility," 50.

48. Washington, *Working with the Hands*, 183, 187; Neverdon-Morton, *Afro-American Women of the South*, 35.

49. Mrs. Booker T. Washington, "What Girls Are Taught," 74.

50. Washington, *Working with the Hands*, 98.

51. Washington, "Cotton States and International Exposition Address, 1895," *BTWP* 3: 583–87.

52. Washington, *Up from Slavery*, 114–15.

53. Washington, 115.

54. Willard, "Timing Impossible Subjects," 647.

55. Logan, "Resources and Material Equipment," 38.

56. Weiss, *Robert R. Taylor*, 177; Davis, *Guest of Honor*, 100–101.

57. Washington, *Up from Slavery*, 153.

58. Willard, "Timing Impossible Subjects," 647.

59. "An Item in the *Tuskegee Student*," October 29, 1910, *BTWP*, 10:428–29.

60. Pierce, *Dinners*, 11, 25.

61. Gillette and Ziemann, *White House Cookbook*, 279.

62. Washington to Margaret Murray Washington, May 14, 1906, BTWP-LOC, reel 499.

63. Washington to Margaret Murray Washington, May 16, 1906, BTWP-LOC, reel 499.

64. Margaret Murray Washington concurred with Washington's ideas about food reform and was certainly charged with the task of helping implement his program. She was the president of the local Tuskegee Women's Club, which hosted discussions related to food reform. Meeting minutes are included in the Margaret Murray Washington Notebook, Tuskegee University Archives.

65. Norrell, *Up from History*, 394. Although Washington promoted beef as a symbolically significant meat, pork never disappeared from Tuskegee or from Washington's private table. In *Working with the Hands*, he criticized rural African Americans for not raising pork scientifically. See *Working with the Hands*, 155–56.

66. "An Invitation to a Possum Supper for Teachers," October 6, 1914, *BTWP*, 13:142.

67. "James Carroll Napier to Washington," November 27, 1912; "Washington to Jeannette Tod Ewing Bertram," November 15, 1913; "Charles William Anderson to Emmett Jay Scott," November 21, 1913, all in *BTWP*, 12:60, 334–35.

68. "Washington to Jeannette Tod Ewing Bertram," November 15, 1913, *BTWP*, 12:334.

69. Washington, *Working with the Hands*, 190.

70. "Washington to Ernest Ten Eyck Attwell," July 15, 1912, *BTWP*, 11:559.

71. "A Sunday Evening Talk," March 27, 1910, *BTWP*, 12:299.

72. Washington, *Working with the Hands*, 80; "A Tuskegee Student Bill of Fare," *BTWP*, 6:428.

73. Washington, "Teaching Domestic Economy at Tuskegee," *Good Housekeeping Magazine* (November 1910): 623–24. Washington also instructed his staff to serve as much food as possible that had been produced at Tuskegee. See E. T. Atwell to Washington, May 2, 1905, BTWP-LOC, reel 432.

74. J. H. Washington to E. T. Atwell, June 13, 1906, BTWP-LOC, reel 432; J. H. Washington to Booker T. Washington, May 1, 1911, BTWP-LOC, reel 496.

75. Washington to Warren Logan, June 15, 1902, BTWP-TA, box 001.004, folder 1902.

76. "Canning," in Tuskegee Institute, *Tuskegee Normal and Industrial Institute Catalogue*; J. H. Washington, "Our Canning Establishment," *Tuskegee Student*, July 20, 1900.

77. Hersey, *My Work Is That of Conservation*, 86–87, 99. See also Rafia Zafar, "Carver's Food Movement."

78. Daniel C. Smith to Washington, February 7, 1902, George Washington Carver Collection, Tuskegee University Archives, box 4, folder 1.

79. Hersey, 109; Campbell, *Moveable School*, 67–68.

80. Campbell, *Moveable School*, 67.

81. *Tuskegee Student*, December 30, 1899.

82. Campbell, *Moveable School*, 67.

83. Washington, "Cotton States and International Exposition Address, 1895," *BTWP* 3: 583–87.

84. Hersey, *My Work Is That of Conservation*, 150.

85. "Tuskegee Negro Conference Notes," January 6, 1900, *Tuskegee Student*.

86. Washington, *Working with the Hands*, 32.

87. Washington, 149–50.

88. Hershey, *My Work Is That of Conservation*, 114.

89. Reid, *Reaping a Greater Harvest*, 31.

90. Neverdon-Morton, *Afro-American Women of the South*, 124.

CHAPTER 3

1. Du Bois to Yolande Du Bois, February 13, 1923, DBP, mums312-b021-i090.

2. Du Bois to Yolande Du Bois, January 24, 1923, DBP, mums312-b021-i084; Du Bois to Yolande Du Bois, February 2, 1923, DBP, mums312-b021-i085; Du Bois to Yolande Du Bois, February 13, 1923, DBP, mums312-b021-i090.

3. Du Bois to Yolande Du Bois, February 13, 1923, DBP, mums312-b021-i090.

4. Green, *Code of Etiquette*, 6.

5. For more about etiquette guides, see K. Smith, "Childhood."

6. Green, *Code of Etiquette*, 124–25.

7. Green, 22–28, 137–38.

8. Green, 23.

9. C. H. Brown, "*Mammy*," 41.

10. Gatewood, *Aristocrats*, 256.

11. Ritterhouse, *Growing Up Jim Crow*, 85.

12. Delany and Delany, *Having Our Say*, 50.

13. Shaw, *What A Woman Ought to Be*, 16.

14. Ritterhouse, *Growing Up Jim Crow*, 88.

15. Delany and Delany, *Having Our Say*, 57.

16. Quoted in Higginbotham, *Righteous Discontent*, 202.

17. Hackley, *Colored Girl Beautiful*, 194.

18. "Fighting Your Health Battles," *New York Amsterdam News*, December 1, 1926, 20; "Health in Harlem," *New York Amsterdam News*, December 2, 1926, 14.

19. Hackley, *Colored Girl Beautiful*, 102.

20. Hackley, 34–35.

21. "Faces are Altered by Food," *CD*, June 17, 1911.

22. For more information about the history of the *Brownies' Book*, see Vaughn-Roberson and Hill, "*Brownies' Book*"; Phillips, "Children of Double Consciousness"; V. Harris, "Race Consciousness"; Young, "*Brownies' Book*"; and Kory, "Once upon a Time."

23. *Crisis*, October 1919, 285–86.

24. "The Judge," *Brownies' Book*, November 1920, 337.

25. "To Mothers," *Brownies' Book*, March 1920, 82.

26. Peggy Poe, "Pumpkin Land," *Brownies' Book*, January 20, 1920, 3–6.

27. "The Judge: What Is the Most Fun?," *Brownies' Book*, April 1920, 108.

28. "Food for 'Lazy Betty,'" *Brownies' Book*, February 1920, 60–62.

29. "Doughnuts," *CD*, July 2, 1910, 7.

30. Sinitierre's presentation "A Place at the Table" helped further cement my growing certainty that Du Bois's ideas about food were worthy of investigation.

31. Levenstein, *Fear of Food*, 107–8; Kellogg, *Miracle of Life*, 207–8.

32. Du Bois, "Frightened," March 16, 1891, DBP, mums312-b230-i085.

33. Levenstein, *Revolution at the Table*, 21.

34. Other references to a "dyspeptic nation" include Remondino, "Questions," 122; Nootnagel, "General Considerations"; and "Talmage's Advice to Home Getters," *Sanitary News*, May 17, 1890, 398.

35. Levenstein, *Revolution at the Table*, 21.

36. "National Society to Conserve Life: Life Extension Institute Formed to Teach Hygiene and Prevention of Disease," *New York Times*, December 13, 1913, 2.

37. Life Extension Examiners, *Life Extension Examiners Life Extension Institute Fortieth Anniversary*. A number of reports about Du Bois's urine are cataloged among the DBP. See, for example, "Life Extension Institute Analysis of Urine, 1929," DBP, mums312-b049-i361.

38. Du Bois, *Against Racism*, 301.

39. Du Bois to Louis Wright, January 9, 1930, DBP, mums312-b057-i153; Du Bois to Richard M. Carey, September 22, 1953, DBP, mums312-b139-i273.

40. Life Extension Institute to Du Bois, September 15, 1935, DBP, mums312-b029-i458; Du Bois to Louis Wright, January 9, 1930, DBP, mums312-b057-i153.

41. Life Extension Institute, Health Survey Summary, July 26, 1922, DBP, mums312-b019-i405.

42. Comparative Report on Periodic Health Survey, July 26, 1922, DBP, mums312-b019-i404.

43. Avery, *Dyspeptics Monitor*; Chambers, *Indigestions of Diseases*.

44. Vester, "Regime Change," 41.

45. For more information about Du Bois's ideas about "true manhood," see Booker, "*I Will Wear No Chain!*", 121–23; and Carby, *Race Men*, 9–44.

46. Levenstein, *Revolution at the Table*, 12; Duncan, *How to Be Plump*.

47. Veit, *Modern Food*, 157–80; Levenstein, *Revolution at the Table*, 176–77.

48. Veit, *Modern Food*, 158–59; Bordo, *Feminism*, 185–212; Biltekoff, *Eating Right*, 119.

49. "Homeopathic Medical Society of the County of Kings," *North American Journal of Homeopathy*, ed. Eugene H. Porter, 46 (1898), 5.

50. "The Medical Treatment of Cancer," *Journal of the American Institute of Homeopathy*, 12 (1919–20): 770. See also Heller, *American Homeopathy*.

51. Du Bois to Edmund Devol, June 9, 1926, DBP, mums312-b033-i094; Du Bois to Edmond Devol, June 16 1926, DBP, mums312-b033-i095.

52. Du Bois to Alexina C. Barrell, March 1, 1935, DBP, mums312-b073-i182.

53. Du Bois to Nina Du Bois, January 29, 1938, DBP, mums312-b085-i097.

54. Knadler, "Dis-abled Citizenship"; Baynton, "Disability."

55. Wolff, "Myth of the Actuary."

56. Hoffman, *Race Traits*, 175–76.

57. Hoffman, 170–71.

58. J. Miller, "Effects of Emancipation."

59. See Provenzo, *Du Bois's Exhibit*, for examples of these photographs.

60. Knadler, "Dis-abled Citizenship," 103–4; Du Bois, *Souls of Black Folk*, 60–74.

61. Knadler, 104.

62. Du Bois, *Souls of Black Folk*, 70–74.

63. Du Bois, 70, 72, 73.

64. Du Bois, review of *Race Traits*, 130–31.

65. Du Bois, "Talented Tenth."

66. Rudwick, "Du Bois and the Atlanta University Studies"; Du Bois, *Health and Physique*.

67. Du Bois, *Health and Physique*, 90–91. Historian Jim Downs argues that the hardships of emancipation did negatively impact the health of the freed people. See Downs, *Sick from Freedom*, 7.

68. Du Bois, *Health and Physique*, 90–91.

69. Lewis, *W. E. B. Du Bois*, 106.

70. Du Bois to Yolande Du Bois, February 13, 1923, DBP, mums312-b021-i090.

71. Memo from Yolande Du Bois to nurse, 1935, DBP, mums312-b076-i361.

72. Sullivan-Fowler, "Doubtful Theories."

73. Armstrong, *Modernism*, 3.

74. Kellogg, *Itinerary of a Breakfast*, 100.

75. Dr. A. Wilberforce Williams, "Keep Healthy: Constipation-Hemorrhoids," *CD*, November 15, 1913, 4.

76. Whorton, *Inner Hygiene*, 86.

77. See Hunter, *To 'Joy My Freedom*, 187–218, for more information about the association of working-class blacks with tuberculosis. For an argument that constipation was gendered female, see Herbert, "Digestive Femininity."

78. Whorton, *Inner Hygiene*, 211; Hastings, *Physical Culture*, 89; Lowe, *Health Rules*, 59.

79. "Food for 'Lazy Betty,'" *Brownies' Book*, February 1920, 60–62.

80. Whorton, *Inner Hygiene*, 40–41; Wallach, *How America Eats*, 144–48; Sokolow, *Eros and Modernization*; Nissenbaum, *Sex, Diet, and Debility*.

81. Wallach, *How America Eats*, 13–18.

82. Tompkins, "Sylvester Graham's Imperial Dietetics," 51.

83. Graham, *Treatise*, 55

84. Gant, *Constipation*, 138.

85. Whorton, *Inner Hygiene*, 20.

86. "Dr. A. Wilberforce William Talks on Preventative Measures, First Aid Remedies, Hygienics and Sanitation, Complexion," *CD*, October 10, 1914, 8.

87. Quoted in Whorton, *Crusaders for Fitness*, 223.

88. Graham, *Treatise*, 105

89. Herbert, "Digestive Femininity," 9.

90. White, *Arn't I a Woman?*, 7.

91. Lowe, *Health Rules*, 61–63.

92. Hornibrook, *Stand Up*, 15.

93. Peters, *Diet and Health*, 11.

94. Brumberg, *Fasting Girls*, 236.

95. Kellogg, *Autointoxication*, 266.

96. Conrad and Barker, "Social Construction of Illness"; Foucault, *Birth of the Clinic*.

97. Conrad and Barker, "Social Construction of Illness," 73.

98. In *The Birth of the Clinic* Michel Foucault describes the "clinical gaze" that members of the medical establishment use to establish their authority over the bodies of their patients and over ideas about the nature of and treatment of illness.

99. Du Bois to Yolande Du Bois, February 13, 1923, DBP, mums312-b021-i090.

100. Du Bois to Yolande Du Bois Williams, March 23, 1935, DBP, mums312-b076-i355.

101. Shaw, *What a Woman Ought to Be*, 2.

CHAPTER 4

1. Peggy Poe, "The Watermelon Dance," *Brownies' Book*, September 1920, 263–64. The character "Happy" reappears in stories written by Peggy Poe in the January 1920 and January 1921 issues.

2. See, for example, the following in the *Brownies' Book*: Augusta Bird, "A Criss-Cross Thanksgiving," November 1920, 326–30; Langston Hughes, "Those Who Have No Turkey," November 1921, 324–28; Minna B. Boyles, "Lolly-Pop Land," April 1921, 112–13; and Maud Wilcox Nidermeyer, "The Pink Banana," October 1921, 99–300.

3. Jessie Fauset, "Turkey Drumsticks," *Brownies' Book*, November 1920, 342–46.

4. Du Bois, memorandum to Mr. Isaac Beton, secretary of the Pan-African Congress, with regard to the economic situation of the black race in the United States of America, May 22, 1923, DBP, mums312-b022-i378.

5. Literary luminary Langston Hughes made a more positive distinction between what he imagined as two different regional ways of life in his short story "Those Who Have No Turkey." The narrator of the story suggests that sophisticated black northerners should embrace a form of race loyalty that transcends class demarcations. See Hughes, "Those Who Have No Turkey," *Brownies' Book*, November 1921, 324–28.

6. Julia Price Burrell, "The Quaintness of St. Helena," *Brownies' Book*, August 1920, 245–47.

7. Lillian A. Turner, "How Lilimay 'Kilt' the Chicken," *Brownies' Book*, September 1921, 251–52.

8. Pocahontas Foster, "The Chocolate Cake," *Brownies' Book*, April 1921, 114–20.

9. Foster, 120.

10. Augusta Bird, "A Criss-Cross Thanksgiving," *Brownies' Book*, November 1920, 326–29.

11. Bird, 327.

12. Du Bois, *Souls of Black Folk*, 62; Du Bois, *College-Bred Negro*, 37.

13. Hobbs and Stoops, "Demographic Trends."

14. Hilliard, *Hog Meat and Hoecake*, 48.

15. Hilliard, 162.

16. Warman, *Corn and Capitalism*, 160.

17. Ferris, *Edible South*, 128.

18. C. Wilson, "Cornbread," 152–54..

19. Ferris, *Edible South*, 129.

20. Hilliard, *Hog Meat and Hoecake*, 92.

21. Covey and Eisnach, *What the Slaves Ate*, 21; Taylor, *Eating, Drinking, and Visiting*, 104.

22. Hilliard, *Hog Meat and Hoecake*, 105.

23. Hilliard, 62.

24. J. Wilson, "Over-Eating."

25. J. Wilson, "Over-Eating."

26. Levenstein, *Revolution at the Table*, 21.

27. Ferris, *Edible South*, 126–27.

28. Beardsley, *History of Neglect*, 54–58; Ferris, *Edible South*, 128–31.

29. Beardsley, *History of Neglect*, 57.

30. Davis, Gardner, and Gardner, *Deep South*, 384.

31. Bourdieu, *Distinction*, 173.

32. Atwater and Woods, *Dietary Studies*, 18.

33. "What Negro Families Ate on Day of Interview," Neighborhood Union Collection, Atlanta University Center Archives Research Center, box 7, folder 15.

34. Du Bois, *Negro American Family*, 135–36.

35. Du Bois, 137–48.

36. Du Bois, 138, 140.

37. Du Bois, 146–47.

38. Bourdieu, *Distinction*, 173.

39. Delany and Delany, *Having Our Say*, 89.

40. Hughes, *Not without Laughter*, 14.

41. Hughes, 155.

42. Hughes, 171.

43. Hughes, 171.

44. Hughes, 171.

45. U.S. Census Bureau, "Great Migration."

46. Bégin, *Taste of the Nation*, 76.

47. Layson and Warren, "Chicago and the Great Migration."

48. "Loud Talking in the Pekin," *CD*, April 23, 1910, 1.

49. Poe, "Origins of Soul Food," 9. A. Wilberforce Williams, a physician who served as the health editor for the *Chicago Defender* from 1911 to 1929, published numerous articles advising readers on proper nutrition and on topics such as how to avoid obesity. See, for example, A. Wilberforce Williams, "What to Eat in Cold Weather," *CD*, March 11, 1922, 12, and "Obesity," *CD*, October 11, 1924, 12.

50. Poe, "Origins of Soul Food," 17.

51. "Rogers' Pig Ankle College Burns," *CD*, June 17, 1911, 1.

52. William H. A. Moore, "And Christ Came," *CD*, December 30, 1939, 13.

53. "Pig Ankle Joints," *CD*, May 29, 1915, 4.

54. Chicago Commission on Race Relations, *Negro in Chicago*, 264.

55. Du Bois, *Philadelphia Negro*, 161.

56. Du Bois, 178.

57. Du Bois, 161.

58. Davis, Gardner, and Gardner, *Deep South*, 234.

59. Higginbotham, *Righteous Discontent*, 187.

60. Delany and Delany, *Having Our Say*, 45.

61. Delany and Delany, 46.

62. Du Bois, *Efforts for Social Betterment*, 50, 59, 73.

63. "Report of Major Activities of the Atlanta Urban League for 1931," NULP, part 1: E8, folder "Historical Information, Atlanta, GA, 1928–1938"; "The Columbus Urban League and Departments, Fourteenth Annual Report, January 1932," NULP, part 1: E9, folder "Historical Information, Columbus U.L., 1927–1932."

64. "To All Friends of the Organization," NULP, part 1: E9, folder "Historical Information Brooklyn, New York, National Urban League, 1929–1931."

65. Neverdon-Morton, *Afro-American Women of the South*, 35, 117.

66. Mr. John E. Milholland, "Talks about Women," *Crisis*, April 1911, 27.

67. "The Negro Worker in the World," *Crisis*, November 1923, 23.

68. Higginbotham, *Righteous Discontent*, 178.

69. Higginbotham, 211–21.

70. Quoted in Higginbotham, 213.

71. For numerous examples of tests taken by domestic science students at the National Training School, see NHBP, box 311, folder 1, "National Trade and Professional School Curricula and Teaching Procedures, Examination Questions, 1920–1921."

72. Lasch-Quinn, *Black Neighbors*, 40.

73. "Scientific Cooking Taught," *CD*, October 4, 1919, 17.

74. "Report of a Committee Appointed to Review the Work of Memorial Center

and Urban League, Incorporated, 1929–1930," NULP, part 1: E9, folder "Historical Information: Buffalo, New York, National Urban League, 1929–1931."

75. "Urban League's Home Making Class Interests," *Pittsburgh Courier*, February 21, 1931; "Urban League Offers Food and Nutrition Classes," *Pittsburgh Courier*, July 28, 1934.

76. "Citizens Endorse Urban League Food Show," *Pittsburgh Courier*, June 1, 1929.

77. Shaw, *What a Woman Ought to Be*, 169; Neverdon-Morton, *Afro-American Women of the South*, 146.

78. "Lesson IV, Meat, Fish and Eggs," Neighborhood Union Collections, box 7, folder 43.

79. Shapiro, *Perfection Salad*, 86.

80. Shapiro, 89.

81. Williams-Forson, *Building Houses*, 96.

82. "Hard Problem for Women," *CD*, September 9, 1911, 2.

83. "Police! Fire! Murder! Pork Chops! Pigs' Feet!," *CD*, October 14, 1911, 1.

84. "Second Annual Report of the Chicago Urban League on Urban Conditions among Negroes, Inc. for the Fiscal Year Ended October 31, 1918," NULP, part 1: E9, folder "Historical Info, 1918–1931, Chicago, IL."

85. Gaines, *Uplifting the Race*, 158.

86. McKay, *Home to Harlem*, 142.

87. McKay, 270.

88. Hughes, *Ways of White Folks*, 37.

89. Drake and Cayton, *Black Metropolis*, 572.

90. Drake and Cayton, 250.

91. "The Store . . . ," *CD*, July 4, 1914.

92. Poe, "African American Meals," 180.

93. "The Southern Menu," *Christian Recorder*, January 31, 1895.

CHAPTER 5

1. Du Bois, "Close Ranks."

2. Tunc, "Less Sugar."

3. Dickson, *Food Front*, 75.

4. Keene, "Images of Racial Pride," 213; Scott, *Scott's Official History*, 362.

5. Dickson, *Food Front*, 73.

6. Mjagkij, *Loyalty in Time of Trial*, 139–40; Dickson, *Food Front*, 73–77.

7. Hamp Williams to County Food Administrators, June 11, 1918, U.S. Food Administration Records, Record Group 4, State and Local Food Administrators, Arkansas Reports, HM 2005, box 1, AR7, National Archives, Fort Worth, Tex.

8. Keene, "Images of Racial Pride," 214.

9. Undated press release, USFA-NPS, box 589, folder "Press Releases."

10. Quoted in N. Brown, *Private Politics*, 41.

11. Untitled and undated document, USFA-NPS, box 589, folder "Press Releases."

12. "Sunday Is Food Conservation Day," *Kansas City Advocate*, October 19, 1917, 1.

13. R. R. Wright to A. U. Craig, November 2, 1917, USFA-NPS, box 592, folder "Schools, Colleges, and Universities."

14. Ezra C. Roberts to A. U. Craig, June 11, 1918, USFA-NPS, box 592, folder "Summer Schools/Stereopticon slides."

15. E. A. Long to A. U. Craig, May 9, 1918, USFA-NPS, box 592, folder "Denominational Bds; Educational and Religious."

16. Hilda M. Nasmyth to United States Food Administration, October 17, 1918, USFA-NPS, box 590, folder "Food Guide Information."

17. Quoted in Keene, "Images of Racial Pride," 221–22.

18. Ferris, *Edible South*, 128–31.

19. U.S. Food Administration, *Eat Cane Syrup and Molasses, Save Sugar by Using Best Louisiana Molasses and Sugar Cane Syrup*, lithograph, 1918, Prints and Photographs Division, Library of Congress, Washington, D.C., https://www.loc.gov/pictures/resource/cph.3g07917/ (accessed November 13, 2017); Ferris, *Edible South*, 129.

20. Wallach, *How America Eats*, 156; Ferris, *Edible South*, 128–29.

21. Ferris, *Edible South*, 127.

22. Mullendore, *United States Food Administration*, 116.

23. Wallach, *How America Eats*, 155; U.S. Food Administration, *Annual Report*, 197–98.

24. Beardsley, *History of Neglect*, 54–58; Hardeman, *Shucks*, 149–50.

25. Taylor, *Eating, Drinking, and Visiting*, 145.

26. Study cited in Beardsley, *History of Neglect*, 18.

27. Levenstein, *Revolution at the Table*, 145; Bentley, *Eating for Victory*, 20–21.

28. Levenstein, *Revolution at the Table*, 137–46.

29. Levenstein, 145.

30. B. C. Pickens to Hamp Williams, February 20, 1918, U.S. Food Administration Records, , box 1, folder P, National Archives, Fort Worth.

31. Veit, *Modern Food*, 23.

32. Du Bois, "Food."

33. Du Bois, 165.

34. C. Wilson, "Cornbread," 152–54; C. Wilson, "Biscuits," 122–25; Taylor and Edge, "Southern Foodways," 1–13; Ferris, *Edible South*, 128.

35. Engelhardt, *Mess of Greens*, 52.

36. Veit, *Modern Food*, 110.

37. "Rev. Turpeau's Statistics," *Washington Bee*, January 26, 1918, 1.

38. "Rag-Time Doin's," *Topeka Plaindealer*, March 7, 1902.

39. "Farm and Garden: Money in Melons," *BAA*, April 29, 1905, 3.

40. Dirks and Duran, "African American Dietary Patterns."

41. "Negroes and Their Food," Margaret Mead Papers, box 25, folder 11, Library of Congress, Manuscript Division, Washington, D.C.

42. "Hoecake and Corn Dodgers," *Richmond Dispatch*, October 31, 1897, 4.

43. "Breakfast Dainties," *Washington Bee*, October 10, 1907, 2.

44. "Talk: Chinese Bread," *BAA*, October 22, 1904, 3; "Household Talks: System in Housekeeping," *BAA*, March 18, 1905, 3; "Johnny Cake's Name," *BAA*, July 9, 1911, 5.

45. Editorial, *Indianapolis Freeman*, May 2, 1914, 4.

46. "Cornbread and Biscuit . . . ," *Indianapolis Freeman*, December 19, 1896.

47. For example, the menu for a meeting of the Negro Democratic Union in 1937 featured roast chicken and dressing, dredged potatoes, creamed peas, fruit, salad, radishes, rolls, corn bread, butter, and pie. See "'Demo' Union Holds Regular Meeting," *Kansas City Plaindealer*, May 7, 1937, 5. See also "Woman's Column," *Philadelphia Tribune*, February 27, 1915, 2; Marian Parker, "Home and Kitchen Suggestions: The Secret of

Making Good Biscuits," *Norfolk (Va.) New Journal and Guide*, June 4, 1927; and "For the Cook to Try: Recipes That Offer Agreeable Variety for Summer," *CD*, July 22, 1911, 7.

48. See, for example, "A Pre-nuptial Announcement," *CD*, October 14, 1911, 1; "Pythians Hold Demonstration: St. James Lodge Gives a Swell Banquet and Reception," *BAA*, May 8, 1909, 4; "About the City," *BAA*, April 16, 1910, 8; and "Mr. Genf Howard Has Birthday Surprise," *CD*, February 17, 1912, 1.

49. Untitled document, USFA-NPS, box 590, folder "Releases, Negro Press."

50. Press release, USFA-NPS, box 589, folder "Press Releases"; "The Woman's World: Food Administration," *Philadelphia Tribune*, February 16, 1918, 2.

51. Veit, *Modern Food*, 110–11.

52. "*The Blue Grass Cook Book* by Minnie C. Fox," *New Orleans Times-Picayune*, April 21, 1918, 46.

53. Newspaper clippings, USFA-NPS, box 590, folder "Loose Newspaper Clippings."

54. Veit, *Modern Food*, 101–2.

55. Lloyd Harrison, *Corn—the Food of the Nation*, lithograph, 1918, Prints and Photographs Division, Library of Congress, Washington, D.C., http://www.loc.gov/pictures/item/2002711987/ (accessed November 13, 2017).

56. Lynch, *"Win the War" Cookbook*, 43, 105.

57. W. E. B. Du Bois, "Segregation," *Crisis*, January 1934, 20.

58. Lewis, *W. E. B. Du Bois*, 300.

59. Moore, *Booker T. Washington*, 117.

60. Harlan, *Wizard of Tuskegee*, 439.

61. Harlan, 438–40; "An Account of the First Meeting of the National Conference on Race Betterment," *Battle Creek Idea* 7 (1914): 12.

62. Du Bois, "Forum of Fact and Opinion: The Group," *Pittsburgh Courier*, May 22, 1937, 11.

63. Du Bois, *Economic Co-operation*, 10.

64. Du Bois to Burt M. Roddy, March 6, 1918, DBP, mums312-b012-i402.

65. Du Bois, "Forum of Fact and Opinion: Co-operation Without," *Pittsburgh Courier*, June 12, 1936, 11. For more information about Du Bois and economic cooperation, see Carreiro, "Consumers' Cooperation."

66. Nembhard, *Collective Courage*.

67. George Schuyler, "An Appeal to Young Negroes," Ella Baker Papers box 2, folder 2, Schomburg Center for Research in Black Culture, New York Public Library.

68. Ransby, *Ella Baker*, 82.

69. Quoted in Ransby, 84.

70. Nembhard, *Collective Courage*, 113.

71. Ferguson, *Sage of Sugar Hill*, 122.

72. Ella Baker, "A Penny a Day for Economic Security," Ella Baker Papers, box 2, folder 3.

73. Ransby, *Ella Baker*, 85.

74. Ransby, 91–94.

75. "Four Million Dozens of Eggs," *Philadelphia Tribune*, June 4, 1936, 4.

76. "Race Owns Stores," *CD*, July 13, 1935, 3; "First Chain Store Unit Organized," *Atlanta Daily World*, March 9, 1934, 1; Clarence Jackson Jr., "Consumers' Cooperative Store Opens," *Philadelphia Tribune*, October 31, 1935, 1; "Capital Launches First Consumers'

Cooperative Group," *BAA*, December 5, 1936, 8; "The Richmond Cooperative," *Norfolk New Journal and Guide*, October 29, 1938, 8.

77. "Dunbar Co-op Sells 100,000 Quarts of Milk," *Atlanta Daily World*, June 26, 1937, 8.

78. Nembhard, *Collective Courage*, 133; "Harlem's Own Cooperative, Inc.," Ella Baker Papers,, box 2, folder 6.

79. "Buffalo's Cooperative Store Successful; Whites Astonished," *Norfolk New Journal and Guide*, September 26, 1931, 3.

80. "A Notable Economic Experiment," *Norfolk New Journal and Guide*, May 14, 1932, 7.

81. "For Grocery Store Owners," *Atlanta Daily World*, June 10, 1932, 6.

82. "Buying Club in Philly Does Big Business," *Pittsburgh Courier*, February 6, 1932, 3.

83. Beulah Young, "Detroit Housewives Use the System of Cooperative Buying," *Philadelphia Tribune*, September 24, 1931, 5; "Consumer Cooperatives Urged as Best Bet for American Negroes: Chicago Co-op Leaders Reveal Club Findings," *Atlanta Daily World*, July 20, 1942, 1.

84. "Mississippi Farmers Save by Co-Operative Marketing," *CD*, July 19, 1930, 4.

85. Moye, *Ella Baker*, 35.

86. Moye, 36; Ransby, *Ella Baker*, 89–90.

CHAPTER 6

1. De Knight, *Date with a Dish*, xiii. For an excellent analysis of De Knight's cookbook, see Katharina Vester, "*Date with a Dish*."

2. For an explication of the phrase "classical phase of the civil rights movement," see Hall, "Long Civil Rights Movement," 1234.

3. De Knight, *Date with a Dish*, xiv.

4. Van Deburg, *New Day in Babylon*, 203–4.

5. Russell, *Domestic Cook Book*, 5.

6. Charles Gayarré, "A Louisiana Sugar Plantation of the Old Régime," *Harper's*, March 1887, 606–21.

7. Russell, *Domestic Cook Book*, 22–23.

8. Russell, 7, 15, 23, 24.

9. Molly O'Neill, "A 19th Century Ghost Awakens to Redefine Soul," *New York Times*, November 21, 2007.

10. Russell, *Domestic Cook Book*, 5

11. Bill Daley, "Pioneer Shared 'Old Southern Cooking,'" *Chicago Tribune*, June 19, 2013; A. Fisher, *What Mrs. Fisher Knows*, 50.

12. A. Fisher, *What Mrs. Fisher Knows*, 28, 138, 144.

13. A. Fisher, 9, 41, 42, 76.

14. A. Fisher, 50.

15. Estes, *Good Things to Eat*, 19.

16. Estes, 40–41.

17. Estes, 58, 68, 85.

18. Montana Federation of Negro Women's Clubs, *Cook Book*, 8–9. The "southern" recipes are for a "Southern Pound Cake" and for "Southern Fried Chicken." The Mexican ones are for "Mexican Patties," made with veal, salt pork, green peppers, onion, and tomatoes, and for a "Mexican Sauce," made with peppers and tomatoes.

19. "Household Notes: Watercress Sandwiches," *BAA*, November 7, 1908; "Corn and Rice Pone," *BAA*, April 26, 1918, 7.

20. Dirks and Duran, "African American Dietary Patterns," 1881.

21. Dirks and Duran, 1881–89; see also Dirks, "African Americans and Soul Food."

22. For evidence of "hog and hominy"–based diets, see especially Atwater and Woods, *Dietary Studies*; and Frissell and Bevier, *Negroes in Eastern Virginia*. For evidence of more diversity, see Richards and Shapleigh, "Dietary Studies."

23. Dirks and Duran, "African American Dietary Patterns," 1887. See also Horowitz, *Putting Meat on the America Table*.

24. Dirks and Duran, "African American Dietary Patterns," 1887.

25. Dirks and Duran, 1887.

26. Dirks and Duran, 1886. Some of the data about dietary patterns was collected from the Institute for Colored Youth in Philadelphia. Obviously, these students did not have the same level of control over their dietary choices as others, a fact that adds an additional complication to the task of making generalizations about food preferences.

27. "Negroes and their Food," Margaret Mead Papers, box 125, folder 11.

28. "Negroes and their Food," box 127.

29. Committee on Food Habits, *Problem of Changing Food Habits*, 102.

30. Hughes, "Simple's Christmas Wish."

31. Hughes, "Simple Says."

32. Baker, "Bigger Than a Hamburger," 120.

33. Baker, 121.

34. Andy Warhol, *Green Coca Cola Bottles*, 1962, acrylic, screenprint, and graphite pencil on canvas, Whitney Museum of American Art, http://collection.whitney.org/object/3253, (accessed November 13, 2017).

35. Pendergrast, *For God, Country, and Coca-Cola*, 8; see also Elmore, *Citizen Coke*.

36. Weiner, "Democracy."

37. Coca-Cola Company, "Our Story."

38. Ozersky, *Hamburger*, 2.

39. De Knight, *Date with a Dish*, 326–27.

40. Andy Warhol, *Hamburger*, 1985–1986, acrylic paint and silkscreen on two canvases, Tate National Galleries of Scotland, http://www.tate.org.uk/art/artworks/warhol-hamburger-ar00233 (accessed November 13, 2017); Leth, "Andy Warhol Eating."

41. Gross, *Forbes*, 176–93.

42. J. Farmer, *Lay Bare the Heart*, 31–32.

43. "Just Take Me to Jail."

44. Lewis and D'Orso, *Walking with the Wind*, 4.

45. W. Brown, *Colin Powell*, 35.

46. Holsaert et al., *Hands on the Freedom Plow*, 498.

47. Holsaert et al., 499.

48. Carmichael and Thelwell, *Ready for Revolution*, 530.

49. Althea Smith, "A Farewell to Chitterlings: Vegetarianism Is on the Rise among Diet Conscious Blacks," *Ebony*, September 1974, 112.

50. The literature about the ideological transformations of civil rights activists is extensive. As a starting point, see Joseph, *Waiting 'til the Midnight Hour*.

51. Van Deburg, *New Day in Babylon*, 195.

52. Stanonis, "Feast of the Mau Mau," 94.

53. "Wrinkles Top Scarf Where Hank Ballard Is Concerned," *Pittsburgh Courier*, May 2, 1961, A23.

54. Gertrude Gibson, "Candid Comments," *Los Angeles Sentinel*, December 29, 1960, A15.

55. J. Gillison, "They Call It 'Soul' Music: 'Down Home' Jazz Feeling Scoring a 'Swinging' Hot with the Public," *Philadelphia Tribune*, May 16, 1961.

56. Masco Young, "Philly after Dark," *Philadelphia Tribune*, March 25, 1961, 5.

57. Masco Young, "If You Don't Dig 'Soul Jive,'" *Cleveland Call and Post*, April 15, 1961, 7.

58. Craig Claiborne, "Cooking with Soul," *New York Times*, November 3, 1968.

59. Jones/Baraka, "Soul Food," *Home: Social Essays*, 121–23.

60. "Off the Main Stem," *Philadelphia Tribune*, December 6, 1960, 5.

61. "Soul Food Moves Downtown," *Sepia*, May 1969, 46–49.

62. "Through the Looking Glass with Cookie," *Sacramento Observer*, February 25, 1969, 25.

63. Gates, *Colored People*, 38, 18.

64. Hughes, *Best of Simple*, 200–201. For a more detailed discussion of the role of food in the Simple/Semple stories, see Williams-Forson, *Building Houses*, 100–105.

65. Hughes, *Best of Simple*, 122.

66. Hughes, 126.

67. Freedman, *Ten Restaurants*, 279.

68. Carol Barnett interviewed by Ray Allen, April 8, 1993, African-American Migration and Southern Folkways Oral History Project.

69. Since the concept of "soul food" is a product of the 1960s, it is anachronistic to refer to black food expression prior to that time period as "soul food." Although this is a common convention in much food writing, it distorts the way that generations of black eaters thought about their dietary habits.

70. Vester, *"Date with a Dish,"* 52–53. For other thoughtful discussions of "soul food," see Williams-Forson, "Take the Chicken Out"; Piatti-Farnell, *Food and Culture*; Palmie, "Intangible Cultural Property," 57; and J. Harris, *High on the Hog*, 208.

71. Hobsbawm, "Introduction," 4.

72. Hobsbawm, 2.

73. A. Miller, *Soul Food*, 4.

74. Quoted in Denise Gee, "The Gospel of Great Southern Food," *Southern Living*, June 1996, 126–28.

75. "Berkeley Board of Education Plans Soul Food Menu," *Oakland Post*, October 23, 1968, 16.

76. "Marin Co-op Staged Black Spectacular," *Oakland Post*, April 10, 1969, 11; "Black Culture Day Set," *Oakland Post*, April 30, 1970, 1; "International Cooking School," *San Francisco Sun Reporter*, March 15, 1969, 17; "YWCA Horoscope for 1970," *San Francisco Sun Reporter*, January 10, 1970, 16.

77. "Southern Gourmet Cooking Sarah's Forte," *Oakland Post*, August 15, 1973, 6.

78. "Blacks Want Jobs," *San Francisco Sun Reporter*, February 15, 1969, 11.

79. "Berkeley's Longfellow School Had 'Young Black Experience,'" *Oakland Post*, May 5, 1971, 2.

80. "Berkeley Board of Education Plans Soul Food Menu," *Oakland Post*, October 23, 1968, 16.

81. "Soul Food, Eat Hearty," *Oakland Post*, March 31, 1971, 18.

82. Hearon, *Cooking with Soul*, 5.

83. Student Nonviolent Coordinating Committee, "Excerpts from Paper."

84. Jackson and Wishart, *Integrated Cookbook*, 1–2.

85. Quoted in Tipton-Martin, *Jemima Code*, 96.

86. Mother Waddles, *Mother Waddles Soul Food Cookbook*, 20.

87. Grosvenor, "Soul Food," 72.

88. Grosvenor, 72.

89. This was not universally true. In their *Soul Food Cook Book*, Harwood and Callahan specifically acknowledged the European, Native American, and African influences on southern cuisine. See Tipton-Martin, *Jemima Code*, 93.

90. See R. Green, "Mother Corn," 117.

91. Palmie, "Intangible Cultural Property," 57.

92. A. Miller, *Soul Food*, 45.

93. For a history of Sylvia's, see Freedman, *Ten Restaurants*, 251–88.

94. Yentsch, "Excavating the South's African American Food History," 59–60.

CHAPTER 7

1. "Soul Food Moves Downtown," *Sepia*, May 1969, 48.

2. "Through the Looking Glass with Cookie," *Sacramento Observer*, February 27, 1969, 25.

3. Cleaver, *Soul on Ice*, 49.

4. Craig Claiborne, "Cooking with Soul," *New York Times*, November 3, 1968; "Sacramento's the Place to Go for 'Soul Food,'" *Sacramento Observer*, May 8, 1969, 15.

5. Konadu, *View from the East*, xxii.

6. Mendes, *African Heritage Cookbook*, 85.

7. Dorothy Johnson, "Authentic and Meaningful Data," *San Francisco Sun Reporter*, June 10, 1972, 36.

8. Grosvenor, *Vibration Cooking*, xiv.

9. Evelyn Williams, "Travel Report," *San Francisco Sun Reporter*, October 10, 1970, 42.

10. "Black Solidarity Day Activities Planned," *Bay State Banner* (Boston), May 14, 1970, 7.

11. J. Harris, *High on the Hog*, 218.

12. Charles Aikens, "African Cookbook Tempts with Ghana Stew, Punch," *Oakland Post*, May 25, 1972, 9.

13. "Thanksgiving Afro-American Style," *Bay State Banner*, November 30, 1967, 3.

14. For information about US, see S. Brown, *Fighting for US*.

15. Pleck, "Kwanzaa"; Karenga, *Kwanzaa*; Mayes, *Kwanzaa*, 7.

16. Congress of African People, *Kwanza*.

17. Mayes, *Kwanzaa*, 95–96.

18. Opie, *Hog and Hominy*, 155–74.

19. Rickford, "'Kazi Is the Blackest of All,'" 112.

20. Ahidiana Work/Study Center, *Food Guide*, 4.

21. For an analysis of Coca-Cola as a symbol of Americanization, see the previous chapter of this book as well as Weiner, "Democracy."

22. Many recent studies of the civil rights movement have sought to challenge the ideas that the movement ended successfully with the passage of landmark national legislation such as the Civil Rights Act of 1964 and that the activists conceptualized the goals of the movement in identical ways. A useful starting point for examining these perspectives is Joseph, *Waiting 'til the Midnight Hour*.

23. Banet-Weiser, *Authentic*, 137. For other analyses of the sit-ins and their relationship to consumer culture, see L. Cohen, *Consumers' Republic*; and Weems, *Desegregating the Dollar*.

24. Semmes, "Entrepreneur of Health"; Semmes, "Role of African-American Health Beliefs."

25. Semmes, "Role of African-African Health Beliefs," 55.

26. Curtis, "Islamizing the Black Body," 174. The Nation of Islam claimed that the circulation of the newspaper was 650,000 copies a week, a figure that Curtis claims was likely exaggerated, though exact circulation figures cannot be precisely known. See Curtis, *Encyclopedia of Muslim-American History*, 403.

27. Witt, *Black Hunger*, 107.

28. Muhammad, *How to Eat to Live, Book No. 1*, 70.

29. Muhammad, 4–5.

30. Curtis, "Islamizing the Black Body," 169.

31. Clegg, *Original Man*, 115; Curtis, *Black Muslim Religion*, 190. Although the NOI claimed to have about 100,000 members at the organization's peak in the early 1960s, historian Claude Clegg estimates that the figure was probably closer to 20,000. Many more were in sympathy with the organization.

32. Malcolm X, "Afro-American History, 22–23."

33. Muhammad, *How to Eat to Live, Book No. 1*, 2.

34. Malcolm X, "Afro-American History, 22–23."

35. Muhammad, *How to Eat to Live, Book No. 2*, 31, 64.

36. Muhammad, 134.

37. "Get Behind Muhammad's Program," *Muhammad Speaks*, January 21, 1971.

38. Curtis, *Encyclopedia of Muslim-American History*, 89, 403.

39. L. Cohen, *Consumers' Republic*, 371.

40. Student Nonviolent Coordinating Committee, "Annual Report, 1964"; "In Pine Bluff Leaders Call Truce: Dick Gregory Released from Jail," *Student Voice*, February 25, 1964, 1.

41. "Open City Drive Begins," *Student Voice*, January 14, 1964, 3; "Restaurant Chain Integrates," *Student Voice*, January 20, 1964, 2; "Dobbs House Desegregates in Some Southern Cities," *BAA*, January 25, 1964; Gregory and Moses, *Callus on My Soul*, 90–91.

42. Dobbs House menu, 1955, New York Public Library, http://menus.nypl.org/menu_pages/56811 (accessed January 2, 2014).

43. Gregory, *Natural Diet*, 14–15.

44. Gregory, 16; Kay Bourne, "Dick Gregory Campaigns for Human Rights," *Bay State Banner*, October 24, 1968, 1.

45. Fiddes, *Meat*, 65.

46. Gregory, *Natural Diet*, 16.

47. Gregory, 81.

48. Gregory, 10.

49. The guidelines Gregory followed while fasting are detailed in Fulton, *Fasting Primer*.

50. Fulton, *Vegetarianism*, 11.

51. Fulton, 9–10.

52. Jones/Baraka, "Soul Food," *Home: Social Essays*, 121–23.

53. Witt, *Black Hunger*, 30.

54. Opie, *Hog and Hominy*, 159.

55. Baraka, *Autobiography of LeRoi Jones*, 422.

56. Jones/Baraka, "Soul Food," 123; Joseph, *Waiting 'Til the Midnight Hour*, 254–55; Woodard, "Amiri Baraka," 63. Woodard speculates that the vegetarian diet of the Committee for Unified Newark members might also be the result of the influence of the vegetarian Moorish Temple Science movement. Noble Drew Ali established a temple in Newark in 1913.

57. See Baraka, *African Congress*.

58. Imamu Amiri Baraka, "The Political School of Kawaida," in Bracey and Harley, *Black Power Movement, Part I*, reel 1.

59. Baraka, "Political School of Kawaida."

60. Hohle, "The Body and Citizenship," 286.

61. Baraka, "Political School of Kawaida."

62. Fulton, *Vegetarianism*, 12.

63. Levenstein, *Fear of Food*, 145–49. Although my research has not uncovered a statement from a culinary nationalist making this association, the steep increase in sugar consumption in Europe and European colonies beginning in the sixteenth and seventeenth centuries was made possible by slave labor. Thus sugar too was a food item that could be historically linked to slavery. See Mintz, *Sweetness and Power*.

64. Baraka, "Political School of Kawaida."

65. Mumininas, "Mwanamke Mwanahci (The Nationalist Woman)," in Bracey and Harley, *Black Power Movement, Part I*, reel 1, 11.

66. Mumininas, "Mwanamke Mwanahci," 12.

67. Konadu, *View from the East*, xxxii–xxxiv.

68. Uhuru Sasa Shule, daily schedules, reprinted in Konadu, 167.

69. Tkweme, "The Black Experience in Sound."

70. Konadu, *View from the East*, 76–77.

71. Tkweme, "The Black Experience in Sound," 53; Konadu, *View from the East*, 77.

72. Konadu, *View from the East*, 77.

73. Cone and Land, "Resolutions," 274.

74. "The Brotherhood Code," reprinted in Konadu, *View from the East*, 153.

75. C. Williams, *Destruction of Black Civilization*, 54.

76. Amini, *Commonsense Approach to Eating*, 9.

77. Simanga, "Congress of African People," 61.

78. Cone and Land, "Resolutions," 262.

79. Cone and Land, 264.

80. Cone and Land, 265.

81. Cone and Land, 265–66.

82. Mayes, "Holiday of Our Own," 241.

83. For a detailed discussion of this transition, see Frazier, "Congress of African People."

84. Amiri Baraka, "Comments on Resignations of Haki Madhubuti and Jitu Weusi (IPE & The East)," in Bracey and Harley, *Black Power Movement, Part I*, reel 2, 23.

85. Baraka, 24.

86. Baraka, 25.

87. Jennings, *Malcolm X*, 174, 186.

88. Lee (Madhubuti), *From Plan to Planet*, 87.

89. Lee (Madhubuti), 88.

90. Lee (Madhubuti), 88.

91. Judy Klemsrud, "Vegetarianism: Growing Way of Life, Especially among the Young," *New York Times*, March 21, 1975, 43.

92. Maya Pines, "Meatless, Guiltless," *New York Times*, November 24, 1974, 296; William Serrin, "Experts Find the U.S. Diet Rich in Fats, Sugars, and Salts," *New York Times*, June 13, 1980, A18, 122.

93. Belasco, *Appetite for Change*, 27. See also Iacobbo and Iacobbo, *Vegetarian America*.

94. Belasco, *Appetite for Change*, 47.

95. "Medkeba," *CD*, March 9, 1972, 10.

96. Grosvenor, *Vibration Cooking*, xv.

97. "A Look East," *Ebony*, August 1969, 170.

98. Fitzgerald, "Southern Folks' Eating Habits," 20.

99. Gwen P. Harvey, "Watch What You Eat," *Black Ink*, October 1972, 4.

100. Ralph Johnson and Patricia Reed, "What's Wrong with Soul Food?," *Black Collegian*, December 1980/January 1981, 20.

101. Opie, *Hog and Hominy*, 169.

102. Althea Smith, "A Farewell to Chitterlings: Vegetarianism Is on the Rise among Diet Conscious Blacks," *Ebony*, September 1974, 104.

103. See the following works by Florence Somerville in the *CD*: "Where It's At for a Vegetarian," January 11, 1973, 25; "Vegetarian Diets Are Exciting," June 21, 1973, 23; "Trying to Get in Shape? Go on a Vegetable Diet," January 31, 1974, 19; "Meat Strikes Out with Vegetarians," May 18, 1972, 19.

104. Burgess, *Soul to Soul*, 15.

105. Belasco, *Appetite for Change*.

106. Johnston and Baumann define foodscape as "a dynamic social construction that relates food to specific places, people, and meanings." Johnston and Baumann, *Foodies*, 3.

CONCLUSION

1. Kay Greaves, "Sims Spoke at Urban League Dinner," *Oakland Post*, May 5, 1971, 14.

2. Greaves, 14.

BIBLIOGRAPHY

MANUSCRIPT COLLECTIONS

Amherst, Mass.
 University of Massachusetts Library, Special Collections and University Archives
  W. E. B. Du Bois Papers, 1868–1963
Atlanta, Ga.
 Atlanta University Center Archives Research Center
  Neighborhood Union Collection
Cambridge, Mass.
 Schlesinger Library
  Women's Educational and Industrial Union Papers
Fort Worth, Tex.
 National Archives
  United States Food Administration Records
Kansas City, Mo.
 National Archives
  United States Food Administration Records, Negro Press Section
New York, N.Y.
 New York Public Library, Schomburg Center for Research in Black Culture
  African-American Migration and Southern Folkways Oral History Project
  Ella Baker Papers
Tuskegee, Ala.
 Tuskegee University Archives
  Booker T. Washington Papers
  George Washington Carver Collection
  Margaret Murray Washington Notebook
Washington, D.C.
 Library of Congress, Manuscript Division
  Booker T. Washington Papers
  Margaret Mead Papers
  Nannie Helen Burroughs Papers
  National Urban League Papers

PERIODICALS

Atlanta Daily World
Baltimore Afro-American
Battle Creek Idea
Black Collegian
Black Ink
Boston Bay State Banner
Brownies' Book
Cambridge Tribune
Chicago Defender
Chicago Tribune
Christian Recorder
Cleveland Call and Post
Colored American
The Crisis
Ebony
Good Housekeeping Magazine
Harper's
Indianapolis Freeman
Kansas City Advocate
Kansas City Plaindealer
Los Angeles Sentinel
Muhammad Speaks
New England Kitchen Magazine
New Orleans Times-Picayune
New York Amsterdam News
New York Times
Norfolk (Va.) New Journal and Guide
North American Journal of Homeopathy
Oakland Post
Philadelphia Tribune
Pittsburgh Courier
Richmond Dispatch
Sacramento Observer
San Francisco Sun Reporter
Sanitary News
Sepia
Southern Living
Student Voice
Topeka Plaindealer
Tuskegee Student
Washington Bee

Abel, Mary Hinman. *Practical Sanitary and Economic Cooking Adapted for Persons of Moderate and Small Means.* Rochester, N.Y.: E. R. Andrews, 1889.

Addams, Jane. *Twenty Years at Hull House.* 1910. New York: Signet, 1999.

Ahidiana Work Study Center. *A Food Guide for Afrikan People.* New Orleans: Ahidiana Work Study Center, 1973.

Amini, Johari A. *Commonsense Approach to Eating: The Need to Become a Vegetarian.* Chicago: Institute for Positive Education, 1972.

Atkinson, Anna J. "Atlanta University: Student Dietaries." *New England Kitchen Magazine,* July 1896, 162.

Atkinson, Edward. *The Science of Nutrition.* Boston: Damrell and Upton, 1896.

Atwater W. O., and Chas. D. Woods. *Dietary Studies with Reference to the Food of the Negro in Alabama, 1895 and 1896.* Washington, D.C.: Government Printing Office, 1897.

Avery, W. S. *The Dyspeptics Monitor.* New York: E. Bliss, 1830.

Baker, Ella. "Bigger Than a Hamburger." In *The Eyes on the Prize Civil Rights Reader,* edited by Clayborne Carson et al., 120–22. New York: Penguin Books, 1991.

Baraka, Amiri (LeRoi Jones). *The Autobiography of LeRoi Jones.* Chicago: Lawrence Hill Books, 1984.

———, ed. *African Congress: A Documentary of the First Modern Pan-African Congress.* New York: Morrow, 1972.

Bracey, John H., Jr., and Sharon Harley, eds. *The Black Power Movement, Part I: Amiri Baraka from Black Arts to Black Radicalism.* Bethesda, Md.: University Publications of America, 2001.

Brillat-Savarin, Jean Anthelme. *The Physiology of Taste: Or, Meditations on Transcendental Gastronomy.* 1825. Translated by M. F. K. Fisher. Berkeley, Calif.: Counterpoint, 2000.

Brown, Charlotte Hawkins. *"Mammy": An Appeal to the Heart of the South and the Correct Thing to Do—To Say—To Wear.* 1919 and 1941. New York: G. K. Hall, 1995.

Bruce, Roscoe Conkling. "The Tuskegee Institute." In *From Servitude to Service,* edited by the Boston American Unitarian Association, 81–114. Cambridge, Mass.: University Press, 1905.

Burgess, Mary Keyes. *Soul to Soul: A Soul Food Vegetarian Cookbook.* Santa Barbara, Calif.: Woodbridge Press, 1976.

Campbell, Thomas Monroe. *The Moveable School Goes to the Negro Farmer.* New York: Arno Press and The New York Times, 1969.

Carmichael, Stokely, with Ekwueme Michael Thelwell. *Ready for Revolution: The Life and Struggles of Stokely Carmichael (Kwame Ture).* New York: Scribner's, 2005.

Chambers, Thomas King. *The Indigestions of Diseases of the Digestive Organs Successfully Treated.* London: John Churchill, 1867.

Chicago Commission on Race Relations. *The Negro in Chicago: A Study of Race Relations and a Race Riot.* Chicago: University of Chicago Press, 1922.

Cleaver, Eldridge. *Soul on Ice.* New York: Delta Trade Paperbacks, 1999.

Coca-Cola Company. "Our Story: Going Global." http://www.coca-cola.co.uk/stories/our-story-1960-1981--going-global. Accessed November 13, 2017.

Committee on Food Habits. *The Problem of Changing Food Habits: Report on the Committee on Food Habits, 1941–1943.* Washington, D.C.: National Research Council, 1943.

Cone, James, and Bill Land. "Resolutions." In *African Congress: A Documentary of the First Modern Pan-African Congress*, edited by Amiri Baraka, 262–75. New York: Morrow, 1972.

Congress of African People. *Kwanza: The First Fruits, an African Holiday*. Chicago: Institute of Positive Education, 1972.

Davis, Allison, Burleigh B. Gardner, and Mary R. Gardner. *Deep South: A Social Anthropological Study of Caste and Class*. 1941. Columbia: University of South Carolina Press, 2009.

DeKnight, Freda. *A Date with a Dish: A Cook Book of American Negro Recipes*. New York: Hermitage Press, 1948.

Delany, Sarah A., and A. Elizabeth Delany with Amy Hill Hearth. *Having Our Say: The Delany Sisters' First 100 Years*. New York: Dell, 1994.

Dickson, Maxcy Robson. *The Food Front in World War I*. Washington, D.C.: American Council on Public Affairs, 1944.

Drake, St. Clair, and Horace Cayton, *Black Metropolis: A Study of Negro Life in a Northern City*. 1945. Chicago: University of Chicago Press, 1993.

Du Bois, W. E. B. *Against Racism: Unpublished Essays, Papers, and Addresses, 1867–1961*. Amherst: University of Massachusetts Press, 1988.

———. "Close Ranks." *The Crisis*, July 1918, 111.

———. "Food." *The Crisis*, August 1918, 165.

———. *The Philadelphia Negro*. 1899. New York: Schocken Books, 1967.

———. *The Quest of the Silver Fleece*. Chicago: A. C. McClurg, 1911.

———. Review of *Race Traits and Tendencies of the American Negro*, by Frederick L. Hoffman. *Annals of the American Academy of Political and Social Science* 9 (January 1897): 127–33.

———. *The Souls of Black Folk*. 1903. New York: Bantam, 1989.

———. "The Talented Tenth." September 1903. TeachingAmericanHistory.org. http://teachingamericanhistory.org/library/document/the-talented-tenth/. Accessed November 13, 2017.

———, ed. *The College-Bred Negro*. Atlanta: Atlanta University Press, 1900.

———. *Economic Co-operation among Negro Americans*. Atlanta: Atlanta University Press, 1907.

———. *Efforts for Social Betterment among Negro Americans*. Atlanta: Atlanta University Press, 1909.

———. *The Health and Physique of the Negro America*. Atlanta: Atlanta University Press, 1906.

———. *The Negro American Family*. Atlanta: Atlanta University Press, 1908.

Duncan, T. C. *How to Be Plump: Or Talks on Physiological Feeding*. Chicago: Duncan Brothers, 1878.

Ellis, Pearl Idelia. *Americanization through Homemaking*. Los Angeles: Wetzel, 1929.

Estes, Rufus. *Rufus Estes' Good Things to Eat*. 1911. Mineola, N.Y.: Dover, 2004.

Farmer, Fannie. *The Boston Cooking-School Cook Book*. Boston: Little Brown, 1917.

Farmer, James. *Lay Bare the Heart: An Autobiography of the Civil Rights Movement*. Fort Worth: Texas Christian University Press, 1998.

Fisher, Abby. *What Mrs. Fisher Knows about Old Southern Cooking, Soups, Pickles, Preserves, Etc.* San Francisco: Women's Cooperative Printing Office, 1881.

Frissell, H. B., and Isabel Bevier. *Dietary Studies of Negroes in Eastern Virginia in 1897 and 1898*. Washington, D.C.: Government Printing Office, 1899.

Fulton, Alvenia M. *The Fasting Primer: The Book That Tells You What You Always Wanted to Know about Fasting*. Chicago: B. C. A. Publishing, 1978.

———. *Vegetarianism: Fact or Myth? Eating to Live*. Chicago: B. C. A. Publishing, 1978.

Gant, Samuel Goodwin. *Constipation, Obstipation, and Intestinal Stasis*. Philadelphia: W. B. Saunders, 1916.

Gates, Henry Louis, Jr. *Colored People: A Memoir*. New York: Vintage, 1995.

Gillette, Mrs. F. L., and Hugo Ziemann. *The White House Cookbook*. Washington, D.C., 1887.

Graham, Sylvester. *A Treatise on Bread and Bread-Making*. Boston: Light and Stearns, 1837.

Green, Edward S. *National Capital Code of Etiquette*. Washington, D.C.: Austin Jenkins, 1920.

Gregory, Dick. *Dick Gregory's Natural Diet for Folks Who Eat: Cookin' with Mother Nature*. New York: Harper and Row, 1973.

Gregory, Dick, and Shelia P. Moses. *Callus on My Soul: A Memoir*. Atlanta: Longstreet Press, 2000.

Hackley, E. Azalia. *The Colored Girl Beautiful*. Kansas City: Burton, 1916.

Harlan, Louis R., ed. *The Booker T. Washington Papers*. Vol. 3. Urbana: University of Illinois Press, 1974.

———. *The Booker T. Washington Papers*. Vol. 4. Chicago: University of Illinois Press, 1975.

Harlan, Louis R. and Raymond W. Smock, eds. *The Booker T. Washington Papers*. Vol. 5. Urbana: University of Illinois Press, 1976.

———. *The Booker T. Washington Papers*. Vol. 6. Urbana: University of Illinois Press, 1977.

———. *The Booker T. Washington Papers*. Vol. 9. Urbana: University of Illinois Press, 1980.

———. *The Booker T. Washington Papers*. Vol. 10. Urbana: University of Illinois Press, 1981.

———. *The Booker T. Washington Papers*. Vol. 11. Urbana: University of Illinois Press, 1981.

———. *The Booker T. Washington Papers*. Vol. 12. Urbana: University of Illinois Press, 1982.

———. *The Booker T. Washington Papers*. Vol. 13. Urbana: University of Illinois Press, 1984.

Harwood, Jim, and Ed Callahan. *Soul Food Cook Book*. San Francisco: Nitty Gritty Publications, 1972.

Hastings, Milo. *Physical Culture Food Directory: A Rating of Foods for Vitality, Growth, Reduction and Energy and for the Prevention of Constipation*. New York: MacFadden, 1929.

Hearon, Ethel Brown. *Cooking with Soul: Favorite Recipes of Negro Homemakers*. Milwaukee: Rufus King High School, 1968.

Hobbs, Frank, and Nicole Stoops. "Demographic Trends in the Twentieth Century." U.S. Census Bureau, 2002. https://www.census.gov/prod/2002pubs/censr-4.pdf. Accessed November 13, 2017.

Hoffman, Frederick L. *The Race Traits and Tendencies of the American Negro*. New York: Macmillan, 1896.

Holsaert, Faith S., Martha Prescod Norman Noonan, Judy Richardson, Betty Garman Robinson, Jean Smith Young, and Dorothy M. Zellner, eds. *Hands on the Freedom Plow: Personal Accounts by Women in SNCC*. Champaign-Urbana: University of Illinois Press, 2012.

Hornibrook, Ettie A. *Stand Up and Slim Down*. New York: Doubleday, 1934.

Hughes, Langston. *The Best of Simple*. New York: Hill and Wang, 1990.

———. *Not without Laughter*. 1930. New York: Dover, 2008.

———. "Simple Says for Thanksgiving There Are Some Things Better than Turkey." *Chicago Defender*, November 26, 1949, 6.

———. "Simple's Christmas Wish." *Chicago Defender*, December 22, 1945, 12.

———. *The Ways of White Folks*. New York: Vintage, 1990.

Jackson, Mary, and Lelia Wishart. *The Integrated Cookbook: Or, the Soul of Good Cooking*. Chicago: Johnson, 1971.

Jones, LeRoi (Amiri Baraka). *Home: Social Essays*. 1966. New York: Akashi Classics, 2009.

"Just Take Me to Jail: Remembering Muhammad Ali's Refusal to Fight in Vietnam." June 6, 2016. Democracy Now! https://www.democracynow.org/2016/6/6/just_take_me_to_jail_remembering. Accessed November 13, 2017.

Karenga, Maulena. *Kwanzaa: A Celebration of Family, Community, and Culture*. Los Angeles: University of Sankore Press, 1998.

Kellogg, John Harvey. *Autointoxication of Intestinal Toxemia*. Battle Creek, Mich.: Modern Medicine, 1919.

———. *The Itinerary of a Breakfast*. Battle Creek, Mich.: Modern Medicine, 1918.

———. *The Miracle of Life*. Battle Creek, Mich.: Good Health, 1904.

Lee, Don L. (Haki Madhubuti). *From Plan to Planet: Life Studies: The Need for Afrikan Minds and Institutions*. Detroit: Broadside, 1973.

Leth, Jørgen, dir. "Andy Warhol Eating a Hamburger, 1981." In *66 Scenes from America*, 1982. Art Babble. http://www.artbabble.org/video/louisiana/j-rgen-leth-andy-warhol-eating-a-hamburger. Accessed November 13, 2017.

Lewis, John, and Michael D'Orso. *Walking with the Wind: A Memoir of the Movement*. New York: Mariner Books, 1999.

Life Extension Examiners. *Life Extension Examiners Life Extension Institute Fortieth Anniversary, 1914–1954*. Pamphlet, 1954. Truth Tobacco Industry Documents, University of California at San Francisco Library. https://industrydocuments.library.ucsf.edu/tobacco/docs/#id=lsbd0124. Accessed November 13, 2017.

Lincoln, Mary J., Sarah Tyson Rorer, Lida Ames Willis, Helen Armstrong, and Marion Harland. *Home Helps: A Pure Food Cookbook*. Chicago: N. K. Fairbank, 1910.

Logan, Warren. "Resources and Material Equipment." In *Tuskegee and Its People*, edited by Booker T. Washington, 35–55. New York: D. Appleton, 1905.

Lowe, Edna Eugenia. *Health Rules and Danger Signals*. New Hampton, Iowa: Edna Eugenia Lewis, 1919.

Lynch, Reah Jeannette. *"Win the War" Cookbook*. St. Louis, Mo.: St. Louis Unit of the Women's Committee of the National Council for Defense, 1918.

Malcolm X. "Afro-American History." *International Socialist Review* 28 (March–April 1967): 3–48.

McKay, Claude. *Home to Harlem*. New York: Harper, 1928.

Mendes, Helen. *The African Heritage Cookbook*. New York: Macmillan, 1971.

Miller, J. F. "The Effects of Emancipation upon the Mental and Physical Health of the Negro of the South." Paper read before the Southern Medico-Psychological Association, Asheville, N.C., September 16, 1896. http://docsouth.unc.edu/nc/miller/miller.html. Accessed November 13, 2017.

Montana Federation of Negro Women's Clubs. *Montana Federation of Negro Women's Clubs Cook Book*. Billings: Montana Federation of Women's Clubs, 1926.

Mother Waddles. *The Mother Waddles Soul Food Cookbook*. Detroit: Perpetual Soul Saving Mission for All Nations, 1970.

Muhammad, Elijah. *How to Eat to Live, Book No. 1*. Phoenix: Secretarious MEMPS Publications, 1967.

———. *How to Eat to Live, Book No. 2*. Phoenix: Secretarious MEMPS Publications, 1972.

New England Cotton Manufacturers' Association. *Transactions of the New England Cotton Manufacturers' Association*. Waltham, Mass.: E. L. Barry, 1903.

Nootnagel, Charles. "General Considerations of the Stomach." *Medical Brief: A Monthly Journal of Scientific Medicine and Surgery* 35 (1907): 287–92.

Peters, Lulu Hunt. *Diet and Health with Key to the Calories*. Chicago: Reilly and Lee, 1918.

Pierce, Paul. *Dinners and Luncheons: Novel Suggestions for Social Occasions*. Chicago: Brewer, Barse, 1907.

Remondino, P. C. "Questions of the Day: The Stomach and Dyspepsia or the Lady and the Tiger." In *National Popular Review: An Illustrated Journal of Preventative Medicine and Applied Sociology*, March 1893, 113–25.

Richards, Ellen H. *Euthenics: The Science of Controllable Environment*. Boston: Whitcomb and Barrows, 1912.

Richards, Ellen H., and A. Shapleigh. "Dietary Studies in Philadelphia and Chicago, 1892–93." In *Dietary Studies in Boston and Springfield, Mass., Philadelphia, Pa., and Chicago, Ill.*, edited by R. D. Milner, 37–98. Washington, D.C.: Government Printing Office, 1903.

Riis, Jacob. *The Battle with the Slum*. New York: Macmillan, 1902.

———. *How the Other Half Lives: Studies among the Tenements of New York*. New York: Charles Scribner's Sons, 1890.

Russell, Malinda. *Domestic Cook Book: Containing a Careful Selection of Useful Recipes for the Kitchen*. 1866. Ann Arbor, Mich.: William L. Clements Library, 2007.

Scott, Emmett J. *Scott's Official History of the American Negro in the World War*. Washington, D.C., 1919.

Smart-Grosvenor, Vertamae Smart. "Soul Food." *McCall's*, September 1970, 72–75.

———. *Vibration Cooking: Or the Travel Notes of a Geechee Girl*. New York: Doubleday, 1970.

Student Nonviolent Coordinating Committee. "Annual Report, 1964." In *Arsnick: The Student Nonviolent Coordinating Committee in Arkansas*, edited by Jennifer Jensen Wallach and John A. Kirk, 200. Fayetteville: University of Arkansas Press, 2011.

———. "Excerpts from Paper on which 'Black Power' Philosophy Is Based." *New York Times*, August 5, 1966, 10.

Terrell, Mary Church. *A Colored Woman in a White World*. New York: G. K. Hall, 1996.

"Toddle House Menu." *Memphis Magazine*, November 2010. http://www.memphismagazine.com/November-2010/Toddle-House/. Accessed January 2, 2014.

Tuskegee Institute. *Tuskegee Institute Catalogue, 1909–1910*. Tuskegee, Ala.: Tuskegee Institute, 1909.

U.S. Census Bureau. "The Great Migration, 1910–1970." September 13, 2012. https://www.census.gov/dataviz/visualizations/020/. Accessed November 13, 2017.

U.S. Food Administration. *Annual Report of the United States Food Administration for the Year 1918*. Washington, D.C.: Government Printing Office, 1919.

Washington, Booker T. "Negro Homes." *Colored American Magazine*, September 1902. Reprinted in *Booker T. Washington Rediscovered*, edited by Michael Scott Bieze and Marybeth Gasman, 153. Baltimore: Johns Hopkins University Press, 2012.

———. "Twenty-Five Years of Tuskegee." *World's Work*, April 1906, 7433–50.

———. *Up from Slavery*. New York: Doubleday, 1901.

———. *Working with the Hands*. New York: Doubleday, 1904.

Washington, Mrs. Booker T. "What Girls Are Taught." In *Tuskegee and Its People*, edited by Booker T. Washington, 68–86. New York: D. Appleton, 1905.

West, Dorothy. *The Living Is Easy*. 1948. New York: Arno Press, 1969.

Whitwell, William S., ed. "Axioms from Dr. George M. Beard's 'Sexual Neurasthenia.'" In *Pacific Medical and Surgical Journal*, 203–4. San Francisco: W. S. Duncombe Publishers, 1885.

Williams, A. Wilberforce. "Obesity." *Chicago Defender*, October 11, 1924, 12.

———. "What to Eat in Cold Weather." *Chicago Defender*, March 11, 1922, 12.

Williams, Chancellor James. *The Destruction of Black Civilization*. 1971. Chicago: Third World Press, 1974.

Wilson, John Stainback. "Over-Eating—Grease—Baths—Hydropathy & etc." In *The Southern Cultivator*, edited by D. Redmond and C. W. Howard, 295. Augusta, Ga: J. W. and J. S. Jones, 1860.

Winter, Terence, creator and writer. *Boardwalk Empire*. Directed by Ed Bianchi. Season 2, Episode 16, "What Does the Bee Do?" Aired October 16, 2011, on HBO.

Women's Educational and Industrial Trade Union. *Bulletin of the Domestic Reform League*. December 1907. http://babel.hathitrust.org/cgi/pt?id=uc1. b3102040;view=1up;seq=14. Accessed November 15, 2017.

Work, Monroe N. *Negro Yearbook: An Annual Encyclopedia of the Negro*. Tuskegee, Ala.: Negro Yearbook, 1914.

SECONDARY SOURCES

Aberjhani and Sandra L. West. *The Encyclopedia of the Harlem Renaissance*. New York: Facts on File, 2003.

Anderson, Benedict. 1983. *Imagined Communities: Reflections on the Origins and Spread of Nationalism*. New York: Verso, 2016.

Anderson, James D. *The Education of Blacks in the South, 1869–1935*. Chapel Hill: University of North Carolina Press, 1988.

Appadurai, Arjun. "How to Make a National Cuisine: Cookbooks in Contemporary India." *Comparative Studies in Society and History* 30, no. 1 (January 1988): 3–24.

Armstrong, Tim. *Modernism, Technology, and the Body: A Cultural Study*. Cambridge: Cambridge University Press, 1998.

Banet-Weiser, Sarah. *Authentic: The Politics of Ambivalence in a Brand Culture*. New York: New York University Press, 2012.

Baynton, Douglas C. "Disability and the Justification of Inequality in American History." In *The New Disability History: American Perspectives*, edited by Paul G. Longmore and Lauri Umansky, 33–57. New York: New York University Press, 2001.

Beardsley, Edward H. *A History of Neglect: Health Care for Blacks and Mill Workers in the Twentieth-Century South*. Knoxville: University of Tennessee Press, 1987.

Bégin, Camille. *Taste of the Nation: The New Deal Search for America's Food.* Urbana: University of Illinois Press, 2016.

Belasco, Warren. *Appetite for Change: How the Counterculture Took On the Food Industry, 1966–1988.* New York: Pantheon Books, 1988.

Bentley, Amy. *Eating for Victory: Food Rationing and the Politics of Domesticity.* Champaign-Urbana: University of Illinois Press, 1998.

Biltekoff, Charlotte. *Eating Right in America: The Cultural Politics of Food and Health.* Durham: Duke University Press, 2013.

Bobrow-Strain, Aaron. *White Bread: A Social History of the Store-Bought Loaf.* Boston: Beacon Press, 2013.

Booker, Christopher B. *"I Will Wear No Chain!": A Social History of African American Males.* Westport, Conn.: Praeger, 2000.

Bordo, Susan. *Feminism, Western Culture, and the Body.* Berkeley: University of California Press, 2004.

Bourdieu, Pierre. *Distinction: A Social Critique of the Judgment of Taste.* London: Routledge, 1984.

Bracey, John H., Jr., August Meier, and Elliot Rudwick. *Black Nationalism in America.* Indianapolis: Bobbs-Merrill, 1970.

Bresnahan, Roger J. "The Implied Readers of Booker T. Washington's Autobiographies." *Black American Literature Forum* 14, no. 1 (Spring 1980): 15–20.

Brown, Christopher M. "The Politics of Industrial Education: Booker T. Washington and Tuskegee State Normal School, 1880–1915." *Negro Educational Review* 50 (July/October 1999): 123–28.

Brown, Nikki. *Private Politics and Public Voice: Black Women's Activism from World War I to the New Deal.* Bloomington: Indiana University Press, 2006.

Brown, Scot. *Fighting for US: Maulena Karenga, the US Organization, and Black Cultural Nationalism.* New York: New York University Press, 2003.

Brown, Warren. *Colin Powell: Soldier and Statesman.* Philadelphia: Chelsea House, 2005.

Brumberg, Joan Jacobs. *Fasting Girls: A History of Anorexia Nervosa.* New York: Vintage Books, 2000.

Brundage, W. Fitzhugh. "Introduction." In *Up from Slavery: With Related Documents,* by Booker T. Washington. Edited by W. Fitzhugh Brundage, 1–35. Boston: Bedford/St. Martin's, 2003.

Carby, Hazel. *Race Men.* Cambridge, Mass.: Harvard University Press, 1998.

Carreiro, Joshua L. "Consumers' Cooperation in the Early Twentieth Century: An Analysis of Race, Class and Consumption." Ph.D. diss., University of Massachusetts, 2015.

Clegg, Claude. *An Original Man: The Life and Times of Elijah Muhammad.* New York: St. Martin's, 1998.

Coclanis, Peter. "What Made Booker Wash(ington)? The Wizard of Tuskegee in Economic Context." In *Booker T. Washington and Black Progress: Up from Slavery 100 Years Later,* edited by W. Fitzhugh Brundage, 81–106. Gainesville: University Press of Florida, 2003.

Cohen, Lizabeth. *A Consumers' Republic: The Politics of Mass Consumption in Postwar America.* New York: Knopf, 2003.

Cohen, Sol. "The Industrial Education Movement, 1906–17." *American Quarterly* 20, no. 1 (1968): 95–110.

Conrad, Peter, and Kristen K. Barker. "The Social Construction of Illness: Key Insights and Policy Implications." *Journal of Health and Social Behavior* 51 (2010): 67–79.

Cooley, Angela Jill. *To Live and Dine in Dixie: The Evolution of Urban Food Culture in the Jim Crow South*. Athens: University of Georgia Press, 2015.

Coombs, Danielle, and Bob Batchelor, eds. *We Are What We Sell: How Advertising Shapes American Life . . . and Always Has*. Santa Barbara: Praeger, 2014.

Covey, Herbert C., and Dwight Eisnach. *What the Slaves Ate: Recollections of African American Foods and Foodways from the Slave Narratives*. Santa Barbara: ABC-Clio, 2009.

Curtis, Edward E., IV. *Black Muslim Religion in the Nation of Islam, 1960–1975*. Chapel Hill: University of North Carolina Press, 2006.

———. "Islamizing the Black Body: Ritual and Power in Elijah Muhammad's Nation of Islam." *Religion and American Culture: A Journal of Interpretation* 12 (Summer 2002): 167–96.

———, ed. *Encyclopedia of Muslim-American History*. New York: Facts on File, 2010.

Davis, Deborah. *Guest of Honor: Booker T. Washington, Theodore Roosevelt, and the White House Dinner That Shocked a Nation*. New York: Atria Books, 2012.

Dirks, Robert. "African Americans and Soul Food." 2016. The Sophie Coe Prize. https://sophiecoeprize.files.wordpress.com/2012/12/dirks-soul-food-chapter1.pdf. Accessed November 16, 2017.

Dirks, Robert T., and Nancy Duran. "African American Dietary Patterns at the Beginning of the 20th Century." *Journal of Nutrition* 31, no. 7 (July 2001): 1881–89.

Downs, Jim. *Sick from Freedom: African American Illness and Suffering during the Civil War and Reconstruction*. Oxford: Oxford University Press, 2012.

Elias, Megan. *Stir It Up: Home Economics in American Culture*. Philadelphia: University of Pennsylvania Press, 2010.

Elias, Norbert. *The Civilizing Process: The History of Manners*. New York: Urizen Books, 1978.

Elmore, Bartow J. *Citizen Coke: The Making of Coca-Cola Capitalism*. New York: W. W. Norton, 2016.

Enck, Henry S. "Tuskegee Institute and Northern White Philanthropy: A Case Study in Fund Raising, 1900–1915." *Journal of Negro History* 65, no. 4 (Autumn 1980): 336–48.

Engelhardt, Elizabeth S. D. *A Mess of Greens: Southern Gender and Southern Food*. Athens: University of Georgia Press, 2011.

Engs, Robert Francis. *Educating the Disfranchised and Disinherited: Samuel Chapman Armstrong and Hampton Institute, 1839–1893*. Knoxville: University of Tennessee Press, 1999.

Ferguson, Jeffrey. *The Sage of Sugar Hill: George S. Schuyler and the Harlem Renaissance*. New Haven: Yale University Press, 2005.

Ferris, Marcie Cohen. *The Edible South: The Power of Food and the Making of an American Region*. Chapel Hill: University of North Carolina Press, 2014.

Fiddes, Nick. *Meat: A Natural Symbol*. London: Routledge, 1991.

Fisher, Claude. "Food, Self, Identity." *Social Science Information* 27, no. 2 (1988): 275–92.

Fitzgerald, Thomas K. "Southern Folks' Eating Habits Ain't What They Used to Be If They Ever Were." *Nutrition Today* 14 (June 1979): 16–21.

Foucault, Michel. *The Birth of the Clinic: An Archaeology of Medical Perception*. Translated by A. M. Sheridan Smith. New York: Pantheon Books, 1973.

Frazier, Robeson Taj P. "The Congress of African People: Baraka, Mao, and the Year of '74." *Souls* 8 (2006): 142–59.

Freedman, Paul. *Ten Restaurants That Changed America*. New York: Liveright, 2016.

Gaines, Kevin. *Uplifting the Race: Black Leadership, Politics, and Culture in the Twentieth Century*. Chapel Hill: University of North Carolina Press, 1993.

Gatewood, Willard. *Aristocrats of Color: The Black Elite, 1880–1920*. Fayetteville: University of Arkansas Press, 2000.

Gerstle, Gary. *American Crucible: Race and Nation in the Twentieth Century*. Princeton: Princeton University Press, 2001.

Gilmore, Glenda. *Gender and Jim Crow: Women and the Politics of White Supremacy in North Carolina, 1896–1920*. Chapel Hill: University of North Carolina Press, 1996.

Goffman, Erving. *The Presentation of Self in Everyday Life*. New York: Doubleday, 1959.

Goings, Kenneth W. *Mammy and Uncle Mose: Black Collectibles and American Stereotyping*. Bloomington: Indiana University Press, 1994.

Green, Rayna. "Mother Corn and the Dixie Pig: Native Food in the Native South." *Southern Cultures* 14 (Winter 2008): 114–26.

Gross, Daniel. *Forbes Greatest Business Stories of All Time*. Hoboken, N.J.: Wiley, 1997.

Hall, Jacquelyn Dowd. "The Long Civil Rights Movement." *Journal of American History* 91 (2005): 1233–63.

Hamilton, Shane. "The Twentieth Century." In *The Routledge History of American Foodways*, edited by Michael D. Wise and Jennifer Jensen Wallach, 48–58. New York: Routledge, 2016.

Hardeman, Nicholas P. *Shucks, Shocks, and Hominy Blocks: Corn as a Way of Life in Pioneer America*. Baton Rouge: Louisiana State University Press, 1981.

Harlan, Louis R. *Booker T. Washington: The Making of a Black Leader, 1856–1901*. New York: Oxford University Press, 1972.

———. *Booker T. Washington: The Wizard of Tuskegee, 1901–1915*. New York: Oxford University Press, 1986.

Harley, Sharon. "For the Good of Family and Race: Gender, Work, and Domestic Roles in the Black Community, 1880–1930." *Signs* 15, no. 2 (1990): 336–49.

Harris, Jessica. *High on the Hog: A Culinary Journey from Africa to America*. New York: Bloomsbury, 2012.

Harris, Violet J. "Race Consciousness, Refinement, and Radicalism: Socialization in *The Brownies' Book*." *Children's Literature* 29 (2001): 91–112.

Haynes, Elizabeth Ross. "Negroes in Domestic Service in the United States." *Journal of Negro History* 8, no. 4 (1923): 384–442.

Heller, John S. *The History of American Homeopathy: The Academic Years, 1840–1935*. Binghamton, N.Y.: Haworth Press, 2005.

Heneghan, Bridget T. *Whitewashing America: Material Culture and Race in the Antebellum Imagination*. Jackson: University Press of Mississippi, 2003.

Herbert, Elizabeth. "Digestive Femininity: Constipation and Womanhood in the Progressive Era." Master's thesis, St. Louis University, 2013.

Hersey, Mark D. *My Work Is That of Conservation: An Environmental Biography of George Washington Carver*. Athens: University of Georgia Press, 2011.

Higginbotham, Evelyn Brooks. *Righteous Discontent: The Women's Movement in the Black Baptist Church, 1880–1920*. Cambridge, Mass.: Harvard University Press, 1992.

Hilliard, Sam Bower. *Hog Meat and Hoecake: Food Supply in the Old South, 1840–1860.* Athens: University of Georgia Press, 2014.

Hobsbawm, Eric. "Introduction: Inventing Traditions." In *The Invention of Tradition,* edited by Eric Hobsbawm and Terrence Ranger, 1–14. Cambridge: Cambridge University Press, 1983.

Hohle, Randolph. "The Body and Citizenship in Social Movement Research: Embodied Performances and the Deracialized Self in the Black Civil Rights Movement, 1961–1965." *Sociological Quarterly* 50 (Spring 2009): 283–307.

Horowitz, Roger. *Putting Meat on the American Table.* Baltimore: Johns Hopkins University Press, 2006.

Hunter, Tera. *To 'Joy My Freedom: Southern Black Women's Lives and Labors after the Civil War.* Cambridge, Mass.: Harvard University Press, 1997.

Iacobbo, Karen, and Michael Iacobbo. *Vegetarian America: A History.* Westport, Conn.: Praeger, 2004.

Ingold, Tim. *The Perception of the Environment: Essays in Livelihood, Dwelling, and Skill.* London: Routledge, 2000.

Jennings, Regina. *Malcolm X and the Poetics of Maki Hadhubuti.* Jefferson, N.C.: McFarland, 2006.

Johnston, Josée, and Shyon Baumann. *Foodies: Democracy and Distinction in the Gourmet Foodscape.* New York: Routledge, 2010.

Joseph, Peniel E. *Waiting 'til the Midnight Hour: A Narrative History of Black Power in America.* New York: Holt, 2007.

Keene, Jennifer D. "Images of Racial Pride: African American Propaganda Posters and the First World War." In *Picture This: World War I Posters and Visual Culture,* edited by Pearl James, 207–40. Lincoln: University of Nebraska Press, 2009.

Knadler, Stephen. "Dis-abled Citizenship: Narrating the Extraordinary Body in Racial Uplift." *Arizona Quarterly: A Journal of American Literature, Culture, and Theory* 69 (Autumn 2013): 99–128.

Konadu, Kwasi. *A View from the East: Black Cultural Nationalism and Education in New York City.* Syracuse: Syracuse University Press, 2009.

Kory, Fern. "Once upon a Time in AfraAmerica: The 'Peculiar' Significance of Fairies in *The Brownies' Book.*" *Children's Literature* 29 (2001): 91–112.

Lakoff, George, and Mark Johnson. *Philosophy in the Flesh: The Embodied Mind and Its Challenge to Western Thought.* New York: Basic Books, 1999.

Lasch-Quinn, Elizabeth. *Black Neighbors: Race and the Limits of Reform in the American Settlement House Movement, 1890–1945.* Chapel Hill: University of North Carolina Press, 1993.

Layson, Hana, and Kenneth Warren. "Chicago and the Great Migration, 1910–1950." Digital collection. Newberry Library. http://dcc.newberry.org/collections/chicago-and-the-great-migration. Accessed November 13, 2017.

Leeds, Maxine Craig, "Racialized Bodies." In *The Routledge Handbook of Body Studies,* edited by Bryan S. Turner, 321–32. New York: Routledge, 2012.

Levenstein, Harvey. *Fear of Food: A History of Why We Worry about What We Eat.* Chicago: University of Chicago Press, 2012.

———. *Revolution at the Table: The Transformation of the American Diet.* Berkeley: University of California Press, 2003.

Lewis, David Levering. *W. E. B. Du Bois: The Fight for Equality and the American Century, 1919–1963*. New York: Henry Holt, 2000.

———. *When Harlem Was in Vogue*. New York: Penguin Books, 1997.

Litwack, Leon. *Been in the Storm So Long: The Aftermath of Slavery*. New York: Vintage, 1980.

Manring, M. M. *A Slave in a Box: The Strange Career of Aunt Jemima*. Charlottesville: University of Virginia Press, 1997.

May, Vanessa. "'Obtaining a Decent Livelihood': Food Work, Race, and Gender in W. E. B. Du Bois's *The Philadelphia Negro*." *Labor: Studies in Working-Class History of the Americas* 12 (2015): 115–26.

Mayes, Keith A. "A Holiday of Our Own: Kwanzaa, Cultural Nationalism, and the Promotion of a Black Power Holiday, 1966–1985." In *The Black Power Movement: Rethinking the Civil Rights–Black Power Era*, edited by Peniel Joseph, 229–50. New York: Routledge, 2006.

———. *Kwanzaa: Black Power and the Making of an African-American Holiday Tradition*. New York: Routledge, 2009.

Meier, August. *Negro Thought in America: 1880–1915*. Ann Arbor: University of Michigan Press, 1988.

Miller, Adrian. *Soul Food: The Surprising Story of an American Cuisine One Plate at a Time*. Chapel Hill: University of North Carolina Press, 2013.

Mintz, Sidney. *Sweetness and Power: The Place of Sugar in Modern History*. New York: Penguin Books, 1985.

Mitchell, Michele. *Righteous Propagation: African Americans and the Politics of Racial Identity after Reconstruction*. Chapel Hill: University of North Carolina Press, 2004.

Mjagkij, Nina. *Loyalty in Time of Trial: The African American Experience during World War I*. Lanham, Md.: Rowman and Littlefield, 2011.

Moore, Jacqueline N. *Booker T. Washington, W. E. B. Du Bois, and the Struggle for Racial Uplift*. Lanham, Md.: Rowman and Littlefield, 2003.

Moses, Wilson Jeremiah. *Classical Black Nationalism: From the American Revolution to Marcus Garvey*. New York: New York University Press, 1996.

Moye, J. Todd. *Ella Baker: Community Organizer of the Civil Rights Movement*. Lanham, Md.: Rowman and Littlefield, 2015.

Mullendore, William Clinton. *History of the United States Food Administration, 1917–1919*. Stanford: Stanford University Press, 1941.

Nembhard, Jessica Gordon. *Collective Courage: A History of African American Cooperative Economic Thought and Practice*. University Park: Pennsylvania State University Press, 2014.

Neverdon-Morton, Cynthia. *Afro-American Women of the South and the Advancement of the Race, 1895–1925*. Knoxville: University of Tennessee Press, 1989.

Nissenbaum, Stephen. *Sex, Diet, and Debility in Jacksonian America: Sylvester Graham and Health Reform*. Westport, Conn.: Greenwood Press, 1980.

Norrell, Robert J. *Up from History: The Life of Booker T. Washington*. Cambridge, Mass.: Belknap Press, 2009.

Opie, Frederick Douglass. *Hog and Hominy: Soul Food from Africa to America*. New York: Columbia University Press, 2010.

Ozersky, Josh. *The Hamburger: A History*. New Haven: Yale University Press, 2009.

Palmie, Stephan. "Intangible Cultural Property, Semiotic Ideology, and the Vagaries of Ethnoculinary Recognition." *African Arts* 42 (Winter 2009): 54–61.

Parker, Alison M. "'The Picture of Health': The Public Life and Private Ailments of Mary Church Terrell." *Journal of Historical Biography* 13 (Spring 2013): 164–207.

Pendergrast, Mark. *For God, Country, and Coca-Cola*. New York: Basic Books, 2013.

Peterson, Patti McGill. "Colonialism and Education: The Case of the Afro-American." *Comparative Education Review* 15, no. 2 (June 1971): 146–57.

Phillips, Michelle H. "The Children of Double Consciousness: From *The Souls of Black Folk* to the *Brownies' Book*." *PMLA* 128 (2013): 590–607.

Piatti-Farnell, Lorna. *Food and Culture in Contemporary American Fiction*. New York: Routledge, 2011.

Pilcher, Jeffrey M. "The Embodied Imagination in Recent Writings in US Food History." *American Historical Review* 121 (June 2016): 861–87.

Pleck, Elizabeth. "Kwanzaa: The Making of a Black Nationalist Tradition, 1966–1990." *Journal of American Ethnic History* 20 (Summer 2001): 3–28.

Poe, Tracy. "African American Meals from Slavery to Soul Food." In *The Meal: Proceedings of the Oxford Symposium on Food and Cookery*, edited by Harlan Walker, 179–90. Devon, Eng.: Prospect Books, 2002.

———. "The Origins of Soul Food in Black Urban Identity: Chicago, 1915–1947." *American Studies International* 37 (February 1999): 4–17.

Porter, Roy. "History of the Body." In *New Perspectives on Historical Writing*, edited by Peter Burke, 206–31. University Park: Pennsylvania State University Press, 1991.

Provenzo, Eugene F. *W. E. B. Du Bois's Exhibit of American Negroes: African Americans at the Beginning of the Twentieth Century*. Lanham, Md.: Rowman and Littlefield, 2013.

Purkiss, Ava. "'Beauty Secrets: Fight Fat': Black Women's Aesthetics, Exercise, and Fat Stigma, 1900–1930s." *Journal of Women's History* 29 (Summer 2017): 14–37.

Ransby, Barbara. *Ella Baker and the Black Freedom Movement: A Radical Democratic Vision*. Chapel Hill: University of North Carolina Press, 2005.

Reid, Debra A. *Reaping a Greater Harvest: African Americans, the Extension Service, and Rural Reform in Jim Crow Texas*. College Station: Texas A&M University Press, 2007.

Rickford, Russell. "'Kazi Is the Blackest of All': Pan-African Nationalism and the Making of the 'New Man.'" *Journal of African American History* 101 (Winter–Spring 2016): 87–125.

Ritterhouse, Jennifer. *Growing Up Jim Crow: How Black and White Children Learned about Race*. Chapel Hill: University of North Carolina Press, 2006.

Robinson, Dean E. *Black Nationalism in American Politics and Thought*. Cambridge: Cambridge University Press, 2001.

Ross, Marlon B. "Aggressive Mobility and Sexual Transgression in the Construction of the New Negro Modernity." In *Modernism, Inc.: Body, Memory, Capitol*, edited by

Rudwick, Elliot M. "W. E. B. Du Bois and the Atlanta University Studies on the Negro." *Journal of Negro Education* 26, no. 4 (Autumn 1957): 466–76.

Salmon, Lucy Maynard. *Domestic Service*. New York: Macmillan, 1901.

Semmes, Clovis. "Entrepreneur of Health: Dick Gregory, Black Consciousness, and the Human Potential of Movement." *Journal of African American Studies* 16 (2012): 537–49.

———. "The Role of African-American Health Beliefs and Practices in Social Movements." *Minority Voices* 6 (1990): 45–57.

Shapiro, Laura. *Perfection Salad: Women and Cooking at the Turn of the Twentieth Century.* Berkeley: University of California Press, 1986.

Sharpless, Rebecca. *Cooking in Other Women's Kitchens.* Chapel Hill: University of North Carolina Press, 2013.

Shaw, Stephanie. *What a Woman Ought to Be and Do: Black Professional Women Workers during the Jim Crow Era.* Chicago: University of Chicago Press, 1996.

Simanga, Michael. "The Congress of African People (1970–1980): History and Memory of an Ideological Journey." Ph.D. diss., Union Institute and University, 2008.

Sinitierre, Phillip Luke. "A Place at the Table: W. E. B. Du Bois, Nature, and Food History." Paper delivered at the University of North Texas Moral Cultures of Food Conference, April 4, 2015.

Slocum, Rachel. "Race in the Study of Food." *Progress in Human Geography* 35, no. 3 (2010): 303–27.

Smith, Alison K. "National Cuisines." In *The Oxford Handbook of Food History*, edited by Jeffrey M. Pilcher, 444–60. New York: Oxford, 2012.

Smith, Katharine Capshaw. "Childhood, the Body, and Race Performance: Early 20th-Century Etiquette Books for Black Children." *African American Review* 40, no. 4 (Winter 2006): 795–811.

Sokolow, Jayme A. *Eros and Modernization: Sylvester Graham, Health Reform, and the Origins of Victorian Sexuality in America.* Rutherford, N.J.: Fairleigh Dickinson University Press, 1983.

Spencer, Colin. *British Food: An Extraordinary Thousand Years of History.* New York: Columbia University Press, 2002.

Spivey, Donald. *Schooling for the New Slavery: Black Industrial Education, 1868–1915.* Westport, Conn.: Praeger, 1978.

Stanonis, Anthony J. "The Feast of the Mau Mau: Christianity, Conjure, and the Origins of Soul Food." In *Dethroning the Deceitful Pork Chop: Rethinking African American Foodways from Slavery to Obama*, edited by Jennifer Jensen Wallach, 93–106. Fayetteville: University of Arkansas Press, 2015.

Strasser, Susan. *Satisfaction Guaranteed: The Making of the American Mass Market.* New York: Pantheon, 1989.

Sullivan-Fowler, Micaela. "Doubtful Theories, Drastic Therapies: Autointoxication and Faddism in the Late Nineteenth and Early Twentieth Centuries." *Journal of the History of Medicine and Allied Sciences* 50 (1995): 364–90.

Szanto, David, Carmen Wong, and Jennifer Brady. "Stirring the Pot: The Performativities of Making Food Texts." In *Conversations in Food Studies*, edited by Colin R. Anderson, Jennifer Brady, and Charles Z. Levkoe, 52–74. Winnipeg: University of Manitoba Press, 2016.

Taylor, Joe Gray. *Eating, Drinking, and Visiting in the South: An Informal History.* Baton Rouge: Louisiana State University Press, 1988.

Taylor, Joe Gray, and John T. Edge. "Southern Foodways." In *The New Encyclopedia of Southern Culture: Foodways*, edited by John T. Edge, 152–54. Chapel Hill: University of North Carolina Press, 2007.

Tipton-Martin, Toni. *The Jemima Code: Two Centuries of Africa American Cookbooks.* Austin: University of Texas Press, 2015.

Tkweme, W. S. "The Black Experience in Sound: Jazz and African-American

Communities during the Black Arts Movement Era." *International Journal of Africana Studies* 13, no. 2 (2007): 46–54.

Tompkins, Kayla Wazana. *Racial Indigestion: Eating Bodies in the Nineteenth Century*. New York: New York University Press, 2012.

———. "Sylvester Graham's Imperial Dietetics." *Gastronomica* 9 (2009): 50–60.

Tunc, Tanfer Emin. "Less Sugar, More Warships: Food as American Propaganda in the First World War." *War in History* 19 (2012): 193–216.

Turner, Bryan S. "The Turn of the Body." In *The Routledge Handbook of Body Studies*, edited by Bryan S. Turner, 1–18. New York: Routledge, 2012.

Turner, Patricia A. *Ceramic Uncles and Celluloid Mammies: Black Images and Their Influence on American Culture*. Charlottesville: University of Virginia Press, 2002.

Van Deburg, William L. *Modern Black Nationalism: From Marcus Garvey to Louis Farrakhan*. New York: New York University Press, 1986.

———. *New Day in Babylon: The Black Power Movement and American Culture, 1965–1975*. Chicago: University of Chicago Press, 1992.

Vapnek, Lara. *Working Women and Economic Independence, 1865–1920*. Champaign-Urbana: University of Illinois Press, 2009

Vaughn-Roberson, Courtney, and Brenda Hill. "*The Brownies' Book* and *Ebony Jr.!* Literature as a Mirror of the Afro-American Experience." *Journal of Negro Education* 58 (1989): 494–510.

Veit, Helen Zoe. *Modern Food, Moral Food: Self-Control, Science, and the Rise of Modern American Eating in the Early Twentieth Century*. Chapel Hill: University of North Carolina Press, 2015.

Vester, Katharina. "*A Date with a Dish*: Revisiting Freda DeKnight's African American Cuisine." In *Dethroning the Deceitful Pork Chop: Rethinking African American Foodways from Slavery to Obama*, edited by Jennifer Jensen Wallach, 47–60. Fayetteville: University of Arkansas Press, 2015.

———. "Regime Change: Gender, Class, and the Invention of Dieting in Post-Bellum America," *Journal of Social History* 44 (2010): 39–70.

Wallach, Jennifer Jensen. "Food and Race." In *The Routledge History of American Foodways*, edited by Michael D. Wise and Jennifer Jensen Wallach, 293–310. New York: Routledge, 2016.

———. *How America Eats: A Social History of U.S. Food and Culture*. Lanham, Md.: Rowman and Littlefield, 2013.

Warman, Arturo. *Corn and Capitalism: How a Botanical Bastard Grew to Global Dominance*. Chapel Hill: University of North Carolina Press, 2003.

Warner, Mark S. *Eating in the Side Room: Food, Archaeology, and African American Identity*. Gainesville: University Press of Florida, 2015.

Warnes, Andrew. *Hunger Overcome: Food and Resistance in Twentieth-Century African American Literature*. Athens: University of Georgia Press, 2004.

Weems, Robert E., Jr. *Desegregating the Dollar*. New York: New York University Press, 1998.

Weiner, Mark. "Democracy, Consumer Culture, and Political Community: The Story of Coca Cola during World War II." *Food and Foodways* 6 (1996): 109–29.

Weiss, Ellen. *Robert R. Taylor and Tuskegee*. Montgomery: New South Books, 2012.

Wells, Jeremy. "Up from Savagery: Booker T. Washington and the Civilizing Mission." *Southern Quarterly* 42, no. 1 (Fall 2003): 53–74.

White, Deborah Gray. *Arn't I a Woman? Female Slaves in the Plantation South*. New York: W. W. Norton, 1999.

Whorton, James C. *Crusaders for Fitness: The History of American Health Reformers*. Princeton: Princeton University Press, 1982.

———. *Inner Hygiene: Constipation and the Pursuit of Health in Modern Society*. Oxford: Oxford University Press, 2000.

Willard, Carla. "Timing Impossible Subjects: The Marketing Style of Booker T. Washington." *American Quarterly* 53 (December 2001): 624–69.

Williams, Heather Andrea. *Self Taught: African American Education in Slavery and Freedom*. Chapel Hill: University of North Carolina Press, 2007.

Williams-Forson, Psyche. *Building Houses Out of Chicken Legs: Black Women, Food, and Power*. Chapel Hill: University of North Carolina Press, 2006.

———. "Chickens and Chains: Using African American Foodways to Understand Black Identities." In *African American Foodways: Explorations of History and Culture*, edited by Anne L. Bower, 126–38. Urbana: University of Illinois Press, 2007.

———. "Take the Chicken Out of the Box: Demystifying the Sameness of African American Culinary Heritage in the U.S." In *Edible Identities: Food as Cultural Heritage*, edited by Rhonda L. Brulotte and Michael A. D. Giovine, 93–108. New York: Routledge, 2016.

Wilson, Charles Reagan. "Biscuits." In *The New Encyclopedia of Southern Culture: Foodways*, edited by John T. Edge, 122–25. Chapel Hill: University of North Carolina Press, 2007.

———. "Cornbread." In *The New Encyclopedia of Southern Culture: Foodways*, edited by John T. Edge, 152–54. Chapel Hill: University of North Carolina Press, 2007.

Witt, Doris. *Black Hunger: Soul Food and America*. Minneapolis: University of Minnesota Press, 2004.

———. "The Intersections of Literary and Culinary Studies." In *African American Foodways: Explorations of History and Culture*, edited by Anne L. Bower, 101–25. Urbana: University of Illinois Press, 2007.

Wolff, Megan J. "The Myth of the Actuary: Life Insurance and Frederick L. Hoffmans's *Race Traits and Tendencies of the American Negro*." *Public Health Report* 121 (January–February 2006): 84–91.

Woodard, Komozi. "Amiri Baraka, the Congress of African People, and Black Power Politics from the 1961 United Nations Protest to the 1972 Gary Convention." In *The Black Power Movement: Rethinking the Civil Rights–Black Power Era*, edited by Peniel Joseph, 55–77. New York: Routledge, 2006.

Woodward, C. Vann. *Origins of the New South, 1877–1913*. Baton Rouge: Louisiana State University Press, 1951.

Wright, Clarissa Dickson. *A History of English Food*. London: Random House UK, 2011.

Yentsch, Ann. "Excavating the South's African American Food History." In *African American Foodways: Explorations of History and Culture*, edited by Anne L. Bower, 59–100. Urbana: University of Illinois Press, 2007.

Young, Patricia A. "*The Brownies' Book* (1920–1921): Exploring the Past to Elucidate the Future of Instructional Design." *Journal of Language, Identity and Education* 8 (2009): 1–20.

Zafar, Rafia. "Carver's Food Movement." *The Common Reader: A Journal of the Essay,* May 15, 2015. https://commonreader.wustl.edu/c/carvers-food-movement/. Accessed October 18, 2017.

INDEX

food habits, 21, 37, 40–41, 45, 55, 107–9, 125, 131–32, 154, 171, 173, 192; middle-class norms, 8, 19, 26, 59; performance of, 39–47; reform initiatives and, 20, 21, 45, 95, 137; servitude and, 25, 34, 41, 114; white middle class, 27, 30, 40, 56, 68, 82, 93, 104; white working class, 30; working-class food habits, 98, 102, 105–12, 120, 131, 135, 137, 153, 195

Somerville, Florence, 192

soul food, 11, 147, 158, 172; Amiri Baraka and, 164, 183; Bay Area, Calif., and, 167–69; consumption of prior to 1960s, 150, 151–55; Craig Claiborne and, 182; creation of concept, 144, 146, 162–70; definitions of, 169–70; Dick Gregory and, 182; Edna Lewis and, 167; Great Migration and, 120; origins of term, 162; rejection of, 2, 173–74, 177–83, 186, 188, 191, 192; relationship to African diaspora, 174–77; slavery and, 172; vegetarian, 192. *See also* southern food

South Carolina, 99, 126, 129, 148

Southern Christian Leadership Conference, 143

southern food, 20, 21, 43, 101–8, 117, 120, 132, 146–47, 150, 162–66, 168–69, 175; Abby Fisher and, 148; Booker T. Washington and, 62–64; *Brownies' Book* and, 98–101; Edna Lewis and, 167; Great Migration and, 109, 110, 120; Jesse B. Semple and, 155; Nannie Helen Burroughs and, 203n72; rejection of, 119, 121, 170–71, 174–75, 183. *See also* soul food

Spelman College, 31, 34, 114, 116

spinach, 192

stereotypes, 26, 27, 43, 74; cultural inferiority and, 38; fried chicken and, 42; gluttony and, 27, 40, 43, 82; innate cooking skills and, 134, 146, 147, 204n17; larceny and, 42; mammy and, 135; physicality and, 77, 85; servility and, 25; social class and, 111, 150; watermelon and, 98

Student Nonviolent Coordinating Committee, 143, 159, 160, 169

sugar, 99, 123, 127, 129, 156, 157, 177, 185–89 passim, 220n63

sweet potatoes, 50, 67, 99; candied, 61, 203n72; pie and, 112, 146, 168, 175, 183, 187; pudding and, 148; rejection of, 179; soul food and, 167, 168, 169; southern food and, 151; working class and, 107

Sylvia's restaurant, 172

symbolism, 13, 18, 46, 64, 68, 137, 140, 160, 196; agriculture and, 66; "American" food and, 21, 99, 156–62, 170, 172, 197; beef and, 19, 52, 53–54, 57, 101, 124, 138, 206n65; body size and, 82; Civic Club and, 2; Coca-Cola and, 21, 156–59, 161, 177; communion and, 14; corn and, 21, 103, 130–36; hamburger and, 21, 158–59, 161, 177, 181; literacy and, 32; meat and, 181; napkin and, 2, 9; pork and, 21, 103, 110; pure food and, 37; soul food and, 158, 173, 195; Thanksgiving and, 24; wheat and, 19, 54–57, 90, 101, 124, 130–36, 138; white sauce and, 116

Taft, William H., 81

Talbert, Mary Burnett, 126

talented tenth, 86, 102, 137, 139

Tennessee, 147; Memphis, 139

Terrell, Mary Church, 23–25, 26, 27, 28, 29, 34, 35, 37, 44, 196, 201n5

Texas, 169

Thanksgiving, 24, 98, 100, 112, 155, 175

three M's diet. *See* pork and corn diet

Turner, Lillian A., 99

turnips, 153, 203n72

Tuskegee Institute, 19, 44, 49–70, 114, 130, 138; campus meals, 7, 49, 53–56, 205n42, 205n65; curriculum, 8, 31, 34, 36, 114, 116; fund-raising, 33, 53, 57, 64; United States Department of Agriculture and, 106; wartime food conservation and, 125, 126. *See also* beef; Carver, George Washington; corn bread; dining etiquette; pork; Washington, Booker T.; wheat

Tuskegee Women's Club, 56, 206n64